REVUE"

. **Music by Walter**
gh

certainly does not
ld hands make light
. — Miss Her-
references among the
a, I shall merely say
: a race in which all
consist of Derby
choice, even if it
, would be the two
a, devised, and acted
fell. These mono-
thing in their kind
per. I have the
miration for Mr.
ion Miss Hermione
g Miss Grenfell to
and miles of this.

Wilcox of ...... n
flutterings of those
t women with whom
d be endurable, and
untryside would be
on has done more
ed and trusty col-
set of sketches, most
ate. He has also
ces to other than his

fell, for example,
ches and impersona-
nto the very bosom
itute and of three
ood. The awful
ss, patronage, and
it in her talk on
tire, and a further
well shown in her
nal dilemmas. Miss
v

In this show Miss JOYCE
GRENFELL walks alone. She
has two scenes to herself, and,
in a momentarily quieter atmosphere, can achieve subtle
effects which stand out against
the noisier burlesque which is
the note of most of the evening.
Her imitation of a lecturer
addressing a Women's Institute
audience and telling them how
to make such useful things as
a decorative waste-paper basket
out of an old biscuit-tin, or an
animal calendar out of two
pieces of india-rubber and some
matches, producing "a little
bird who will keep you up to
date," took immediate rank as
one of the high spots of the
evening, until she eclipsed it in
the second part with character-
sketches of three different
mothers. One of these should become
for ever memorable—the understanding
English mother, being as nice as she
can, as sympathetic, and as secretly
optimistic as she dares, talking to her
daughter and explaining that "your
father and I quite understand," but
they do not object to Ernest just
because he is a conjurer, and an elderly
Russian conjurer at that, but has the
daughter really thought whether she
will really be happy living the life of
a conjurer's wife?

JOYCE GRENFELL, APPEARING IN FARJEON'S "LITTLE REVUE."

This very clever and witty revue, which is drawing all London to
the Little Theatre, has as one of its leads Joyce Grenfell, who, up till
now, has never appeared on the stage. She owes her good fortune
to Herbert Farjeon, who met her at a party and immediately offered
her a part, and she has made a great and instantaneous success.
She contributes two turns of her own composition, which are quite as
the best items in the programme

cricket, folk-dance, and Joyce Grenfell gave brilliant slices
nd very combative of type impersonation.
based on knowledge
Farjeon shows that
cess by omitting to
the decorative items,
business. n a night of
nfell for strikingly
nes and lore of Mr.
g? All edious bur-
fell and ught never
t of the because the
too obvious.
dergraduate
better. The rest of
brand of pith and
a great little Little

IVOR BROWN.

Mr. Farjeon has followed up " Nine Sharp " with a " LITTLE REVUE "
AT THE LITTLE THEATRE, and brought back into delightful partnership Miss Hermione Baddeley, Mr. Cyril Ritchard, Miss Charlotte Leigh,
Mr. George Benson, and others. He has found an excellent newcomer
in Miss Joyce Grenfell, who does a little " Drapering " without inviting

too close compari-
sons with the one
and only Ruth. Her
invasion of the Vil-
lage Institute and
her studies of
modern maternity
ring the bell de-
cisively, and so does
Mr. Bernard Miles,
with his earnest,

---

at party, is star of revue

The Little Revue.
Authors: Herbert Farjeon and some others.
Theatre: Little.

MR. FARJEON'S previous
revue, "Nine Sharp," was
a success. I believe this will be
a success, too.
My tally last night was that of
e thirty-one scenes twenty came
f, which means that the even-
g was about 67 per cent. enter-
ining. For a revue I think that
pretty good.
Mr. Farjeon is always at his best
nen he has a guy to aim at.
This time he has chosen plays
out crazy families, of which we
d a plague not long ago : um-
ellas ; Chekov's three sisters,
o, here, are always wanting to
to Manchester ; Glyndebourne,
e principle that the further
u have to go to hear opera the
tter it is ; and cricket, village,
and club.
Of the scenes which don't quite
come off, the most reprehensible is
one called Looking at Lightning,
for which the only excuse is that
lightning rhymes with frightening.

Top performances

Individually, the performances
are first-rate. Joyce Grenfell, who
was discovered at a private party,
delivers some uproariously funny
monologues.
Hermione Baddeley is an old lady
wintering at Torquay, and later on
Cyril
e.
ather
ing at
ngs a
A skit
on folk-dancing is good fun precisely
because it keeps so near to the truth of
rapt activity and earnest endeavour. Miss
Joyce Grenfell scores twice with her
monologues. In a song about a tired and
frightened schoolgirl Miss Betty Ann
Davies succeeds in doing what can seldom
be done in revue : she draws the audience
into a tragic emotion and holds it with
absolute control.

To 'Rene -
with love -
from
Michael.
November 1976.

Llewellyn

Joyce Grenfell Requests the Pleasure

Joyce Grenfell Requests the Pleasure

M

SBN 333 19428 4

First published 1976 by

MACMILLAN LONDON LIMITED
*4 Little Essex Street London WC2R 3LF
and Basingstoke
Associated companies in New York Dublin
Melbourne Johannesburg and Delhi*

Printed in Great Britain by
BUTLER AND TANNER LIMITED
Frome and London

For My Husband

Contents

List of Illustrations

List of Illustrations

Besides the photographers mentioned above, the publishers would like to make acknowledgement to any they have failed to trace or whose photographs they unwittingly reproduced. They would also like to thank Mr John Ward, R.A., for permission to reproduce his watercolour portraits, and Mr Peter Letts for copying photographs and press cuttings in albums. The photograph on page 105 was accidentally miscaptioned in the first impression of *The Past Masters* by Harold Macmillan and its appearance here may help to set the record straight.

My mother

CHAPTER ONE

My Mother

I was born in Montpelier Square, London, in 1910, the elder child of Nora and Paul Phipps. The background to my mother is light. All the rooms she lived in were light. Pale rooms with notes of strong colour: geranium-pink, 'lipstick'-red, chalk-blue, saffron-yellow. No top lighting; pools of light from lamps with wide white shades painted pink inside, to her order; pools of light on tables. Low bowls of massed, solid-coloured flowers: geraniums, primroses, gardenias, roses. Uncluttered, lived-in rooms, warm in winter, cool in summer. A wicker basket full of polished apples and, when she could get them, the tiny scarlet and white Lady apples from Virginia. Not many pictures on the walls but always leaves: branches of beech-leaves beginning to unpleat; laurel, shined with salad oil to prolong its brilliance; sometimes bare winter branches; all of them standing in large glass tanks or white pottery urns. Wherever she lived these things appeared – in London, North Carolina and New York. The times we lived in Canada came too early for me to remember clearly, but I have the same impression of light in Vancouver and Winnipeg before I was aware of detail.

Light and warmth – or, as she spelt it, warmpth. The *p* added another degree or two to the temperature.

She has been gone for twenty-two years but the qualities that drew people to her still ring in the air like music for those who knew and loved her; and they are many. The patterns she made on the memory are clear, funny, exasperating, lovable. Her weaknesses brought pain, but her essence, and this is what has endured, is light, luminous and illuminating.

The earliest photograph I have of her shows her sitting on the knee of her nanny, Aunt Eliza Pie. My mother is about a year old and solemn. Aunt Eliza Pie is black and serene. As she grew older my mother and Aunt Eliza sang together and that is how she learned the songs she was later to sing to me and which I have sung all my life and now recorded.

My mother was the youngest of eleven children born to Nancy Witcher Keene and Dabney Langhorne of Richmond, Virginia, and solemn is not what she became. She was a small skinny child, who could somersault over a rail with the best of the boys when she was five, and was the only girl, and the only white child on the block, who could 'eef'. 'Eefing' is a Negro sound made by holding the hands over the mouth to make a cup and then opening and closing the cup to let out the 'eef'. You make the sound by saying 'eeth-e' and 'ithe-e' on the chest, on a quick breath, in and out. It is done in a strong rhythm, and one little black boy 'eefed' while the rest of them danced barefoot in the dust. Or my mother did the 'eefing' while everyone else danced. She could throw a ball overarm, like a boy, and was a pitcher in the local children's baseball game. She was lively all right: wild as the wind. She became very feminine and pretty; quick as a whip but with no concentration and not much staying power if she lost interest. She always had a loving heart.

She had very little formal education and never did learn to spell. But she was a creative bad speller. 'Also' became 'alsough'. 'Roads' had echoes of Africa – 'Rhodes'. She 'raped' her Christmas presents and made a delicious coffee 'mouse' in her refrigerator.

Her mother, Nancy, was musical and played the piano by ear, seldom the most reliable of methods, but it served to give a lot of pleasure to the family. My grandmother Langhorne's taste was for romantic music and opera, and it seems she was able to come home from the theatre and remember the melodies well enough to reproduce them then and there. Three of the daughters were musical. Irene played the piano, using the music: she sang in French as well as English and was sent to Paris to study. Legend says that my grandfather was proud of Irene and when she got back from France he asked her to sing 'Go Tell Aunt Nancy', a folk song all of them (and later their children) were raised on. He pronounced it as Irene had done before she left home 'Ant Nancy'. She is said to have taken a statuesque position, breathed deeply, and sung in a French accent; 'Go telle Arnt-e Nar-ncy'. This was not well received in the family circle.

Phyllis played the piano with real talent and from the music, too; and my mother sang to her own serviceable if limited accompaniment on the guitar. She could not change key but she knew five or six useful chords and looked enchanting, sitting on the steps leading up to the front door at Mirador, where they lived after the move from Richmond, playing and singing to her instrument hung with coloured ribbons. Her

*My ma
with Aunt
Eliza Pie*

voice was true and light and she knew all the songs of the day as well as the Negro spirituals she had sung with Aunt Eliza Pie.

Another legend says that when the singer Jean Darewski heard my mother sing he offered to give her lessons, but there was never time for them. Years later Chaliapin was at a party in London when she sang and they ended the evening singing together to her accompaniment. She taught him to sing 'Way Down Yonder in the Cornfield' and made him 'hold the tune' while she put in the harmonies.

The Langhorne sisters were considerable belles. When my mother was growing up it was impossible for anyone to take a bath the day after a local ball because the tub would be full of flowers sent to the older girls. Lizzie, the eldest girl, was so close to her father that he said he never remembered a time when she wasn't there. All of them were handsome, and Irene and Nancy were beauties. Irene, the only tall and stately one, led the Mardi Gras Ball in New Orleans, an envied mark of distinction. She married Charles Dana Gibson and became his top Gibson girl; you can see her in the books of his drawings. She is always the most beautiful. (My mother is there, too, as a Gibson teenager in a Peter Thompson suit, middy blouse and pleated skirt, with a big black bow at the back of her head.) Nancy, with the profile of a goddess on a medallion, was the strongest character, and Phyllis was the gentlest. These two rode well and from contemporary photographs we can see they sat their horses side-saddle like queens, straight-backed and elegant. They cut a dash in their London-made habits and short top hats with veils, and were much admired. Both made second marriages in England.

There were handsome brothers, too: all dead, except Buck, before I had time to remember them. Buck was a character, a man of charm given to roaming, and was drawn as by a magnet to any crap game within travelling distance. It was said that when his youngest child was being taught the Lord's Prayer and had to repeat after his mother: 'Our Father, which art in Heaven', he looked up and said: 'Mama, where's Papa gone now?'

My mother was fourteen when her mother died, suddenly, after collapsing in the street. The shock was stunning. All the Langhorne children believed they came first with their mother, and in some remarkable way she had managed to have a special relationship with each of them. My mother, born last, was much cherished. She described coming home after her mother's funeral, drained of all feeling, and how she went up to her mother's room and opened the closet. There she saw her small shoes neatly arranged in rows. The sight of a pair of familiar worn red house-slippers with rosettes was the moment of realisation that she would never, never see her mother again.

'When I die,' she used to say to my brother Tommy and me, '*promise* me you won't grieve. You *know* I'll be all right. *Promise* me you'll go to the movies and know I'll be glad you've gone. I couldn't bear you to grieve.' We remembered this and we never grieved, but nor did we go to the movies. It was impossible to believe that she was eclipsed by death. I am not prepared to go into it now but my belief is that Life is continuity.

No photograph I have ever seen of her has caught the vitality and the quality of light that were her essence. There are characteristic snapshots of her standing, hands on hips, legs apart, head slightly tilted; but close-ups, particularly professional portraits, are usually lifeless and even heavy; two things she never was. When Sargent did a charcoal drawing of her he said it was difficult not to make her look sad because her heavy eyelids said sadness, although her lively presence contradicted it. She, the most natural of creatures, became self-conscious in the presence of a painter or a camera, and at once put on a special posing face. She had one for trying on hats, too, and Tommy and I teased her about it. 'You *never* look like that *really*.' 'Of *course* I do,' looking at herself half-sideways, with her mouth pursed and eyebrows up. 'I promise you, you *don't*, ever.'

My mind goes blank when I read descriptions of people's looks; I just cannot see those dancing eyes and mouths too wide for beauty that novelists used to give their tousle-headed heroines. But I think I had better try and describe my mother because if I get it right it must be more like her than the photographs. She was slight but not small; her hair was bright brown but not golden. She had, as all Langhornes had, good bones and therefore an interesting profile. Her nose was arched; not Roman or broken but bony with wide nostrils. No, she didn't look like a horse. She looked more eighteenth-century than twentieth; high cheek-bones with apple-round cheeks when she smiled; small pointed chin, rounded not sharp, and a curling mouth. Her head was a good shape but her very fine hair was hard to manage (I've inherited it). It suited her best when she wore it piled up, showing her ears, but after she had it bobbed it was waved and soft, parted on one side.

It's no good. I can't get her into focus that way. Perhaps her legs may help. She was always proud of them; well shaped with pretty ankles and neat narrow feet. The last time she was in England, a year before she died at sixty-five, she was walking across Grosvenor Square near the U.S. Embassy and an American sailor wolf-whistled at her from behind. She was pleased about this, 'I'm afraid you're fifty years too late.' 'No, ma'am,' said the sailor; 'it's never too late with legs like those.'

Early on she settled certain dress-rules for herself. When possible wear crisp white collars and cuffs with everything. Always try and have something white next to the face. Her favourite hats were tam-o-shanters and she had them, in cloth and velvet, all through her life. She changed the exact angle according to fashion, but the big beret was *her* hat and she kept her trust in it. She preferred navy blue to black and I never saw her wear red. She wore beige and grey but thought brown was gloomy.

When she was a girl flirtation was a commonplace exercise, anyway in Virginia. My mother did it naturally. She also fell in love, or thought she was in love, so often that, like Matilda, nobody believed her. One of her beaux described her as 'hung on wires with a heart like an hotel'. The summer she was eighteen she became engaged to five young men at the same time and somehow none of them knew about the others. After her death one of them wrote to her sister Nancy:

I met her first when I had just graduated from Harvard and to say I had never seen anything like her before is putting it mildly. She was unique and of course I, like so many other boys, became engaged to her. From that point on you pretty well know all that happened and you may remember you employed me to argue with her on various occasions.

But arguing never worked with my mother. Persuasion and an appeal to her heart had a better chance of success.

Late in 1908 she was sent to England to stay with Nancy and her husband Waldorf Astor at Cliveden, their house in Buckinghamshire. There had been a lot of life lived since my mother left school and it was hoped she might calm down in the damper climate. Nancy was expecting her second child; it would be a quiet country house life. But my mama soon collected English admirers and one was an ardent peer, twenty years older than she was. He took her into a conservatory, got down on both knees among the potted palms and proposed. My mother could not take him seriously and he went elsewhere.

The news of this offer reached her father in Virginia and his hopes were raised. It sounded so promising, an English peer old enough and, pray heaven, strong enough to keep her in check. But things were moving fast and, while her father continued to hope, my mama met a penniless young architect, just starting his career, who had been at Eton and Oxford with Waldorf. He was Paul Phipps and he was my father. They got engaged and a cable was sent off to my grandfather, but in the excitement my mother forgot to put the name of her intended. So Grandpa Langhorne, full of relief, wrote to congratulate her on her engagement to Lord E.

I've got six letters written at this time by my mother to her father, and in one dated 11 March 1909 she writes: 'I am so sorry you have made a mistake. It isn't E. It is Paul Phipps.'

Her father must have taken this badly; I haven't any of his letters but from the tone of my mother's to him she had a lot of convincing to do. Grandpa Langhorne knew his youngest daughter and had been through a great many romantic entanglements with her, so all her certainties that *this* time things were different did not wash with him. But she admits her past weaknesses:

I've been such a failure to you but I want to prove to you I have got some good in me after all. I know all of my weak points and that's a help. I have got that to begin on. Nanny [Nancy] is going to help me and I am going to

My ma in 1911

try with all my strength to succeed and if good doesn't come out in me at this time when I am so happy then there isn't any in me for I am so happy I am frightened.

A week later she writes:

I pray day and night that I may be all he thinks I am. I want to be so different ... I will do right by him or die.... I will be good and true and square. I want a home and children. I know I will be happy.

There is only one letter written by my father at this time, to the wife of his great friend Ducie Antrim:

Well, well, well. I am glad you like the idea – very glad indeed. I tell you it is the *best* idea that ever occurred to anyone. You're quite right, Nora is a fascinating person – but she is much more than that. She has the best heart in the world – which is about as good a thing as one can say of anyone. She is clever too. I told you that before once and I *think* you rather doubted it – but it's true. She's clever in the cleverest way – very original, has her own ideas, and looks at things from her own point of view though she can see other points too and being an extremely sensitive and artistic person, what she don't know she feels. She has an observation which is quite uncanny, and what is not 'harvested' by her 'quiet eye' is not worth garnering. In fact she is the jolliest woman with the nicest point of view and the best companion I know.

Of course you think I am the 'lovelorn loon' but the odd thing is it's all true and if I were a woman I would rather have Nora's point of view and ideas than those of anyone I know.

This is an odd letter – but it is pleasant to explode like this occasionally.

It is moving to be the child of these high hopes, and knowing what came later makes the letters poignant.

The biggest debt I owe my parents is for the happy, stable background they made for my brother Tommy and me to grow up in. At least it seemed happy to us, and stable. It says much for their concern for us that they achieved this confident atmosphere, because they were not happy together, but we never suspected it until much later. I was nineteen, and married, and Tommy was fifteen when they parted.

I don't know when the difficulties began, but I think it was not long before there were problems. I am no longer interested in the sad details . . . let them go. Until I was twelve I felt no tension between them and I was a nosey little girl, observant and critical, and yet all I remember until then was a feeling of safety and happiness. After that I was vaguely aware of their differences. It was understood that my mother liked going to parties and my father didn't. I accepted this. There was no serious worry about their relationship and the warmth and affection that surrounded us were genuine and undisturbed. That is the miracle they achieved. It *was* a happy home in spite of their basic (or was it only a surface?) incompatibility. It never occurred to me that our family could ever come apart.

To write in cold blood that we laughed a lot together is to suggest the merry tinkle of what Beachcomber called 'gladdery and joyage' and the heart sinks to think about it. But it wasn't like that. As a family we were amused by each other more than we were confounded. We laughed more with than at. I think the meeting-place of shared amusement made my parents' marriage last as long as it did. Even in bad times they found the safety-valve, the return to perspective. And the other thing that held them together was their mutual respect for each other. My mother always admired my father; my father was often exasperated by my mother but he went on loving her. I know this because when he was an old man he told me so. It is idle to think 'if only', but I have an idea that if they had been able to come together again years later, 'all passion spent', they might have been congenial because they *liked* each other.

Of course my mother was spoilt. Coming at the end of a big family she was the indulged baby; a bright pretty child, clever and funny, and they made much of her. She grew to accept attention; the centre of the stage was the natural place to be. She didn't have to seek it, it was hers. With her temperament and power to draw people to her it is remarkable that she didn't abuse her gifts more. There was nothing calculated about her expectancy of happy endings; she simply acted as if they were inevitable for everyone. She had little trouble in putting her problems behind her, and beginning again with a clean sheet. She forgave and expected everyone else to forgive too, and she never sulked. But there were back-logs of bills unpaid, engagements forgotten or cut, fibs told, mistakes that were regretted but never fully rooted out, so that they appeared again and again. She had an innate honesty that she refused to use until late in her life, and it built up into remorse. Remorse is bad company. She came to know it well.

My father bore the brunt of the muddles and debts and it weighed heavily on him, for he was punctilious about money and had a strong sense of concern for other people. I think he settled for the lop-sided life he found himself in, troubles not shared but off-loaded, because he decided that if the marriage was to continue at all, this was the only way to maintain it.

It is easy to blame her. Looked at critically she was feckless, irresponsible and self-centred; but to her children she was none of these things. We knew her as one of ourselves and found her funny and enthusiastic and warm. But then she put us first and this strong maternal instinct was a surprise and an irritation to her beaux. There were always plenty of them. We didn't see much of them, but we knew they existed as voices on the telephone and, intuitively, I resented the lot of them. When one of them was rash enough to come to tea I believe I was direct in my attack, asking plain questions such as 'Are you going home now?' Putting her children first sometimes meant leaving her beaux flat. She would rush away before the end of a matinée to be home in time for our regular after-tea sessions of games and singing and stories. She left the hairdresser's only partly waved, dashed from the dressmaker's still buttoning her dress, got a taxi and sat on the edge of the seat to encourage it to go faster, and arrived home only a little late, spilling the change, hurrying up the stairs, arms full of parcels and an excuse on her lips. She was never altogether reliable about time until the last years of her life when she became uncharacteristically over-punctual. It was all part of her never-ending effort to do better.

A friend of mine wrote about my mother: 'She had that particular quality of making ordinary things like getting on to a bus exciting and fun.' This is true; except that my mother never went by bus if she could help it. I think she believed taxis were provided for her special use. She took at least two a day, often unnecessarily, and this extravagance was a source of irritation to my father; and later to me. He took taxis only in exceptional circumstances but she couldn't resist the sight of a For Hire flag. She got to know a number of London taxi-drivers by name and they hailed each other in passing. One toothless old man used to cruise around in his rattling cab waiting for her to come out after lunching at the Berkeley Hotel (then in Piccadilly). He knew she often went to the Grill Room and used the ladies' cloakroom of the hotel as a sort of home from home where she could leave her parcels and change her stockings. (No one laddered stockings and lost just one glove as often as my mother.) Sometimes the toothless old man was sent to pick up her shopping and bring it back to her at home. He came to my wedding, as did the one-legged gardenia-seller who had a stand outside the Berkeley Street entrance to the hotel. He knew she would always buy one, and now and then she bought the whole tray-full and he went home early. Gardenias were her favourite flowers. Years later, at the end of the terrace of Little Orchard, her house in Tryon, North Carolina, my mother planted a gardenia bush and it grew and flourished and flowered and was her great delight.

The capacity for enjoyment never diminished in her. It was infectious and she was good at sharing it, as she was fond of sharing 'things'. Because I have been on the receiving end of so much generosity of every kind all my life I have found it natural to share, because I've been shared with. My mother and all her family were great sharers. She would not only give you the coat off her back (probably not yet paid for) but the hat to go with it; and when Aunt Nancy Astor gave me a new dress, as she frequently did, she always remembered that new dresses go best with new shoes and these were added. My cousin Nancy Perkins had very little money when she was young and my mother shared her clothes with her while they were still fresh and fashionable. Nancy never forgot this (nor a tortoiseshell brush and comb that she admired, so my mother gave them to her), and when she had money she kept the sharing pattern going in spring and autumn, and sent round suitcases of her Paris-made clothes for my mother and me to share.

One of the mysteries of life is that women of very different shapes and sizes can wear each other's clothes. Nancy is a size fourteen, my mother was a twelve and even then I was a large size eighteen. Today

My Mother

I'm sometimes an even larger twenty. Rose Baring, who wrote the
letter saying my mother made getting on a bus exciting and fun, also
said: 'Whatever was happening Nora made it seem like a wonderful
surprise,' and when Nancy's suitcase arrived my mother turned it into
an occasion. We had two or three friends who joined in the Nancy-loot-
sharing and we telephoned and asked them to come round. First we had
tea in the studio. This was a big room on the ground floor, built out at
the back of the tall eighteenth-century brick house in St Leonard's
Terrace, Chelsea, by a horse-painter who needed space for his models.
The horses came in through the narrow back garden and approached
the studio up a ramp through barn-sized doors. By the time we bought
the house the doors and ramp had gone and a big window and window-
seat were in their place. The piano and our Decca gramophone lived
in the studio and we could make plenty of noise down there without
disturbing the neighbours. The walls were bright white, the curtains
strong pinky-red, and it was here that we always had the new branches
of beech-trees in spring, and laurel, at most other times, in a big ac-
cumulator vase. Tea was set out on a round, bottle-green, painted
tea-table. There were small hot, sweet, buttered scones, Tiptree Little
Scarlet strawberry jam and a Fuller's cake, often iced and decorated
with walnuts. Some of us sat on the floor and that is where my mother
best liked to sit, cross-legged. She never got pins and needles and could
get up from that position without using her hands. After tea we went
upstairs, to the second floor, to her bedroom with its view of the Royal
Hospital, across the Guards cricket ground, framed in the smoky blue
of her small patterned damask curtains. All the clothes, hats, scarves
and belts were spread out on my mother's bed. She was our acknowledged arbiter of fashion and helped us to decide who was to have
which clothes. Her enthusiasm was catching. Her idea was that everyone should have a good time and she was, as another friend said, 'a
life enhancer'. We all tried on everything, queuing up to take our
turn looking at ourselves in the long glass hung inside the cupboard
door. Even though my mother rightly knew which garment was best
suited to each one of us, we had to prove it for ourselves.

I see us now, standing in our pink petticoats, straight up-and-down
crêpe-de-chine slips with bands of lace round the top, our peculiar
Twenties figures forced flat by bust-bodices, made from lengths of
stout satin ribbon twelve inches wide, fastened at the back with strong
hooks and eyes. Our hair is water-waved or marcelled in regular un-
dulations. Our legs are uniform in orangey 'flesh'-coloured stockings

23

with seams, probably 'art' silk; our feet in court shoes with the new Cuban heel are from Jack Jacobus in Shaftesbury Avenue. (There you could get satin evening shoes dyed the same day, to match your dress, at one guinea a pair.) We do not use rouge or eye–pencil, but have discovered Tangee lipstick that is supposed to take on our own natural colour, but which stains our lips light purple. Our face-powder is no longer pink but honey-beige. We compare notes about this, and about deodorants that don't make us itch and hair-removers that really do the job but smell horrible, of rotting vegetation. We are all reticent about such things, but barriers come down as we pool discoveries. None of us has ever had a facial but my mother has Madame Maria to come and 'do' her face for special occasions (frequent) and she uses Madame Maria's highly priced hand-made creams and lotions and a liquid rouge that she applies to her cheeks in little blobs from the glass bottle-stopper.

We help each other into Nancy's dresses and suits and exclaim with awe at the labels sewn in them – Chanel, Lanvin, Louise-boulanger and Schiaparelli. These are names we have read about in *Vogue* and *Harper's Bazaar* and none of us had dreamed we would one day own such clothes. We all have small dress-allowances from our parents and rarely buy our clothes from shops, because the dressmakers we go to make them so much more cheaply. All the group go to Mrs Woolgar and Miss Grover; both live in Chelsea and charge thirty shillings to make a dress and two pounds for a coat. Twice a year our country friends engage Miss Grover, the traveller, to come and stay ten days to dressmake for them on the premises. Mrs Woolgar, tethered by the needs of a jobbing-gardener husband, works in the tiny dark Regency cottage she lives in, in Elystan Place, and comes out to give us our fittings at home, bringing the clothes round in a small cardboard suit-case. Everything she makes smells of Gold Flakes until it has been hung out in a draught. Both dressmakers can copy anything, and Nancy's Paris models are borrowed from their new owners and duplicated in S.W.3.

Finally the selection is made. My mother, with common consent, has the navy blue suit with white piqué collar and cuffs, by Chanel. Whatever I get has to be let out and lengthened. No doubt Mrs Woolgar will make it possible for me to breathe freely in the Louise-boulanger flowered chiffon evening dress with its skirt short in front and long at the back.

We part; plans are made to go and sit in the pit to see Edna Best in a new play. My mother is going to the movies after dining at the Berkeley Grill and we all say that she must wear the Chanel.

Sometimes a creative mood came over my mama and she made her own dress. This is how she did it. Taxi to Peter Jones's shop. It is, at most, seven minutes walk from St Leonard's Terrace, but looking out of her bedroom window she could see there were cabs on the rank in the Royal Hospital Road, the other side of Burton Court cricket field, so she might as well use one. She lifted the receiver of her daffodil-shaped telephone and gave the rank's number, as familiar as her own. She kept the taxi ticking outside Peter Jones while she bought four yards of material, and came home. Upstairs the material was folded lengthways in half and laid out on the floor of her bedroom. Then she cut a hole to put her head through, rough hemmed the neck and bottom of the skirt, let the selvedge remain for the edge of the kimono sleeves, giant-stitched the side-seams, and lo! it was a dress to wear out to dinner that evening. In the hand it looked what it was, a hurriedly tacked together shift; but with her inside it, a wide sash (out of her belt-and-sash drawer) tightly tied round her small waist, and a flower (out of the flower-and-ribbon box in the cupboard) tucked in the knot, it was a fetching, original and becoming garment.

Here is a little snob story. My mother went to a party in one of her home-made dresses and Queen Marie of Roumania was there and liked the dress so much that she invited her to come and see her next day at Buckingham Palace where she was visiting her cousin King George V and Queen Mary; my mother was to bring material and cut out a dress for Queen Marie. As I have said, my mama was slight with a small waist: Queen Marie of Roumania was a fine figure of a woman, but waistless. My mother could not do sums any more than she could spell, but something told her that what hung freely on her to be gathered into a wide sash was going to be more exact on the Queen and would not leave any fullness to be gathered and held in anywhere by anything. She felt she had bitten off more than she could chew, but it was exciting to be going to the Palace, and later she was going to have tea with the King and Queen. It was a sharp spring day and, like me, my mother hated being cold, so she had put on a cosy little old white woolly spencer under her light spring coat, planning to take it off before she saw the royals and leave it with the footman. He was understanding and said he would keep it safely for her until the time came for her to leave. All went well with the cutting out of the dress. My mother had never seen a queen in her petticoat before and enjoyed the experience but wished the lady's maid hadn't looked so superior when she put the material on the floor to cut it out. There were, as my mama feared, not many folds when Queen Marie tried the dress on, but she liked herself in it and it was handed to the lady's maid to seam and hem.

Tea with Queen Mary and King George was interesting and jollier than she had expected. One of the princes threw a scone at another and the Queen was only faintly amused and the King not at all. My mother was drawn out by Queen Marie and made to sing a song, but she felt bereft without her guitar and wasn't sure it was a good idea. But they asked for more and she was a success and stayed late. The Prince of Wales, whom she already knew, went down with her in the lift to see her into her taxi. My mother didn't want to lose her little old cosy white woolly spencer, for she was fond of it, but she didn't feel she could ask the footman to give it back and help her into it in front of the Prince. The footman had no intention that she should; he indicated that he had the whole thing under control and gave her a meaningful wink. She took this to mean he would keep the woolly spencer until she could collect it quietly on another occasion. And that is what she did. I remember waiting to hear how this visit had gone, and my mother's account of it had me right in the Palace with her, flying scones and all.

My mother not only made up dresses; she made up games for us to play – and played them with us too. They sprang from her as the occasion demanded. It was a long, wet spring day when she invented the singing-walking game. At that time we were living in a first-floor flat at No 8, Burton Court, Chelsea. I was eight, Tommy was four. We'd been kept indoors by the wet afternoon, Lucy, our nanny, was out and our mama was looking after us. We were bored with our wet-day ploys. Tommy had ridden his 'trike' up and down the little linoleumed passage between our minute day-nursery and where the hall carpet began, turning at high speed into the housemaid's cupboard and off again up the six yards of lino, ringing his bell without ceasing. I had drawn and painted till I'd used up my drawing-book. It wasn't time for tea. To amuse us my mother pushed a big armchair over to the window and we all three sat in it. From here we could watch people going by in the street below. 'Let's see,' said my ma, inventing, 'if we can make that man in the bowler hat keep time to the music,' and she sang 'The Keel Row', making it exactly fit the man's stride. 'Come on – you do it, too.' It was fun. A boy came by on a bicycle and he didn't know it but we had him pedalling to the waltz from *Maid of the Mountains*. In those

My ma, Tommy and I

days the brewers still used horses to pull their beer-drays and it was interesting to discover that the huge fur-fringed feet could be made to keep time to 'Baa, Baa Black Sheep'. The skill of the game lies in following the beat, and you have to vary your tempo to fit the pauses and strides. We used to play it in cars, and I still play it in traffic jams. It is a help against frustration to set pedestrians to music like 'Colonel Bogey' or 'Tea for Two'.

We loved being told stories and my mother was a compelling teller. She sat cross-legged on the floor with her back to the fire (that was only one of the many ways she laddered her fine silk stockings) and whatever children were around at the time collected near her, leaning on her, hanging round her neck until she settled them down. All her stories began in the same way: 'ONCER-PONCER-TIME'. For Tommy she invented an endless saga about a boy called Button Bill who was Tommy's age and reflected his taste for cars and 'proper' boy's clothes. Button Bill had special dispensations from the law that allowed him to drive at the age of four, then five, six, seven. She said that he lived in an actual house in Park Lane. It had blue-tiled window-boxes and I felt a real sense of loss a few years ago when it was pulled down. The serial went on until Tommy went away to school and was wearing the 'proper' grey flannel boy's suit that his *alter ego* had always worn.

My ma found a technique of putting in a question to cover flagging interest. 'And what do you suppose happened then?' The air would vibrate with mystery. I pretended to be above such childish stories, but I was right there with suggestions.

'Button Bill lost his way back from Scotland?'

'No.'

'He met an elephant?'

'No.'

'He went to Switzerland and it snowed?'

'*Yes*,' and off she'd go in the new landscape.

There was another saga for more general use when we were staying away and our cousins swelled the audience. It was about a big family called the Buttonhooks who had adventures, and my mother catered for all the tastes present, introducing characters and situations to match her audience. She invented a girl named Rose, just my age, tailored to fit my dreams, so she had long red pigtails, freckles, wore glasses and had a gold band across her teeth; all appurtenances I wished for. Eventually I did get a gold band intended to straighten some independent lower teeth that had come in at angles, but as it spent most of the time wrapped up in a handkerchief secreted in the elastic band of my school knickers it didn't do much good, and this accounts for the continued irregularity of my lower teeth. I so badly wanted freckles that I painted them on my nose and cheeks with brown watercolour. Then I made the discovery that walking in fine rain without a hat gave me the feeling I had freckles and to this day I can enjoy this fantasy, until I remember what rain does to my kind of hair. I achieved pigtails too, but they weren't red and caused me a bad moment in the lecture theatre of the Victoria and Albert Museum.

On this occasion I had braided my hair into one pigtail and went with my father to hear some Bach. As we went into the hall I noticed there were a lot of schoolboys already seated. I was at the self-conscious stage, about twelve, wishing to be a success with boys and at the same time afraid of them. My father led me into seats directly below a row of schoolboys. The seating rose steeply in tiers from the floor and the knees and feet of the people in the row behind had to be controlled or they nudged the people in the row below. I sit very tall; in fact I almost always sit taller than the man I am next to at dinner. At one moment in the programme Harold Samuel played a dancing *gigue* and I responded by beating time with my head; or trying to. As I moved I realised my pigtail was being held, as in a vice. Those awful boys! I felt myself start to blush from the toes upward. Then discreetly I turned my head to see if I could release my pigtail. The boy behind me had nodded off, his knees together and his feet turned in. Firmly wedged between his knees was my pigtail. I left it there until the *gigue* was ended and applause woke my jailer.

My mother always had instant communication with children and they responded to her immediately. When we were little she discovered that fitting an imaginary coat on us was an endless amusement. We stood there while she pretended to measure the length, the width, the sleeves, the neck. Would we like it a mite easier under the arm? Did we fancy four or six buttons down the front – single-file or double-breasted? She showed us where each button would go, slowly and precisely from top to bottom. 'One here' – a little prod, 'one *here*.' She pretended to drop a button and we helped her look for it. We were completely conned into believing there was a coat and there were buttons. I watched her play this game with countless children down the years and it never failed. 'Do it again,' the accolade of success. Babies grinned toothless grins at her and stopped crying when she took them in her arms. Children in parks, in trains, found her and took her hand.

My cousin Elizabeth Winn remembers being a pretend chicken undergoing preparation for the oven. 'A little salt on the wings and some fat patted in here and just a *tiny* shake of pepper there, you're ready.'

'Do it again, Aunt Nora – do it again.'

My mother was the exact opposite of Anita Loos's Henry in *Gentlemen Prefer Blondes*. All he had to do to ruin a party was to appear at it. All she had to do to make the party a success was be at it. She was, as bachelors are said to be, born welcome. She could always make a party out of the most unpromising occasion; hair-washing night for instance.

At this stage our hair was washed in the bath after we'd been soaped down. Not a very hygienic practice and tough on the customer. We hated it; soap in the eyes and ears; then the preliminary ducking to get the soap out which flooded the ears, and the possibility of slipping under the water altogether. Lucy, our nanny, used a jug to pour water over our heads as a final rinse and this was agreeable, but the whole process was one we found trying. The night for hair-washing varied; we weren't given a chance to dread it for long, Lucy sprang it on us. She simply announced the time had come when she fetched us to go and have our baths. My mother, ever an oiler of ruffled waters, had an idea.

'I tell you what – I'll have a surprise ready for you when you're done.' We went off to be laundered, cheered by the prospect.

We can't have been all that spoilt since we were so pleased by such small delights as buttered scones (drawing-room tea left-overs) topped with a lot of caster sugar, or a surprise 'present' from the cupboard in my mother's bedroom: a piece of ribbon for me and a last year's diary-pencil for Tommy. Our childhood was full of these kinds of 'surprises'. There were always treasures in that cupboard, and in the writing-table drawer: rubber bands, a knob off something, a swatch of silk patterns from Woollands. I came in for flowers off hats, feathers, trimmings, buckles off belts. Sometimes we found surprises under the pillow when we woke up, and there were unmerited rewards for not making a fuss at the dentist. I got sixpence for having a tooth out and an ice-cream for having gas. Bribery, of course, but I don't think it made either of us feel the need to barter for favours when we grew up.

My self-conscious disapproval of any departure from conventional behaviour was irresistible to my mama. She was spontaneous to the point of peril and she enjoyed the element of risk because it caused me to writhe. There never was a more loving mother but she couldn't forbear teasing us. Tommy was much less vulnerable than I was about this. I began to wriggle with embarrassment whenever my ma showed signs of stepping out of the unnoticeable pattern to which I thought all parents should conform. I was sorely tried.

There were not many accents she couldn't imitate, and when we were at home this was fascinating. We encouraged her to go on and on. But in public it was dangerous because she was almost certain to forget halfway through that she had been pretending to be French or Russian or, more likely, some unidentifiable 'mittel-European', speaking in a spoof language made up of authentic-sounding Slav noises. As Ruth Draper did, she could invent sounds that passed for the real thing and convinced strangers, who looked at her with interest, while the travelled ones were seen puzzling out just where she could have come from.

Tommy took it all in his stride, but I remember the three of us being in a train with one other woman passenger when he was as apprehensive as I was. That day our mother was being French and she asked us questions about the countryside. Looking at a cow she said: 'Is zet a gee-gee?' 'Oh *mummee*,' we moaned under our breath, 'don't.' The woman passenger, not hearing us, smiled pleasantly and went back to her book. The train rocked on. Then my mother beckoned us to put our heads closer to hers. 'What do you bet,' she said conspiratorially, 'that I can't drop this piece of paper on her hat without her knowing?' 'No,' we said firmly. 'No – please.' This expected reaction on our part was the spur she needed. 'Oh come on, you all,' she said, 'I bet I can.' We betted she could, too. That was the terror of it.

The woman was sitting on the same side of the carriage as my mother. We sat opposite. I thought that if I closed my eyes I'd be spared the torture but of course I couldn't resist watching. My mother tore up the little piece of paper into four pieces and then, pointing at the landscape racing by on the other side of the woman, said with urgency: 'Look!' The woman turned, we all turned to see and at that moment she dropped the pieces of paper on top of the stranger's hat, where they stayed for the rest of the time we were in her company. We giggled uneasily. I had a reluctant sort of admiration for such risk-taking, even though I didn't like it. I wish I could think my concern was for the victim but I know it was only for my own discomfort. I didn't wish to be identified with such goings-on.

Years later I taxed my mother with having made a fool of an innocent victim. The idea had never crossed her mind. 'I did it because you and Tommy were so afraid I would, and I couldn't resist the look on your faces. I don't suppose the woman ever knew,' she said, 'do you?' I hoped not. 'Oh *dear*,' said my mother.

CHAPTER TWO

My Father

MY father was a confidence-restorer and he looked it; a big man who
stood firm. Big ears (flat), big feet and hands and a long, broad face
with a wide smile. He also had a long strong jaw that could have meant
aggression, but aggression was left out of him, so was rage. Instead he
was tolerant and affectionately amused by the human race: honesty and
faith were natural to him. What he wore looked comfortable and right
rather than dressy, but his hats – black mostly – had dash, with brims
broader than was usual in London W.1, and less showy than in London
S.W.3. He was a bow-tie man and had his made to his own specifi-
cation, long, ribbon-like lengths of bright cottons in checks or stripes
from the West Indies. The ties, and the stiff collars he turned back
himself, more exaggeratedly than did other men, were his own speci-
ality. I hardly ever saw him wear his hat straight on his head, it was
either pushed well back or perched low over his nose. He was not at all
a swashbuckler but he had an air. He had no enemies; his friends loved
him and responded to his individual ideas.

For a man who won a gold watch for his pretty handwriting while
he was at Balliol, and whose caricatures were economic and delicately
drawn, he was unexpectedly bad at tying shoe-laces and knocking
in nails. When he patted me on the shoulder to show affection or
approval he did it with the flat of his hand, gentle but thumping. He
could not pronounce the letter *r*, so that words like tremendous and
Deuteronomy took on extra quality when he used them.

Public image has come to mean a false front to hide the inadequacy
of a man. People who are what they seem to be are not only more
reliable but more comfortable to be with. My pa was what he appeared
to be – good. What do I mean by good? In this instance – generous,
loving, humble, honest. He was an architect, believed wholly in God
as all good; and his influence was central to my growing-up life. He
was born at No 1, Fifth Avenue in New York City when No 1 was a

The young man my mother married

tall town house and not an apartment building as it is now. His father was English, his mother American, so I am three-quarters American by birth, and English by upbringing, education, marriage and residence.

I like this mongrel arrangement and it is stretching to have allegiances on both sides of the ocean.

My first certain memory of my pa makes me about three and he therefore thirty-three. We are in Vancouver and he is jogging me on his knee and my teeth are shuddering in a pleasurable way:

This is the way the farmer goes
Hobble-de-hoy, Hobble-de-hoy.

I nearly fall off as he joggles me more spiritedly, and demand a repeat.

Photographs of this time show us together in an open bull-nosed Hupmobile car. I am serious and blonde with curls, in smocked white cotton; he is beaming, his hat characteristically on the back of his dark curly head. His pipe, stem down, is in the top pocket of his jacket. Soon he was to give up smoking and drinking as an example to the private soldiers in the regiment he came back to England to join in 1914. Such gestures worked in those days. The men were not sending home their pay; instead it went on beer and Woodbines, so a pledge paper was pinned up and my pa was one of the signers. He never meant to give up his port or his pipe for ever, but he never went back to either.

When the First World War broke out we were living in America. He was with a firm of architects, but he left at once for Canada and joined the first regiment going overseas, Princess Patricia's Light Infantry. In England he transferred to the Sherwood Foresters and we moved to Plymouth to be near his camp. The Geordies in his command came from the coal-mines of Durham and Northumberland and dug themselves out of sight in a matter of minutes. But they took slowly to army discipline. My father found them attractive and admirable; small stocky men of unyielding good humour. Coming back into camp one night the guard on duty greeted him with a friendly wave.

'Evenin', Captain Phipps, sir – Nice night.'

My father agreed it was but said he must point out that a guard is not supposed to be friendly, he is supposed to challenge anyone who approaches his post.

'Funny you should say that, sir. That's just what Major White said to me not more than five minutes ago.'

I have no means of finding out much about my father's early life because everyone who knew him then is dead. I know he went away to school at the cruelly early age of eight, as all little boys of his world did, and suffered hell when he lost the card, issued to him by a visiting Bishop, on to which he was supposed to stick stamps in aid of an African mission. The Bishop was due to call again to collect the completed cards and my pa's was nowhere to be found. The waiting time was a nightmare of anxiety he could share with no one. He imagined the possible punishments – expulsion, shame, beatings, his mother's heartbreak. Then the Bishop, an understanding man, arrived; my father dared his confession and was rewarded by forgiveness and no punishment, only another card to be stamped.

He went on to Eton and Balliol and enjoyed both. At Eton he sat between two lords; one distinguished himself by spelling a word without any of its usual letters, wife – *yph*; the other was Ducie, later Lord Antrim, who became his great friend and whom he called Beetle.

I must pause here to record some facts about Beetle. When he was sent away to school at the same pitiful age as my father, his first letter home was very brave:

Dear Mama,
    The boys at this school go about in twos. I go about in ones.
                                 Your loving Ducie.

In the General Strike of 1926 Ducie fulfilled a life's dream and drove a railway engine. He was acting as stoker to a real engine-driver and let it be known that he would very much like to handle the throttle or whatever you handle in trains. The driver said it wasn't permitted, but he'd let Ducie do it just for once. He did it for at least two hundred yards and his cup was full. My father's job in the General Strike was one he would not have chosen, for, like me, he was not at all comfortable in the company of horses. His task was to look after the enormous dray-horses in Paddington Station Goods Depot, and it alarmed him, for he did not know the language. 'Whoa' seemed to mean little to these giants and he kept off 'giddy-up' in case they responded to it. Ducie was the most widely loved man it has been my good fortune to know. It was said of an old mountain man in North Carolina that 'he never met a stranger'. This was true of Ducie.

My parents' generation was able to quote from poems and plays and the Bible, and I wish I could. Instead of my head being full of psalms and sonnets that would be of use to me if I was lost in a desert or held in solitary confinement, all I have tucked away are the words of the songs of my dancing days, a holy quotation or two and one verse of 'I remember, I remember,' by Thomas Hood. I also have a small worthless recitation that my father and the other young men articled to Sir Edwin Lutyens, the architect, used to recite in unison when they should have been working at their drawing-boards. I don't know where it came from, but when we were small my brother and I made our father say it to us over and over again. Eventually we had it by heart too, and the three of us spoke it together, at a run. It had to be said in exactly the same way, with the same 'refained' accent, in the same unctuous melodramatic curate's manner every time we said it;

'Once when I was travelling in South Africa with a very dear friend of mine (he's dead now poor fellow and we all mourned his loss), I was called to the bedside of a poor dying child and, as she looked up into my sweet face, she said: "Oh Mr Clark – Mr Clark – I die happy, oh *so* happy." '

This curiosity is rooted deep in my memory, as it was in my father's, together with 'Farewell and Adieu to you all, Spanish ladies' and a song about food that I continue to find useful when I am called upon to divert small children.

> Oh I'd like to have a pickin'
> Of a little bit of chicken.

I found a copy of the words in my pa's handwriting and at the bottom it says: 'Taught me by a boatman on Loch Rannoch at the turn of the century.'

My father went to France in 1915 with the Sherwood Foresters carrying a copy of *St Paul in the Trenches* and like most men he did not enjoy the experience of war. He was in the mud and the misery and cannot have been sorry when he was invalided out of the army with knee trouble that had been with him since he was a little boy. I was taken to see him in a nursing home in Park Lane, full of glamorous V.A.D.s in muslin veils, many of whom he had danced with in his bachelor days. They told me what a swell he had been, and all my life I have met women who said their young lives were enhanced when Paul Phipps noticed them and asked them to dance. It seems he was a spirited waltzer, and a dab hand at the polka too, and covered the ground as none of their other partners could. He and Waldorf Astor were the first young men to introduce the daring 'reverse' into the ball-rooms of London – until then waltzers went on spinning in the same direction getting giddier and giddier; with the reverse they un-spun from time to time, surely an obvious solution to the problem. But reversing was not approved by the chaperons, and one wonders

My pa

why, unless it was because the young man had to hold his young lady's waist even more firmly when they changed direction. My pa and Waldorf Astor went to Paris, learned the *risqué* manoeuvre and danced it, their coat tails flying, and their patent leather dancing-pumps, trimmed with flat *grosgrain* bows, twinkling as they spun. My pa continued to wear evening pumps all his life and, a source of pride, gave me away at my wedding in the button boots he had been married in twenty years earlier.

As well as not being deft with his hands my father was a clumsy mover, except on the dance floor. His style was chippier than I liked in 1928, when I first began to go to dances – he reversed quite sharply, I thought, but he was a travelling waltzer, so I got round the room at speed with far more agility than with my younger partners. There is a stage – or there was a stage in my youth – when a girl is glad to dance with her father; because it is better to dance with anyone than be left standing alone by the door. Not that I minded this very much. I was so interested in watching people that I soon got over the faint sense of failure at not being asked and would sit by myself completely held by the sights I saw and the developing relationships I witnessed among my friends. My pa still drew admiring glances when he whirled me around at my first dance. There was a period flavour about the way he danced. None of your 'Come Dancing', just-behind-the-beat style, he marked the beat clearly, and using up all the available floor-space navigated neatly, never bumping into other couples.

Not being asked to dance could be painful. But my people-watching activities eased the embarrassment for me. At the back of the page-a-day diaries I've been keeping for years I write in quotations I want to remember; stories I've heard and remarks made. Looking at an old diary I found this, 'On not being married – Irish voice – "When ye get over the disgrace of it, the life is more airy." ' I sometimes felt this at dances. Not being asked to dance gave me a sense of space in which I could observe and imagine. Anyway I felt invisible while I watched.

By any standard I was very green and although I looked grown up I was immature to the point of idiocy. I knew roughly how babies came. A small contemporary, with sniggers, had told me in a Hertfordshire garden and I went straight to my mother and asked if it was true. 'Who told you?' Loyalty very nearly sealed my lips. My mother had guessed who had told me and was sad because she had wanted to tell me herself when the time came for me to ask the question. We didn't go into it very deeply. I wasn't much interested and lived on quite comfortably with hazy visions about sex and very little curiosity. So it never occurred to me even at eighteen, at my own coming-out dance, that it might be misconstrued if I said to a young man, a frequent dancing-partner and a friend, 'I know a marvellously quiet place where we can go,' and I led him up the back stairs of Aunt Nancy's London house to a top passage where the unwanted sofas and chairs from the drawing-rooms had been stacked to make room for dancing. The young man, less green than I was, made as if to kiss me. I was surprised and appalled; it spoilt everything. I got up from the sofa, pushing him away, and ran down to the cloakroom where I found my best friend Virginia Graham filling in time because no one had booked her for that dance.

'The most *terrible* thing has happened – D. tried to kiss me.'

My parents

'He *didn't*.'

'Yes, isn't it ghastly.' We were both shaken.

Going home in the taxi after the party I sat on the tip-up seat facing my parents.

'I've got something awful to tell you. D. tried to kiss me.'

My pa said something like, 'Oh – well – never mind', and my mother, pleased, I expect, that her child had done so well at her coming-out party, didn't say much. In all seriousness I said:

'Do you think I should ever speak to him again?'

My pa thumped me gently and said:
'Oh, I think I should.'
So I did.

At home self-discipline was the rule. We were always given reasons for decisions that irked us, and they usually turned out to be wise and reasonable, so we accepted them. All this was done by my father, for my mother left the disciplining to him. It was in spite of his efforts to prevent it that I was spoilt; so was Tommy. My mother indulged us and sabotaged the formal rules when he wasn't there to see they were carried out; but even she, anxious only for my happiness, would appeal to my better nature, and sometimes this worked. There was a hard core, a framework of discipline that showed us where we stood and I am grateful for it. Gently, with patience, my father raised my standards in all things, from drawing and appreciation of things visible to behaviour. Example is the only really reliable teacher, and he put into practice what he believed in, and because I trusted him and his taste in almost everything (except electric light fittings for walls), I gradually learned that what he stood for measured up to my own ideas as they developed. Indoctrination? Possibly, but based on provable rules. It was his honest reasonableness to which I responded, as most children do to anyone in authority who treats them with respect for their individuality and who they know loves them.

When I went to school in France I was rubbed up the wrong way by the venal grasping behaviour of the natives. 'They actually *ask* you for tips,' I wrote from St Germain-en-Laye, 'just to show you to your seat in the theatre.' I was seventeen and could have signed my letter 'Disgusted'. My pa, who loved France, wrote back suggesting that this wasn't the whole story and it might be wiser if I could try and be like the Psalmist who kept his cattle on a thousand hills – 'That way,' he said, 'nobody can get your goat.'

We started going to concerts together when I was about ten. This was my introduction to Bach and it opened a door for me, just as six years later at the Old Vic Edith Evans playing Rosalind woke me up to the instant power of poetry. Before this Shakespeare was a lesson to be endured, now it became an excitement, an immediate experience. I remember going home from the performance on top of a tram in pouring rain. The lines glistened, and the whole universe was translated into ideas. Sixteen is late for this sort of awakening, but I was a late developer in a lot of ways.

My Father

In the school holidays, and summers were always hot and sunny in those days (blessed memory), my father and I went in August and September to Promenade Concerts at the Queen's Hall and stood to hear the three great Bs, and I discovered Mozart and Handel and Haydn. The impact of Elgar's *Enigma Variations* still reverberates when I hear it now. I don't know how one is supposed to listen to music, although I know I now hear in a different way because I am more knowledgeable through experience, and more perceptive; but then I dreamed dreams and imagined in a Walter Mitty manner and it was not the romantic composers who sent me, it was Bach and Mozart. I have always respected and sometimes been stirred by Beethoven and yet I do not find I love him. It was a reflection of my own feelings that made me put into the mouth of a top-price ticket-holder in a sketch I wrote called 'Artists' Room' in which four different members of the audience go backstage to see the pianist after a recital: 'Beethoven does go on, doesn't he, bless his heart. *Just* when you think he's finished the *entire* thing starts again.'

I do not feel this about the late quartets. It seems to me they are space-age works, difficult but worth the struggle.

My father taught me to look at things with more understanding than I had realised I had. He was strong on form and proportion in all things (not only material but spiritual as well). We explored museums and art galleries. We looked at buildings and objects and he made me see why an object that perfectly does the job it is designed to do has its own beauty – a key, a bridge, a wooden spoon, a pylon, a tea-pot. Some Christmases ago I was given a cooking spoon carved out of bamboo and whenever I use it I think how my father would have delighted in its balance and the satisfying texture of its beautifully handled material.

I was a London-based child. In the First World War we lived in Burton Court, Chelsea, and then we moved across the square to St Leonard's Terrace, and were able to use the same shops and buses. On Saturday afternoons my pa and I went out together to look or listen. Sometimes we climbed to the open top of a number 11 bus and rode down to the City. I learned to recognise Grinling Gibbons carving and developed a feeling for Christopher Wren. My father knew lanes and alleys off the main highways and we wandered, often the only people in the week-end empty streets, looking for special treasures, a moulding round a door, a fine fanlight or the lettering on a tomb that he had earmarked for me to see. He particularly loved St Paul's Cathedral and we would go and stand together under the great dome. He pointed out the harmonious disposition of the tall windows that he found so successful, and I felt the power of balanced symmetry that makes St Paul's so satisfying. In the Second World War he was one of the architects detailed to fire-watch there. He enjoyed exploring the building, climbing up inner stairways to the leads, standing in the dark with London all round him and the skies raked by searchlights.

One summer evening I went with him when he was going to take over the watch from the other architects. It was beginning to get dark when we got there and the only point of light in the cathedral came from a small shaded lantern set on the floor in the exact centre under the dome. The earlier shift was in a room at the back and we were alone in the vast auditorium. We found ourselves walking in on tiptoe out of a sense of awe. It was a dramatic sight, the dark cave of the building yawning about us, and the tiny lamp throwing out low pale stripes of light across the floor. I prayed that the Germans wouldn't hit St Paul's.

Sometimes our Saturday expeditions took the form of a puzzle, a test for my powers of observation.

'Where, on the 19 and 22 bus-route between Sloane Street and Piccadilly Circus, can you find a globe with a crack in it?'

'How high must I look?'

'About as high as your head.'

'Which side of the street?'

'Left – going towards Piccadilly Circus.'

I found it, with the help of hints, 'you're getting warmer – *much* warmer'– it was near the Park Lane Hotel where it proved to be the coat of arms of a house, now destroyed, and appeared on each black iron knob of the area railings.

We went to the National Gallery and the Tate and the Wallace Collection not once but often, just to make sure old favourites were where we had left them. I didn't, then, share his taste for Blake and Turner because I was a slow awakener to ideas and stayed earth-bound for a long time, confident only in facts. The pictures that pleased me as a child all told a story. The Pre-Raphaelites satisfied my passion for faithful detail, although I didn't much like the faces they painted, except for poor Ophelia, lying among the floating flowers; and the apricot-haired girl in 'April Love'. I always went to look at Ophelia. I didn't much like sad pictures, but when I learned that Millais's model had died because she lay too long in the rapidly cooling waters of the tank she posed in, it did add to my interest. 'The Death of Chatterton' was disturbing and I never stayed long to look at his waxen face, only admiring the colour of his trousers so faithfully painted. But I was not morbid and never thought of or wrote poems about death.

Perhaps all small children begin by seeing only primary colours. I remember to the minute when I realised that colours came in variety and were not only plain reds and blues and yellows. My pa and I had gone to Hampton Court in the spring, and for the first time that year I was allowed out of doors without wearing my gaiters. Oh! the liberty of not having to do up all those fiddly buttons and the freedom from being chafed where the gaiters failed to rise high enough to meet my knickers! Fresh air behind the knees was exhilarating and I was young enough to need to run to express my pleasure. The daisies hadn't yet been mown down and the lawns were deep and green – I fetched up beside my father who was looking at the long wall behind the herbaceous border in the palace garden.

'Look at the colour in those bricks.'

'It's red,' I said, seeing it that way.

'Have another look,' said my father, pushing his hat further back on his head.

As I looked again the solid red dissolved and now the bricks were many different colours; some were almost blue, or grey, or mauve, or pink or sandy-yellow. Only a few were brick-red. Revelation! The colours came out at me, subtle in their differences, exciting in their unfamiliarity. From that moment I saw more than primary colours. The discovery was that the colours had been there to be found all the time.

My father was never the life and soul of the party, but he was a quietly funny man with his own very individual delivery and understated wit. He was amused by his own jokes, and I don't see why this is supposed to be a bad thing, unless one overdoes the laughter; for unless you have been amused first there is no incentive to share what has amused you. He didn't laugh all through his telling, but you knew he was enjoying it, and so did his audience. It wasn't that he told many funny stories, it was his general attitude and comment on what he was amused by. As a teller of anecdotes he was concise; he didn't indulge himself in the telling and never attempted imitations. The full measure of a good joke only comes with showing it to someone else who is likely to find it funny too. He and I shared a taste for puns, good and terrible. He held that to be good a pun *should* be pretty terrible. One day, riding on a bus up Sloane Street, he invented a riddle that so pleased him that he was in danger of falling off the platform when the idea struck him.

Q. How do we know that all female fish are constantly uncomfortable?

A. Because of the well-known saying: 'No rose (roes) without a thorn.'

This has all the splendour of a really terrible pun.

My father met his match in punning when he worked for Sir Edwin Lutyens. I always hope the report of Sir Edwin's exchange with the waiter is true. Not that it matters, for it is completely satisfactory, true or untrue.

Sir Edwin – 'Waiter, what *is* this?'

Waiter – 'It's a piece of cod, sir.'

Sir Edwin – 'It must be the piece of cod that passeth all understanding.'

It was always fun telling things to my father. I now realise the luxury of having had a sympathetic and interested ear to pour into. The certainty of knowing you will be heard out with attention is one of the contributing factors to a sense of well-being. I doubt whether this happens as completely in any other relationship as it can between parent and child. My pa never demanded or expected confidences, I gave them freely; but I have never been one to tell all to anyone, because my antennae tell me that those whom one truly loves should be spared burdens. So my confidences were not troubled ones. I was a happy child, anyway, and usually managed by myself to resolve the small miseries that came my way. My pa was proud of Tommy and me, but the most he ever said was, 'Well done.' It conveyed total support and pleasure. I always responded to his reasonableness and lack of excess.

(An echo of his 'Well done' touched me years later in the war when I was in India. I was on a long tour of the Middle East, Iran, Iraq and India, playing in hospital wards. At the end of a day of concerts, a patient in an open-air ward with a thatched roof called out to me as I was crossing the hospital square. The voice was North Country – 'Come 'ere.' I was on my way back to the quarters where I was staying and it had been a long and tiring day. I called back from a hundred yards distance that I'd be in his ward the next day and I'd see him then. 'COME 'ERE,' he commanded louder, so wearily I went over to his hut. He was one of the older soldiers, thick-set and unexcitable. He looked at me closely with no expression on his face. Then with a slow smile he said: 'You'll do.')

I wish I had kept the wise and useful letters my father wrote to me when I was growing up. All I've got left are a few scattered notes. He didn't care much for the telephone and was always conscious of the time-pips, so he wrote little notes. Here is one written to me at boarding school in 1926.

A good conversation tonight. A very nice, very young taxi-driver thought I'd hailed him, so I said, 'Well, I hadn't thought of taking you, but perhaps I'd better.' 'Oh no – don't.' Me: 'I suppose you *were* sent to me from heaven?' Taxi-driver: 'I often feel like that. I did tonight in fact.' Then we said good night. He had a most beautiful taxi.

In quite a different way he communicated with people as easily as did my mother. Without self-consciousness or arrogance she expected to be welcome and acted on this assumption. He never expected to cross thresholds as she did; it was enough for him to hail his fellow-men in passing. They both met with instant rapport in their encounters. One June day he rode on a bus with a cheerful conductor who sang out in an exaggerated la-di-da manner:
'Hayde – Park-er – Corn-ah.'
He paused for effect and then said to my father, as if he were the only one in the world who would understand:
'I always talk like that in Ascot Week. Gives a flavour of the Royal Enclosure.'

After he and my mother parted and the house in St Leonard's Terrace was sold, my father took a gloomy furnished flat off Sloane Square until his new house in Royal Avenue was ready for him. This was a bad period for him and he kept very quiet, not wishing to meet friends who might not yet know about the break-up. I think he wanted to stay out of sight to recover his equilibrium. He was good at disguising un-happiness. His natural confidence was firmly rooted, and all through this sad time he managed to maintain an outward serenity. Even in his heaviest-hearted moments there was something inwardly buoyant about him.

The gloomy hall-porter at the gloomy block of flats must have sensed this and one day he burst out of his depression as if in gratitude and said to my pa: 'You know you always put me in mind of Mendels-sohn's *Spring Song*.'

He was proof of the quotation that may be by Bishop Brent (but I have never been able to verify it): 'Joy does not happen; it is the inevitable result of certain rules followed and laws obeyed.'

My father knew that joy has little to do with happiness.

CHAPTER THREE

Lucy

I GREW up in the days when middle-income families had nannies to look after their children. If the relationship between nanny and child is good it is one of perfect understanding; I had it with my nanny. Her name was Lucy Sampson and she took me 'from the month'; that is from the day the maternity nurse left. We liked each other from the start and this never changed; I remained her first baby till the last. In those days mothers with nannies saw their children only at prescribed times, usually after breakfast and after tea, but my mother was in and out of the nursery at any hour, for she and Lucy were in their early twenties and babies were their interest. Although I loved mv mother at that time, it was in a more remote way than I loved my nanny. Lucy was the ever-fixed star and I was never shaken in my reliance on her.

She was one of four sisters, Edie, Aggie, Amy and Lucy. Their brother, Charlie, had emigrated to America by the time I'd heard of him. Mrs Sampson died when they were young and they were brought up by their father, Jesse, and a widowed aunt called Mrs Povey. I don't know what Mr Sampson did to earn a living but his spare time was spent as a nonconformist lay-preacher, and one cold spring day Lucy took my brother Tommy and me to hear him speak in Hyde Park. It was not at Marble Arch where the speakers shouted and were frightening; it was by a drinking fountain near the east end of the Serpentine in the inner Rotten Row. Mr Sampson didn't shout, nor was he frightening. He praised the Lord in a raised voice to one boy leaning on a bicycle and to Lucy, Tommy and me, thirty feet away. He stood there in a black suit, wearing a beard and gold-rimmed glasses, and holding a big black Bible against his chest. The spring wind wafted his words away from us. I remember a faint sense of embarrassment at knowing him and was glad when it was over and we could say how do you do and good-bye. (For the extrovert I became there was a lot of self-consciousness to be worked through.)

Lucy with me in Canada aged three

By the time I was ten years old I'd grown taller than Lucy. I never thought about her looks, but now I realise she was small, with a rather nondescript face and very bright small blue eyes that she blinked when she was thinking deeply. She had the kind of dark, fine wiry hair that flies in dry weather and goes kinky when it is damp. It was never under control and hairpins fell out of the loose bun she wore at the back of her head. Her legs were short and her feet were set at ten to two. She usually wore what I thought were called 'lace' shoes. I wondered what was lacy about leather but accepted it and never thought to ask. Her hands were so familiar to me that I can still see them with their turned-back finger-tips and curly thumbs. They were small but useful. It irked her that she couldn't stretch them to play an octave on the piano.

To be washed and bathed by a professional is to know precision and style. On Lucy's nights out my mother's gentler handling of the flannel seemed tentative. She didn't use enough soap, and where Lucy rubbed firmly my mother stroked. We complained: 'Oh mum*mee* – do it harder. Do it properly.' Nor did she brush our hair with enough confidence. We were used to short, crisp strokes and elbow-grease.

When she began to be a nanny Lucy wore the nanny's uniform of grey coat and skirt and black hat, but I see her best in a maroon 'costume' tailored for her by her brother-in-law, Mr Harper. It had a three-quarter-length jacket and her wide-brimmed black straw hat was not in the least a nanny hat. It verged on the romantic. She had a silver brooch in the shape of clasped hands, and why these hands were called 'Mizpah' was as much a mystery to me as her 'lace' shoes.

My solo reign in the nursery lasted nearly four years. I had crossed the Atlantic six times by then, and Lucy and her sister Aggie, who became my mother's maid, came too. For a while we lived in Vancouver where the cook was Chinese. Lucy and Aggie had never known a man-cook before, and a Chinese man-cook was a decided novelty. Lucy didn't dislike foreigners but she felt a '*little* funny' about them. She came to like Wing; he made the food look so pretty. Then one day she went into the kitchen while he was preparing for a dinner-party and she discovered he was mixing the soup in what used to be called a domestic article. It was not Wing's fault that he wasn't English but this was going too far. The delicate situation was resolved by my mother, who had to explain a lot of things to the cook. He'd thought the pot was simply a very big cup. Soup came off the menu that night. I dimly remember this episode and used to ask Lucy to tell me about it again. 'Well, dear,' she would finish, 'it wasn't very nice; but another time

Myself about a year old   *In a straw hat in America*

Wing made you a beautiful birthday cake like a pagoda and iced it all over, so he was a nice man really.'

Vancouver was the scene of my only recorded yearning for adventure. I have never gone out looking for adventure, although I can usually cope with it if it comes my way (and I quite like looking back at adventures accomplished). Lucy and I went daily to the beach in Vancouver where she dragged my pushchair on to the soft sand and sat in its shade while I played among the little waves on the edge of the ocean. The skirts of my cotton frock and petticoats were pushed inside my white frilled drawers and I was forbidden to get the frills wet. Someone had told me that my grandmother lived across the sea and I pointed at the huge expanse of water lying between Canada and Russia and asked if she was in that direction. 'That's right, ducky,' said Lucy, whose geographic sense was hazy. 'Yes, Granny is over there.' It occurred to me that there was no need to wait for a boat to take me to see her, I could walk it; so instead of paddling in the little waves I set off into the deep. I was hauled back, wet to the waist, misunderstood and furious. 'I was only going to see Granny,' I sobbed. Lucy was afraid I might try walking west again, so she invented a method that would show whether I had kept my promise *never* to go into the sea above my knees. She drew a line round my legs with an indelible pencil that turned purple if it got wet. Of course the temptation to see the purple appear

49

was as bad as the urge to walk to England. So Lucy put on her thinking cap again, blinked, and came up with another idea. She got a ball of string and tied one end to my ankle. She continued to sit at the top of the beach holding the other end of the string and if I looked like going further into the sea than she wanted me to she jerked the string and I had to hop out backwards. I gave up walking to England.

I think she was ahead of her time in allowing me to eat cheese and salad for tea. These foods were supposed to be unsuitable for children, and other nannies raised their eyebrows when they came to tea and found lettuce, spring onions, watercress, celery and tomatoes on the table. I had to 'start plain', as she called it, with a slice of bread and butter, but then I could choose cheese if I wanted it instead of jam; the other children looked at me with envy while their nannies made 'tst-tst' noises.

Every night when she was giving me my bath we sang hymns together. Often they were by Moody and Sankey, and I equate the delicious taste of sucking warm sponge with 'Jesus bids me shine'. Lucy had a sweet, swooping soprano voice with a quiver in it. 'Count your blessings, name them one by one', she sang, and I learned to join in and enjoyed emphasising the last line, 'And it *will* surprise you what the Lord has done!'

I was always vulnerable to sadness. My mother sang 'Macushla' and I sat under the piano and wept. Certain hymns had the same effect. There was a sense of impending unhappiness about 'Now the day is over' and 'For those in peril on the sea'. A small door opened into a world beyond my own secure scene and I didn't want to look at it.

The presence of God, as Love, was something I liked and accepted as natural, but Jesus and angels made me uneasy because Lucy said there they were all around me; and I couldn't see them. When I was very small we sang 'Jesus, tender Shepherd, hear me'. Lucy sang a line and I had to repeat it.

'Bless Thy little lamb tonight' – 'Come on, ducky.'

'Bless my little lamb tonight.'

'No dear, bless *Thy* little lamb tonight.'

'I haven't got a little lamb.'

'Sh-sh. Bless Thy little lamb tonight. Through the darkness be Thou nee-ar me.'

'No.'

'Yes, Joyce. Be good. Through the darkness be Thou nee-ar me. Keep me safe till morning light.'

Myself about four   *Brother and sister*

Why had she mentioned darkness? I hadn't thought of it till then. Darkness at that stage was a good deal more powerful than morning light. But as long as I knew Lucy was next door in the day-nursery while I was getting off to sleep, all was well.

I suppose I was over-cherished. We were taught to be independent in a lot of ways, but until I was eight years old I had never stayed away by myself. When an invitation came from my friend Jennifer (not her real name) I begged to be allowed to go. She lived in a suburb, then a partly rural area with fields and woods. I got there in the afternoon and it was new and exciting. There was a field full of daisies and we made daisy chains and were allowed to go out again after tea; a treat for me because I lived in a flat and there was nowhere to go once we'd come in from Chelsea Gardens.

It had been broad daylight when I was shown the room I was to sleep in and I hadn't taken in that it was some way from Jennifer's room and the nursery. Now, at bedtime, I saw it was along one passage, down some steps, round a corner, at the far end of another passage and *miles* away from human contact; miles away from home. Jennifer's nanny watched me have a bath, saw that I cleaned my teeth, heard my mumbled prayers, and gave me a bristly kiss. 'Good night, dear,' she said from the door, and turned off the light. I lay there rigid with listening. There were plenty of noises to listen to, rattling window, creaking boards, an owl, a distant train. I pined for a light but I didn't dare move, it was too dark, and the light-switch was too far away. I was as homesick as I have ever been. It was a craving for the familiar, an ache for home and those I knew. I didn't sleep for what seemed like hours.

But the next day was sunny and warm and I forgot about the night before. We played in the field again and spent a lot of time jumping on and off a stile. After lunch we were made to sit quiet in the drawing-room while we digested. Jennifer's mother read to us from a book of fairy tales. I never liked fairy tales. They made me feel spooky and, while I didn't believe in them, they disturbed my calm. I liked down-to-earth stories about little girls I could identify with, like *Anne of Green Gables* and Jo in *Little Women*. Suddenly I remembered the night before. The evening started to come towards me, nearer and nearer, and beyond the dusk that far-away room was waiting for me. I knew I could not stay there another night. Jennifer's mother, a dull woman, read on about someone called Curdy but I'd stopped listening. 'Please,' I said, 'I'd like to telephone my mother.' Mrs Johnson put down the book with some surprise, I imagine. In those days people didn't use the telephone lightly. There was one in the drawing-room, on the writing table. Mrs Johnson got through to my number and handed the telephone to me.

'Mummy?'

'Hello, darling! Are you having a lovely time?'

'I want to come home.'

'Are you alone in the room?'

'No, Jennifer and her mummy are here. I want to come home today.'

'Oh darling – it's so *rude*.'

'I *must* come home. Now.'

My father came and fetched me after his day at the office. I imagine he tried to apologise for me. My hosts cannot have been flattered by my behaviour. I was never invited again. Thank heaven.

Anyone who has been badly homesick will remember that manners, appreciation and consideration do not count one jot while one is suffering.

After Tommy was born we came back to live in England and Lucy left us. She had been ill and needed a change, so Mary Edwards came to us and stayed through the First World War until 1919. She thought as much of Tommy as Lucy had thought of me, and he was king of the nursery all the time Mary was with us. She was very tall and capable and Tommy doted on her. She was always kind to me, but Tommy was *her* baby and I was not to be compared to a paragon called Romola whom Mary had been nanny to before she came to us. My nose was out of joint.

But Lucy came back. It was Mary Edwards's turn for a change and she took on temporary work. By this time we were too old for a nanny, so Lucy turned into a nursery-governess. This was when she took off her nursery grey and went into the maroon costume. She took us to and from our day-schools, supervised our homework and saw that we did our practice on the piano. Once a week we went by bus to Oxford Street and walked through to the Wigmore Hall Piano Galleries where Mrs Dora Milner taught us to play. Lucy sat in the room with us, listening to every word, watching every note. Back in the nursery again she began to teach herself on our upright piano, using our music to learn from, and at one moment all three of us were working on a stirring piece called 'The Jolly Farmer' by Adam Carse. It was Lucy who pedalled first. But she couldn't stretch an octave; not that Adam Carse had put any in his 'Easy Pieces'. She tried hard to make her small hand span the distance between C and C but could only manage C and B flat.

It was decided that Lucy would stay with us until Tommy went away to his prep school and I had had my first monthly period. I didn't even know there was going to be such a thing, although there had been woolly little talks about regular times for purifying of the blood stream and how wonderfully we are made and there was no need to worry about it: and I didn't. Tommy went to school and I was surprised by my first monthly, and then Lucy left. I'd been prepared for the parting and I knew it must happen soon, but when the day came it was a misery. I went to school in the morning and when I came home at tea-time she had gone. It was meant to make it easier for me; no good-byes. I felt a desolation that was hard to bear. The day that Lucy left me and the night I learned my mother had left my father were times of wilderness.

I got used to being without Lucy and I grew up. But as long as she lived we kept in close touch and I cherish her memory.

I saw her quite often because she went as nanny to friends of mine. When I meet people who had Lucy as their nanny we share Lucy stories and remarks. She had all the classic nanny sayings and used them on us all:

'Up the stairs to Bed-fordshire.'

'I'm all behind like the cow's tail.'

'Don't care was *made* to care.'

'Sticks and stones will break my bones, but names will never hurt me.'

'I'll give you what Paddy gave the drum.'

'Cheer up, chicken. You'll soon be hatched.'

An Alsatian dog was brought into her nursery and came over to sniff at the baby on her lap. Lucy eyed him cautiously. 'Is he all right? He looks very S.L.Y. to me.'

When I went into the theatre in 1939 Lucy wasn't sure this was a step in the right direction. She liked the idea of my being on the wireless but there was a Calvinistic streak in her attitude to the stage. 'Oh *dear*,' she said when I first told her I was to be in a revue. Followed by, 'Never mind, ducky.' When she heard me broadcast she always wrote to tell me in case I hadn't known I'd done it. Today with tape recordings you can't tell when your programme is going out, but when we did them all 'live' it was difficult not to be aware of doing a broadcast. 'You were on on Tuesday and it was quite nice.' 'I liked your little songs.' 'Little songs' was the umbrella phrase she used for anything I did on stage or on the air. Any talking, singing or monologues all became 'little songs'. I think this was to keep me down to size; she felt a continuing duty to prevent my head being turned. In 1945 I was in a revue of Noël Coward's called *Sigh No More* and Lucy came to a matinée. By today's standards it was blameless as a vicarage garden party, but it had some worldly dialogue that was not what Lucy was accustomed to. I hoped she'd enjoy the dancing and the costumes but wondered how she'd take the sketches. When she came back-stage afterwards she said it had been quite nice: I'd been quite nice. What she hadn't liked were the girls in the Brazilian number who wore rumba dresses with their midriffs bare and their navels showing. 'It was a pity,' Lucy said, 'they showed their little holes. But I liked your little songs.'

Lucy was one of the few wholly 'good' people I have known. She was good naturally; her instinct for good being more useful, as well as more powerful, seemed to happen without effort. She saw the good in people first; unless they were unkind their faults were less important, and she knew there would be forgiveness in Heaven. Heaven for her was a real place. She never described it but she said she'd recognise it when she got there. The Lord Jesus was her constant companion and she expected to find Him in Heaven ready to welcome her when the time came. He would enfold her in His arms as one of His lambs. Lambs were important to her and she continued to send me little holy cards with verses on them printed in a fancy Biblical script. They were almost always about lambs and the shepherd Jesus. When she was dying she said to me: 'Am I going to die?' She didn't want an answer. Her eyes were as unclouded and trusting as they had always been. 'The Lord Jesus is there waiting for me.'

Some of us who loved her arranged the service at Golders Green and we chose hymns we had learned and sung with her when we were little, and I added 'Lead me, Lord'. The resident quartet sang it very slowly indeed, making the most of the harmonies. She would have enjoyed it.

My grandmother by John S. Sargent

CHAPTER FOUR

My Grandmother

THE most important, lasting influences in my life (sometimes influences of warning) came from my parents and Lucy; very much part of my childhood background was the small, somewhat forbidding figure of my father's mother, my Granny, Jessie Phipps.

The Sargent portrait of her hangs in our living-room in London. It was painted in 1883, three years after the birth of her elder son, my father. She looks from the canvas with calm candour and if you get close you can see that her eyes are of different colours, one green and one brown. She is standing against a black background wearing a white organdie dress under a boned black-and-white striped bodice, tight as a corset. Her short organdie sleeves are tied with black velvet bows above the elbow and there is a black velvet ribbon round her long neck. She has a small neat head, an oval face with regular features, and a very straight back. Her hair is as dark as the background and the only bright colour in the picture is a little cluster of chalk-pink geranium flowers that she holds up in both hands.

If my description of the painting sounds familiar it may be because a reproduction of the picture was once on display all over London as the poster for an exhibition of British portraits at the Royal Academy. I felt a bit guilty about this because I remembered how strongly my grandmother disapproved of 'having one's picture in the paper', and this was even more public. She was to be seen on walls in the Underground, several posters hung along the railings of Burlington House for fully three months, and the picture was also used for the cover of the exhibition catalogue.

She was enchanting to look at even as an old lady and she was obviously remarkably good-looking as a young married woman when her cousin John Sargent painted the portrait. I love the picture but I never got close enough to my grandmother to love her.

She was Jessie Percy Butler Duncan, born in Rhode Island, U.S.A., of Scottish stock in the mid 1850s. She had all the self-discipline and reticence of old New England added to her Dundee inheritance and it made for character but not for warmth: I now realise she was much more of a person than I ever suspected. To me she was always a little forbidding; very dutiful to her grandchildren but keeping them at arm's length, and I never felt I could be myself with her. She commanded special behaviour and this did not encourage spontaneity. At home life was relaxed and Tommy and I were treated as individuals with our own rights, but our grandmother did not encourage us to speak and we were often made to feel in the wrong. I am sure this was not what she meant us to feel, but that is how it came out and, although it was always interesting to me to go almost *anywhere*, visits to Granny were not lit with the hope of enjoyment.

I wish she had talked to us of her childhood in America. Grand-mothers should tell their grandchildren what it was like when they were young. I wonder why I didn't question her. I think I might have been accused of curiosity if I had. I made my mother talk endlessly about her life in Virginia, but Granny was simply a figure in the present with no other background than her tall red-brick house in Culford Gardens, near Sloane Square, and the summer cottage she rented at Chorleywood, then very nearly rural, although Rickmansworth was already beginning to sprawl towards it.

When she married my grandfather Wilton Phipps they came to live in England. Until then she had been with her father in New York, at No 1, Fifth Avenue, and I wonder how easy it was for her to move into the enclosed small and worldly society she found herself in in London. My grandfather was a tea and coffee merchant in the City, and they seem to have led a pretty social life even though they were not rich and didn't entertain on a large scale. Americans were beginning to infiltrate and she was, as a newspaper cutting of 1889 says, 'always the prettiest of the *belles Américaines* in London'.

I found out something of their social life in one of the scrapbooks my grandparents kept between 1889 and 1891. Both wrote in it. He listed shooting parties and the game shot as well as the heights of their four children. She recorded the dinner-parties and some family deaths. Between 12 January and 21 March in 1891 they were invited to thirty-eight dinner-parties, refused fourteen, and went to see Henry Arthur Jones's play *The Dancing Girl* at the Theatre Royal, Haymarket, five times. On 4 April my grandmother went with four friends to the Criterion Theatre to see *The School for Scandal* and wrote that they were 'much amused' at the supper party afterwards given by Charles Wyndham in his room, overlooking Piccadilly Circus, 'furnished like a cabin in a yacht'.

The Wilton Phippses went regularly to 'the play' and there are many theatre programmes stuck in the scrapbook to prove it, and they always had a box. When I knew her my grandmother disapproved of the stage. She had long given up going to 'the play' and was uneasy because my parents had many theatrical friends and I had been stage-struck ever since my first visit to a theatre. (It was a revue at the Hippodrome called *A Box of Tricks*, and I fell in love with the chorus which I thought were all little girls because they did a skipping-rope number and wore ankle-socks.) Granny didn't live long enough to know that two of her grandchildren went on the stage and another flirted with the idea while he was up at Cambridge but decided in the end to go into the church and become a bishop.

Among the grander invitations and family photographs, brown views of Monte Carlo and programmes from Bayreuth, there is a small printed announcement that says in six different kinds of lettering;

Mrs Lichfield
(of Boston U.S.A.)
The New American Lady Whistler
will accept a limited number of engagements,
from private to public, during the season.

Inside, Mrs Lichfield

begs to refer anyone who may wish to patronise her talent to the
Right Reverend
The Bishop of New York.

No comment from Granny or Grandpa, but I think it was he who decided to include Mrs Lichfield in the scrapbook. I have an idea he would have been the more amused at the thought of a lady whistler.

Granny may have remembered Mrs Lichfield when she was so firm with me about my new ability to whistle out as well as in. This was a breakthrough after months of monotonous one-note indrawn whistling. I was seven and heady with the success of it and overdid the performance indoors and out. We were staying at Chorleywood. It was not her way to say, 'Please stop whistling'. Instead she had a little rhyme:

Whistling girls
And crowing hens
Always come
To bad ends.

So boring: such a bad poem too. Hens didn't rhyme with ends. I pointed this out. 'Never mind. What it says is a useful reminder.'

She was right. I have never forgotten it; nor that we are supposed to have a cousin who whistled her husband clean out of the house and never managed to get him back in again.

I don't believe Granny liked children very much and that didn't make for cosiness. She was, as I said, dutiful towards her grandchildren and generous at Christmas and on our birthdays. She was a good present-giver and took the trouble to find out what we really wanted. Now and then, as well as a 'proper' present she gave me a new dress, and my mother who made occasions out of such things sent me round to show Granny how I looked in it. I'd clatter up the stairs at Culford Gardens, two at a time (not for nothing did I have the biggest feet in the form), full of exuberance and pleasure, only to be made to go out of the room and come in again, quietly please. Perhaps she felt it was up to her to teach us rather than love us. She certainly made her mark on me and, witness the whistling girls rhyme, I remember most of her little corrections.

'I say, Granny . . .'

'There is no need to say "I say". I know you are speaking. What did you want to tell me?'

'D'you know what I thought of when I was laying down for my rest?'

'Hens lay. Little girls lie.'

It wasn't worth telling her things. I sensed she wasn't really interested, as my parents were, in what we thought, did, drew, wrote and read. Her task was to see that what we did we did nicely; and quietly.

There were compensations about staying at Chorleywood. Creature comforts like dark yellow butter and thick cream from Lady Ela Russell's Jersey cows. There was sponge cake of the most satisfactory consistency. Unlike the bready stuff that passes for sponge cake today (machine-made, packaged to be stirred up, as seen on TV) it was of a consistency almost impossible to cut because the knife sank down into its light foam-rubbery bulk that dissolved all too soon when you got it into your mouth. After a slice had been wrested from it, the rest of the cake rose back to its original height, at least five inches of it. The outside of Granny's sponge cake was crisp and crumbly but the inside, pale yellow as primroses, was all damp deliciousness, a contradictory blend of chewy weight and melting lightness. We demolished a whole cake at a sitting.

My Grandmother

All the food that Granny's cook, Mrs Creed, produced was special: almost black sticky gingerbread; delicate egg sandwiches, so fresh and dainty that we needed at least four before the edge came off our appetites; chicken croquettes, creamy inside, with tiny spikes of some baked marvel scattered all over the outside – how was that done? I've asked around and no one seems to know. Fools: gooseberry, strawberry, raspberry and blackcurrant, in season, sitting in little Luneville pottery pots with lids; meringues that were just sticky enough not to explode when you bit into them; *crème brulée* and slip-and-go-down – that was my grandmother's name for junket. I learned how to eat a pear without losing the juice. (You cut the top off and spoon out the inside of the pear as you would eat a boiled egg.)

Another compensation was the *Illustrated London News*. There were bound volumes too heavy for me to lift. After tea the 'boy', faceless now but probably a friend at the time, was summoned by a pull-down bell, on the wall beside the fireplace, to fetch one of the huge old volumes and put it on a little mahogany table with two flaps that I was allowed to use when I came down after tea. The books were kept in deep shelves in the dining-room and smelt of damp and dust. I liked the smell. I now own the table.

I suppose there were pictures of current events and occasions. I vaguely remember battleships and Boer War scenes drawn by staff artists; men in pith helmets, and Queen Victoria in her uniform of black crinoline and white-edged bonnet, bun-face and bulk. But what I went for were the advertisements and the fashion pages. Infallible Cures for aches and pains recommended by Professional Men. Iron Jelloids, whatever they were, surely a contradiction in terms; and there were unguents for mastering unruly moustaches and surgical boots to awaken morbid curiosity. Ladies' corsets, long and strong and ending in a point down front, had little to do with the female figure as I knew it. Neither my mother nor Lucy had that sort of shape, and my grandmother, though rigidly corseted around the hips, didn't look so arrowed. I loved the fashion-plates and sat happily poring over every detail of embroidered camisole-top, lace insertion, frill, pleat and the revelation of bustle-cages.

Granny gave me *Reading without Tears* Vol. II when I was staying with her at Chorleywood. It was as sensational as the *News of the World* but with rather more moral tone. Death and disaster overtook most of the children in the short stories. They went to cross the road to pick wild flowers for their mother and great cart-wheels crushed them.

They fell off cliffs and were burnt in fires of their own starting and they tended to say holy things as they breathed their last. Tragedy was commonplace and the Victorian children had their noses rubbed in it from an early age with a terrible sort of glee.

Reading *The Fairchild Family* and Vol. II of *Reading without Tears* didn't toughen my moral fibre. They simply made tragedy cheap. I never dared tell my grandmother what I thought about those books. I had an idea, even then, that life couldn't be as ghastly as all that; anyway not for me.

I didn't much like staying at The Two Gables. I don't think my parents did either. They came and fetched us at the end of our visits and I do have some sepia photographs of my mother in a cotton sunbonnet playing with a bald toothless grinner (me) in the garden, so she must have stayed there now and then. It was a house that needed company. On my own I hated it. There was no electricity and only one bathroom with a high, mahogany-sided bath that you got into by climbing up two linoleum-covered steps. The water was never hot enough, but this didn't worry Granny as she never took a hot bath. Instead a shallow tin hip-bath was put on a white blanket rug in her bedroom and filled with cold water the night before, so it must have been quite parky by the next morning when Granny used it. A housemaid – or could it have been the faceless boy? – carried in the cans of cold water to fill it. Why she didn't take a cold bath in the mahogany tub is not clear. Perhaps it didn't occur to her, brought up as she was in the days before servants were fully considered and treated as people with feelings. According to her lights she was a considerate employer and she saw to it that we behaved to her staff with thoughtfulness and good manners. Unlike some of her contemporaries she never kept her maid up to brush her hair before bed or to undress her after a party. But evidently she didn't think it an imposition to ask for cold water to be carried up to her bedroom. We eyed the hip-bath with interest.

'Granny, how long do you stay in your bath?'

'Long enough to wash properly.'

She used transparent yellow Erasmic soap and it sat in a little shallow dish on the floor. Her flannel, actually made of flannel, lay folded over the side of the bath. The only telephone in the house was in the bathroom and the noise of water running in or out made it impossible to hear what was being said by the caller.

I admired her beautiful nightgowns made of finest nun's veiling with scallop-edged collars and full bishop's sleeves ending in ruffles. On a table by her bed there was a fat silver clock, a limp leather-covered Bible, a plain wooden cross on a stand, and some menthol in a polished wooden holder like a lipstick. I was allowed to rub a litle menthol on my temples and it felt interesting, but we weren't encouraged to loiter in the bedroom and after a good-morning kiss we were told to trot along. As a little girl I was fussy over physical contact and recoiled from the faintest suggestion of human smell. My grandmother smelt deliciously fresh of cologne and she looked, as she undoubtedly was, well washed and cared for. Her cheek was pleasantly cool to kiss. She never allowed water to touch her face. Instead she cleaned it with Daggett and Ramsdell's cold cream bought from a chemist in Sloane Street. She never in her long life had a hole in a tooth.

What I most disliked about staying at Chorleywood were the candles. At dusk lamps came hissing down the grass-matted passage to the small drawing-room as if by magic. Until they were set down the wicks were kept low. The lamps appeared to waft in, for you could not see who was carrying them, but at least, once the wick was turned up, the light was bright and steady. Candles were unstable and faint. I had to go to bed by candlelight and I dreaded it. As I grew older I was given the unwanted privilege of carrying my own candle and allowed to go alone along the sloping passage and up the uneven stairs. It was the unevenness that added to my sense of insecurity. It was only by fixing my eyes firmly on the little blue point in the centre of the flame that I could avoid seeing the way my shadow changed shape as I climbed the stairs and turned the corner at the top. I always ran the last few paces into the sanctuary of the nursery and hot wax fell in drops on the carpet.

If my cousin Ann Phipps (now Holmes) was staying there too things were much better. I always wanted a sister and, although we didn't see a lot of each other, I pretended to myself when we were together that she was my sister. She is two years older than I am and this is a big divide when you are small. I was in awe of her because she was allowed to walk alone to school at Glendower Place. She was a bit squashing to me but I longed to be accepted and came back for more. I expect she was bored with having to play with someone so young, but she endured my company because there was no other. We went blackberrying together on Chorleywood Common, and we walked down to the railway cutting and put pennies on the line to be flattened by the trains. I questioned her about school life. I was still at a very small school in a private house, but Ann wore a purple gymslip and had a school hat. I craved for both. We learned to milk a cow at Lady Ela's farm and I was surprised at how rough udders were and how difficult it was to get the rhythm right so that the milk flowed. The noise of it hitting the pail was encouraging but it took ages to achieve. Ann mastered the knack quite quickly.

Granny owned the orchard on the other side of the road from the house. Even then it was considered to be a dangerous crossing and we were not allowed to make it without supervision. We played in the orchard and it was much better than being in the confines of the garden with its tiny bricked paths and the temptation of popping flowers on the standard fuchsias. This was forbidden, but I sneaked in the odd pop when I could. From the orchard we could see over the hedge to the lawns in front of the Sunshine Home for Blind Babies. It has moved elsewhere now, but then we could stand, solemn and moved, watching the little blind children holding each other's pinafore tails, playing games and squealing as we did. Ann was quickly in tears. She has large eyes and they brimmed over at anything at all sad. She had only to think of orphans and invalids and she cried. We were both weepers, but my tears flowed for less worthy reasons, usually myself, while Ann's took us into other areas. She wept for people's troubles and for 'Those in Peril on the Sea'. This hymn undid her and she had a poor time of it when she grew up and married a sailor because it is a hymn dear to the Navy's heart and she frequently had to cry through it.

We Phipps women are bossy and it took us both a long time to learn how tiresome we were. We are both efficient and can organise. Ann said later, she wished she wasn't – she'd like to be small and helpless and fended for. I haven't minded the capacity to organise, but I wish I could resist the urge to put things right that aren't always my job. Now that I am lazier or more patient and perhaps more sensitive to other people, I can sometimes sit by and let things be fumbled, but I used to feel I *had* to take over.

From my earliest memories of her my grandmother always dressed in black except on very hot summer days in the country when she went into cotton prints patterned in black and white or grey and white. She also wore a high, boned, flesh-coloured net collar with everything. I once saw her in her petticoat with its hand-worked camisole-top and I thought how much prettier she looked in it than in her black widow's clothes. Many of her dresses were made by Madame Marthe, one of the dressmakers of whom it was said: 'She cuts so beautifully.' Maybe she did, but not when she made my white velvet wedding dress. I argued about having to have it made by her, but the chorus of my mother, Granny and Aunt Margaret said that Marthe cuts *so* beautifully, and I

Ann and John Holmes

was defeated. The mistake may have been my determination to design the dress myself. I had strong ideas, often wrong, but after all it was my wedding and I knew what I wanted: a plain, square-necked dress with long sleeves and a full skirt ending in a long train. What I got was roughly this but complicated by much cross-cutting and clever draping, sleeves too tight under the arms even after I complained, and a square neck that didn't sit flat. Madame Marthe made a meal of the dress and I stood patiently for fittings, full of hope that she must know what she was doing. She pulled and pruned, made little French noises and said it was *ravissante*, but then she didn't have to wear it. It must be admitted that I probably wasn't the right shape for cross-cutting, but it was up to Madame Marthe to spot this and contrive. In the photographs, taken in a gale as we left St Margaret's, Westminster, on 12 December 1929, the general effect wasn't too bad, but when I came to try and have it converted into a dress to wear to dinner-parties, the velvet was found to be the kind that marked if you breathed near it and it wouldn't take dye. I kept it in a big cardboard box where it slowly turned yellow and then I hardened my heart and threw it out.

Granny's clothes suited her and seemed to fit very well, so no wonder she stuck to Madame Marthe. She was very trim and neat and lived by certain rules, one of which had to do with gloves. Hers were fine black kid, as delicate as her small, hand-made black-buttoned boots. 'English women,' she told us, 'carry their gloves in the street. American women put their gloves on at the front door. Frenchwomen do not go out of the house until their gloves are on and buttoned.' Nor did my grandmother.

Sunday luncheons at Granny's were good family occasions. Her elder daughter, Margaret, and her husband Edmund Phipps (no relation in spite of the same name) were usually there with their three children, Ann, John, who is my exact contemporary, and Nicholas, who is Tommy's. Aunt Margaret was my favourite relation. I found her approachable, fair, affectionate, reliable and steady. She was large and deep-bosomed; she had a splendid laugh and I knew I could tell her anything and she would take it calmly, whatever it was, and go on loving me. She became Chelsea's first woman Mayor and it was a popular election in the borough. Uncle Edmund, at the Board of Education, was knighted and my cousin Simon Phipps, who was then seven, wrote a family history and this is what he said about Aunt Margaret: 'My Aunt is Lady Phipps. I am not proud – I'm just telling you.'

His observations about our grandmother as an old lady were accurate. Every morning she went straight to the window to read what the thermometer on the wall outside had to say of the temperature. After this she looked through her letters before she picked up *The Times* to read the Deaths, then on the front page. She was pleased when she found she had outlived yet another contemporary and said so. *Then* she ate her egg.

Granny's younger children, Bill and Rachel, were not often at the Sunday luncheons because Bill was in the Navy and he and Aunt Pamela lived wherever he was based, and Aunt Rachel, who was married to Miles Lampson (later Lord Killearn), lived with him in China where he was British Minister in Peking before we had an Embassy there.

I enjoyed those family luncheon parties, not only for the food but for the social life. There was a good deal of gentle teasing of Granny by her own children and this was exhilarating. My father's relationship with his mother was dutiful but not affectionate, I think. He held her in esteem, a chilly place but better than nowhere, and he was proud of her achievements even if he didn't think much of her narrow range of interests. These did not include drains nor, as a topic for the table, the Almighty. 'It isn't suitable,' she said. 'On the contrary,' said my pa, waving the carving knife about, 'drains and God are vital subjects and I can't think of anything more civilised than a discussion in praise of both while we eat this delicious roast beef.'

We joined in the discussions but were soon put down with, 'That's enough, children' from Granny, and as soon as the luncheon was over we all moved into the small library next door to the dining-room. Here Aunt Margaret poured out coffee for the grown-ups and we held out our hands for a spoonful of rocky coffee-sugar, the kind with bits of string going through the crystals; then we were dismissed to the basement to visit Mrs Creed and the rest of the household who were waiting to receive us in the servants' hall.

Here we came into our own. We felt welcome and wanted, our least funny jokes were laughed at, and Mrs Creed, Griffin and Mac had to be our audience whether they wanted to or not. For we went down there to entertain them. We sang songs, asked riddles and did conjuring tricks. We played charades and generally showed off. The household at No 3 certainly appeared to like children and Mrs Creed made encouraging little 'tst-tst' noises to show she was amused. Mr Parker, the butler, never joined us in the 'hall', and the boy and the scullery-maid didn't appear, so the audience of three was outnumbered by the cast. There they sat, Mrs Creed, cook and queen of the staff, Miss Griffin, Granny's lady's maid, and Mac, Miss Macdonald, the housemaid. 'Mrs' Creed (a courtesy title given to all cooks and housekeepers at that time) was little and dark with a moustache and a mole on her chin. She wore a ribbon round her neck like Granny in the Sargent picture and we liked her for laughing easily and feeding us so well. Miss Griffin, sadder, taller and thinner, was always in black and had a jet brooch. She remained on the edge of being shocked and covered her mouth when she laughed. After she retired she went mad, poor woman, and burned all her savings (which she unwisely kept in treasury notes), because she had the delusion she had stolen the money. Mac was plump and rosy and had plump pink morning dresses under her large apron and her caps slid to one side on her grey hair, but she didn't wear a cap on Sundays. Of the three only Mac, I think, was capable of saying what she really felt and thought. She alone had the spirit to contradict us. The other two certainly appeared to accept their imposed station in life without question. ('He made them high or lowly and ordered their estate.' I am relieved to know that even then I knew that verse was a whacking lie, and when we had the hymn at the church on Chorleywood Common, where we gloomily went with our grandmother, I didn't sing those lines.) I am sure Mac knew there was more to life than being a housemaid at No 3 Culford Gardens. There was a pub on the corner of the King's Road nearby where she nipped in from time to time. I'm sure too that Granny never knew this; Mrs Creed was not the one to gossip and Miss Griffin would not have dared tell. I know Mac went to the pub because I sometimes saw her coming out of it and once she saw me and waved in a carefree way. I never told a soul but later it was murmured that Mac was fond of gin. She lasted the course though, and didn't retire till Granny's death.

I should like to know the influences that caused my grandmother to go into local politics, but there is no one alive to tell me and she kept no diaries. I know she was interested in education, and her friend Maude Lawrence must have had something to do with this. Miss Lawrence was deep in educational reforms and enthusiastic. We used to see her at Culford Gardens and she was a contrast to our feminine grandmama. She dressed in severe coats and skirts, a man's hard collar and tie, and she had her grey hair cut short. She also spoke loudly and wasn't to my taste. Anyway Granny rose to be a member of the London County Council and chaired a committee and was made a Dame for it.

A Jewish peer, whose wife had been her friend, loved her in a respectable way and would have married her when they were both widowed, but she remained on her own at Culford Gardens entertaining a few old men friends and I *think* I once met Henry James there. Whoever it was talked in long convoluted sentences and took a long time to say something suitable to a small girl, and I remember wondering when it would finish. Yes – it must have been Henry James. She had many elderly callers and as they all grew older together there was a certain amount of pleasant nodding off after dinner, and my father once found his mama and two gentleman callers so fast asleep that he didn't like to waken any of them and crept away. Usually the parties broke up about ten o'clock and Parker, the butler, saw the gentlemen off the premises and put the chain on the door, and my grandmother went up to her bedroom and cleaned her face with Daggett and Ramsdell's cold cream.

It is strange today to realise that one only moderately well-off old lady lived alone in a seven-bedroomed London house and had six indoor staff and a chauffeur to look after her. At Chorleywood there was another housemaid and a gardener. Nine in all.

Granny must have been considered a good employer because her servants stayed with her for years. But why Mr Parker didn't complain about the place he was given to sleep in is hard to understand. He had a folding bed that he pulled out every night in a windowless area under the stairs in the basement. He was a defeated sort of man all the time I knew him, but he cracked little jokes and was reputed to play the flageolet. His favourite opera, he told us, was *Cavalry Rusty-can-opener*. I didn't get the point until I asked my father to explain. There was nothing of Jeeves about Mr Parker. He wore a celluloid dickey and a food-stained waistcoat and had a brother who was a signalman on the railway at Rickmansworth. On his days off in the summer, when the household moved to Chorleywood, he put on a straw boater and walked across the common to visit the signal-box and take tea.

You can argue about progress and whether it is a blessing, and I'm not sure of the full answer, but I do know that the lot of those in domestic jobs is infinitely better now than when I was young. My mother was appreciated for her genuine friendship and concern for those who worked for her; and she was rewarded by long and affectionate service. Even so, it was a time when a domestic was expected to remember her place and it was unthinkable that a maid should sit down in the presence of her employer unless she had been invited to do so. None of our staff ever called my mother Mrs Phipps; she was either 'Madam' or when the relationship was close, as with my nanny, Lucy, and with Doris Leslie, our very dear house-parlourmaid, it was 'Mm'; 'Good morning, Mm.' My father was always politically well left-of-centre. Remembering his very real concern for people, I was surprised and shaken about thirty years later when I went to look at the staff flat he designed for us to add to our first married house. Like my parents' house, it was in St Leonard's Terrace. Theirs was No 28, ours 21. At the time, 1930, he thought, we thought and so did our two maids, that the addition was the last word in comfort and privacy and gave the maids a new measure of independence because it was self-contained. There were two little bedrooms with h. and c., a bathroom, and a sky-lit sitting-room leading from the kitchen at garden level, so that they could come and go without having to pass through the main part of the house. It was their own separate flat and they were very pleased with it. After the war we let the house on a long lease and the tenants wrote to ask for permission to demolish the staff flat. We were astonished and asked why they wanted to do such an unreasonable thing. Perhaps we would like to come and look at it. When we saw it with our present-day eyes we could hardly believe what we saw. The rooms were really small and poky and the bathroom damp and windowless, with no heating of any kind. It would have been useless to have a television set in the sky-lit sitting-room because it was not possible to get back far enough to see it in focus! We graciously gave our permission for the pulling down of the staff flat.

I've been thinking about the word *service*. It is a good word, like peace and discipline, but it has become debased into meaning subservience, and that is a bad word. Service is a free thing; it has to be given, even when it is paid for, and I will be brave and say I am for it. And for discipline, when it is self-discipline (the only useful kind), and for peace. I can imagine being happy as a very choosey domestic servant in today's world. The hours and pay are now reasonable; the work can be done at one's own good speed and, because there isn't much competition, the choice of employer and environment can be made by the worker. There *are* good employers, who are considerate, kind and generous, and to work for people involved in occupations that leave them no time to do chores could be satisfying. I would not want to be treated as one of the family. I'd demand my privacy, but to share in a family's interests is not a bad thing, and I think I would be loyal, trustworthy, clean in person and work; a good plain cook and a pleasing arranger of flowers; and I'd recommend myself for everything except the cleaning of baths and the ironing.

CHAPTER FIVE

Time of Little Friends

THERE is not much give and take about nursery relationships. Friendship doesn't begin until there is at least a measure of give and take, and in the nursery it is almost always all take. Or so it was with me. Hero-worship is another thing and starts at any time, at any age. Early on I discovered that it is more interesting to pursue than be pursued; it is also more fun to pursue than to capture. I was three when I was aware of my first hero. He was a cousin, slightly younger than I was, called Winkie; handsome but distant. Everything Winkie did he did better than I could. He ran faster, was quicker up trees, much braver, and he pulled his little wooden wagon with strength and purpose, mostly away from me. I didn't like violence then any more than I like it now, so I soon gave up wrestling with him over the wagon and decided climbing trees was not girls' work. I was bad at it, anyhow. It was enough to stand at the bottom of the tree and gaze up at Winkie; enough to admire his gift for running in a curve around the lawn of our grandfather's house in Virginia where we stayed together that summer. He took no notice of me but I didn't suffer. I accepted that my role was that of watcher. I doubt whether he even knew he was being watched. All I asked was to be in his presence. He got no tokens or demonstrations of love from me, but I got warmth from being in his company. Perhaps this undemanding relationship was a kind of love. It was without self, and that is more than I can say about most of the heart-stirrings I went through after that.

There is a period flavour about the names of my little friends between the ages of seven and eleven – Grosvenor, Flavia, Olivia, Yvonne and Iris. Grosvenor de Graywarter fancied me more than I fancied him, and now all I am left with is his unforgettable name and the sight of him bending over the mustard and cress he grew so well on a bit of flannel. Mine came up moth-eaten: Grosvenor's was like a lawn. It was war-time and we went to the same small day-school in the Surrey countryside. There we were put to making rationbook-covers out of dark red American cloth that we had to stitch boldly with white embroidery thread. It was Grosvenor's turn to be the watcher. The watched one wasn't flattered. I have a feeling I was not kind to him. I didn't want his attention, nor the mustard and cress he offered me.

There was no friendship with either Winkie or Grosvenor, but on the first morning at my next school, in London, I began my first give-and-take relationship with a girl called Flavia. We were eight years old, new girls together, and we eyed each other with curiosity. Flavia was a plump child made up of rounds – round face, round nose, round bright eyes and bouncing round dark auburn ringlets, lovingly brushed and curled round someone's finger until they shone like satin. My first friend had been brought to school by her governess. The head-mistress, Miss Burman, a tiny figure not much taller than we were, told us to shake hands. Flavia grabbed my hand and wrung it firmly. She was stocked with energy waiting to be used. With a sudden thought she flung her arms round the governess's neck and whispered in her ear. I thought she was saying 'Don't leave me here,' but the governess unwound her and said: 'We don't tell secrets in front of other people but, yes, you may ask her.' So Flavia said to me: 'Will you come to tea today? It's my birthday.' Thus began the first friendship I remember. For one who became so bossy and self-assured I look back with surprise at this earlier stage when I was ready to be led and anxious to conform. It didn't last long. While it did I looked and listened and even learned a little.

Flavia was a power-house and the acknowledged leader among the group we moved in. Her energies were not only physical. Although she bounced up and down on her mother's sofa on the rare occasions when her mother was not lying down on it (and more often on the sofa in my family's flat), hard-packed energy also drove her opinion, and enthu-siasm carried her on. Her prime interest at that time was the cause of Bonnie Prince Charlie, of whom I had never heard (Alfred and his burnt cakes was as far as I had got). Flavia wore the kilt with a silver safety pin in it and was a passionate Jacobite, aggressive and forceful even at eight. Bonnie Prince Charlie was the centre of her heart and she assumed he must be mine. He had been shamefully treated, she said, and it was up to us to vindicate his memory. To do so she founded a secret society called 'The Followers of Bonnie Prince Charlie', and I was a founder-member. Where we followed him was into the sooty shrubberies of Chelsea Gardens all one long hot summer. There were rules, and secrecy was sworn, and Flavia certainly knew what we were up to and issued orders. How we followed her hero has gone with the wind. All I remember is crouching in the gritty dust, under bushes of privet and spotted laurel, whispering and plotting for whole afternoons on end. The subject of loyalty came up and our characters were examined ruthlessly to make sure we were worthy of being Followers. I felt uneasy because I knew my allegiance to B.P.C. was not deep and that I could be swayed away from him at the first sign of a more realistic objective. Soon one appeared.

A girl called Maisie with a pale moon-face and a sage-green serge dress had not been invited to follow B.P.C., so she founded her own society and it had a more contemporary flavour. She was older than Flavia and I – eight-and-a-half at least. She looked like an illustration to a story by E. Nesbit and was a reliable girl with a social conscience. She lived in Battersea and was serious-minded. The aim of her society was to Help Others. Why it was called the Brown Beans is another mystery lost in time. A brown sateen overall went with membership and the elected were allowed to choose the colour they blanket-stitched round the neck and sleeves.

I was drawn to the practical and it seemed to me there was a better chance of helping others than of reinstating Charlie. History could look after itself. I leaned towards the Brown Beans. Maisie's aims appealed to a tiny seed of a missionary nature in my little flat chest, waiting there, as it does with most children, to be called into use. I was hopeful that wrong could be made right, and while I can't claim that I had any ideas about how this was to be done, I simply record the fact that, as children do, I responded to the suggestion of being useful.

Flavia demanded total allegiance to her cause, and the day came when I had to decide which society beckoned the more strongly. I do not know how I made the final choice but I remember blanket-stitching in yellow wool round the neck of a brown sateen overall. I became a Brown Bean and enlisted to help others. I wish I knew how we set about doing it.

Secret societies flourished in Chelsea Gardens. There was also the Happy Hours Club Magazine, handwritten in a ruby-red exercise book. The author seems to have been me. I am listed humbly as 'Second Editer' but the handwriting is mine. We were a childish lot at eight and whatever else I learned at Miss Burman's school it was not spelling. Here are the Club rules as written:

1. Eacth person useing the following words
Dam, -Fol- Fool, Ass, Lord, Gosh, Devil, Golly, Dash, Hang, Mercy on us,
My stars and stockings, My only aunt, Drat, Golly my aunt, Bally
will pay a penny.
2. No one is to tell lies or sneak.
3. IFF anyone is found bullying a person younger than he or her slef will be
put out.

The banned words are touching today; not even 'bally' packs the
slightest shock-wallop. I was once sent out of a sewing class when I was
fourteen for saying 'blast'. The teacher was a nervous woman whose
best friends had never told her about personal daintiness and the whole
class held its breath when she came near. Apart from this I enjoyed the
sewing class, so when the bell rang at the end of the session I said 'blast'
with feelings of regret, meaning I wanted the class to go on longer. It
was a compliment, if only Mrs Bennett had had the sense to see it, but
she didn't. I was dismissed from the room and told to report what I had
said to the headmistress. 'Unfair, unfair,' I thought as I climbed the
stairs to the headmistress's study. I told my story and as I did so I had
the rare satisfaction of knowing that the headmistress was on my side.
My only punishment was to say to Mrs Bennett, 'I'm sorry I said a bad
word in your class.' Justice existed.

There isn't a hint of original thought in the few pencilled pages of
the Happy Hours Club magazine. Every item is a pale shadow of
something we'd read in *Rainbow* or *Puck*, the twopenny weeklies we
all bought. We inherited traditional jokes and riddles and tried them
out on our parents as if they were newly minted. We, too, asked, as
they had probably done, 'When is a door not a door?' and, 'What do
ships do when they come into harbour?' 'Tie up,' we cried and
daringly flipped our father's tie up to prove it. My brother Tommy was
astonished by carbon paper and was certain no one else had ever
come across it before. In his Sunday letter from his prep school he
described how it worked. It began:

> Take a piss of white paper and put it on a piss of black paper and then take
> another piss of white paper. . . .

We emerged slowly into the world without benefit of 'Dr Who' or
'Blue Peter' and the television news. We were not at all tough and I
was haunted for days by seeing a drunk on a Saturday afternoon lying
in the gutter outside Harvey Nichols in Sloane Street. In those days
blinds were pulled down in shop windows at the end of the working

74

week and this always made me hate Saturdays and Sundays in shopping areas. The combination of drawn blinds and a drunk man shook my sense of security. I didn't want to see it but I couldn't help looking. I thought of his children and how unhappy they would be. It was my first experience of drunkenness and I have never forgotten it. It no longer frightens me but I find it inexcusable and boring.

I do not have total recall, but there are certain indelible snapshots of little friends that have stayed vivid: Olivia, like a portrait by Lely, with her round brown eyes. She had fat knees and did not run well, but she had a good giggle and we were companionable. Ada, at my first school in Surrey, was tiny and freckled like a bird's egg. She looked exactly like her tiny freckled mother, and both did everything at the double. Yvonne, half-French, at the same school, only appeared for a few weeks. She had blonde bubble curls and wore a cross on a fine gold chain. This and her frilly pink silk knickers set her apart. I was allowed to try on the cross and had a holy feeling when I saw it round my neck in the looking-glass. Peggy, in London, blushed, and her firm downy cheeks went a slow pink-to-mauve, interesting to behold. Her name was Wilcox and for some teasing reason my father called her Peggy de Wilsk. She was a steady girl with bright blue eyes that took in everything in our flat. My mother thought she was memorising and said Peggy made her feel unbuttoned. I thought she was splendid because she was unflappable, and tea with the Wilcoxes was so unlike life at home. There were often long silent pauses when we sat at the dining-room table with her parents. At home no one could get a word in edgeways. At the Wilcoxes' I was the one who took it all in, relishing every detail of muted behaviour and taking on their hushed respect for Mrs Wilcox as an act.

Observation was my strong point, and that is the reason I learned so little while I was at school. My mother claimed that she never could hear what her teachers said because she was so busy seeing how they said it. This was true for me too. I could exactly reproduce the tilt of the head and sarcastic rise of the eyebrow that meant that Miss Savoury (at my third school, Francis Holland in Graham Street) was not pleased with my Latin prep. Elderly Miss Kiddle taught us Prayer Book and though it meant a great deal to her she never had my attention. She walked in little rushes on flat feet and had a loose lower lip, both of which I could imitate. She was a dear woman and all the rest of the class dutifully listened to everything she had to tell us, but I was guilty in her presence because I switched off in her lessons and I knew she knew I did. I perpetrated a wickedness over the Prayer Book class. Miss Kiddle wrote a note to my mother complaining that I paid no heed and was not apparently at all interested in the Prayer Book. I guessed that was what the note said and having taken it into the lavatory to read I saw I was right, so I tore it up small, dropped it in and pulled. A few days later Miss Kiddle asked if I had delivered the note. Looking her straight in the eye I said I had and that my mother thanked her for it. Was there no reply, asked Miss Kiddle? Not that I knew of, I said. Miraculously no more was ever said on the subject. It was more than I deserved. I still feel guilty.

Not one word that either Miss Savoury or Miss Kiddle or any other teacher at that time tried to teach me made any impression at all. Only lame Mr Bates who taught us singing caught my ear. His fierceness of manner got through to me and I liked his classes. We sang 'Vi-o-lets' and 'Come out, 'tis now September' and 'Sweet and Low', all new to me and still fresh in my memory.

After five terms it was decided that this school was too High Church. We had too many holidays in aid of the Saints; there was genuflecting and signs of the Cross and knee-bobbing, and while I joined in light-heartedly it wasn't in accordance with my family's view of God. So I was removed.

But before this happened I had found my first 'best' friend. Her name was Betty Bevan and we both joined the Lower Third on the same day, where she pleased both Miss Savoury and Miss Kiddle by doing her prep and paying attention to what they taught her. As well as being good at lessons Betty was imaginative and creative; she drew and painted and wrote poetry. I took to her at once and thought she was just about perfect. She had apricot-gold hair and her pigtails stayed plaited without having to be tied with ribbons because they ended in curls. Also she laughed when I was being funny. The Lower Third were paired off to collaborate on an illustrated story and Betty and I spent hours of homework time at each other's houses working on ours. Her part in this was greater than mine because she was a harder worker and drew better. I had the idea for the story and she developed it. Unlike Happy Hours, there was some originality in our joint work and we were praised for it. Radiance is not a quality children look for. It was what I found in Betty; she gave out joy, and for another ten-year-old to recognise this must have meant its power was considerable. The easy affectionate relationship between Betty and her family was as warm as my own, and going to their house was more fun than any of the others I went to at that time. Betty's father was headmaster of Gibbs's Boys School in Sloane Street, where my parents had thought of sending my brother before he went away to his prep school. (My mother met an eleven-year-old Gibbs boy somewhere and asked him how old you had to be before you could start at the school. 'Well,' said the senior, 'one of our chaps comes in a pram.') Then the Bevans moved away from London and we were sent to different schools.

When I was young there was a form of the Truth Game where you had to say in all honesty how you saw yourself, what period you thought suited you best, what style, what occupation. I never dared play it because my Walter Mitty dreams were so far from possibility that I thought it wiser to keep them to myself. I dreamed not only of ballet dancing but of being a literary genius and, at one time, an athlete. I could *see* myself in these roles even though I knew that to other people the picture might be different. If anyone was not gifted with what is needed for vaulting horses and climbing ropes it was I. But I dreamed and I tried. Every next time was going to be the break-through. The games mistress, short, muscular and patient, stood by the vaulting-horse. 'Next,' she called brightly. I was waiting in line with my gym slip tucked into my dark brown stockinet knickers; eager and hopeful. Thunder of plimsolls on wooden floor, heavy take-off and fumbled clamber. 'Where is your spring?' she wanted to know, helping me over and off. It was only partly consoling that the rest of the class thought I was jolly funny. Then came the rope. The girls in front of me rose up it as if drawn by a wire from the top, lowered themselves with perfect control, gave a little bounce on touching the ground and ran off. 'Next,' called the games mistress without hope, seeing it was I. I ran forward, grasped the rope and gave a little jump as I'd seen the others do. I didn't make it. 'Start again.' Hanging on with every ounce of strength I could raise I managed to get my feet off the ground and clamped them to the knot at the end of the rope. And there they stuck. I was incapable of rising any higher and reluctantly I let go and came down, hard.

I had moments of small triumph in that dull game netball; but that was only because I was so tall I could not always fail to get the ball into the net. And then there was tennis, and I loved it even though I never got further than third couple in the school team. I was not a shaming failure but my play was unreliable with rare flashes of brilliance (I got better after I was fifty).

The only real talent I had was wholly instinctive: I could invent characters and pretend I was someone else. As soon as I could talk I play-acted with my mother, making up conversations about our imaginary children. We sat side by side on the drawing-room sofa and invented together. At first I imitated talk I had heard from her and Lucy. Then I ranged further and became other kinds of talkers with other voices. One invention was an old man, but most of my characters were mothers with children and I imagined them in shops, by the sea, having meals. Apparently my fantasies took me on long journeys, and my ma, feeding me questions, was captivated.

When I was eight and quite portly she came into the bathroom and found me standing at attention in the water, saluting. I had arranged my bath-cap into a peak. My mother always accepted day-dreamings; she had plenty of her own. She asked me with just enough interest in her voice to encourage an answer: 'What are you doing?' 'I'm Princess Mary reviewing the troops on a yacht.'

My parents were encouragers, my father more critically than my mother. Everything we did had for her an aura of miracle about it. In my heart I knew I wasn't 'different' but it was nice to be given confidence and, until I was twenty-five and had been married for six years, I had the feeling that if I tried hard enough I could probably manage to do anything I wanted to – not that I aimed very high. This was not con-ceit; it was the belief that man's potential is total. Our parents helped Tommy and me to feel this. I suppose we were both lightly talented. He was a natural games-player, moved easily and well and had a creative imagination that turned him into a writer. My small talents pulled me in several directions and none of them was clearly marked. For years I accepted that I was going to draw. I have a facility for it and my father encouraged me to work at it but quite early I stopped looking at the way people are made and drew them to a formula. The legs of the children I drew were not capable of supporting the body and generally went one way, sideways, looking left. I evolved a squiggle that had to do for hands and if I could avoid drawing them I did, hiding them in flowing sleeves, or pockets or muffs. Everything I drew was derivative. An exhibition of children's paintings from Vienna came to London in the early 1920s and I was much influenced by it. Soon all my little girls, facing left, had dresses (with pockets) patterned in flowers, and stood in deep grass, their feet hidden by daisies and poppies.

I had little capacity for taking pains until much later, but I had a quick eye for form and my hand responded to it in a slap-dash way. Now and then I brought off an illustration and the colours were fresh, but my school reports for all subjects had a monotony about them: 'Joyce could do better if only she would concentrate.'

In most things I was not as self-assured as I appeared to be. 'Being funny', making up characters, came easily, but it wasn't until I went on the stage that I learned to discipline what I invented; and by then I had some concentration and worked with purpose and some self-criticism. At school I went on observing and reproducing what I observed, and when my friends laughed it egged me on to do more. I never shone in class but I had my moments in playtime, and a few years ago I met a contemporary who remembered me as 'the life and soul of the dorm'.

At the same time as I was enjoying my 'best' friendship with Betty Bevan two more little girls came into my life and have remained there ever since. For three years until I went away to boarding school in late 1924 Dorothy Gillespie, Carley Robinson and I made up a trio. (We are still close friends and since they live out of England we keep in touch by letter.) We were all movie- and stage-mad. Ours was a week-end alliance. Often on Saturdays we lunched together, went to the movies together, had tea in turn at each other's houses and dressed up in our mothers' clothes and acted to music. This meant long sessions experimenting with our hair and our mothers' make-up (face powder, pale rouge, and pale lip-salve with a hint of pink in it). Then we acted. That is to say we took up postures and emoted. We were enclosed in our own private dreams and took very little notice of each other. Music was used to stir us and create a mood, and when I tell you the two most regularly employed records were *Jewels of the Madonna* by Wolf-Ferrari and the overture to *Madame Butterfly* you will see that we were not very like little girls of today.

Dorothy's house had an L-shaped drawing-room and we acted in the L bit of it. We used a brocade-covered pouffe as a stage prop, and I stood on it pretending it was a rock and I was about to be swept away into the sea. Now and then we drew each other's attention. 'Look! – I'm being passionate.' We heaved our faintly indicated bosoms, just beginning to show under our jerseys, and we rolled our eyes. We showed fear as we had seen Alice Terry do it in *Scaramouche*, putting the back of our right hand, fingers stiffly splayed, in front of our open mouths, and leaned against the wall, facing invisible horrors. We did stage faints with great thuds and resulting bruises; we registered tragedy and pain; tried to make ourselves produce real tears by thinking of something sad, but we never, never played at happiness. Our hero-ines in the movies went through hell and, being happy and secure, we enjoyed pretending to suffer as they did. Because of my height I was usually the 'villain'. At Doro's we had no men's clothes but I drew a moustache with burnt cork and spoke low in what I believed to be a suave manner. I would have preferred to play the feminine lead.

The very first time I was conscious of enjoying an audience (other than my parents and Lucy) I was three years old, on board a liner crossing the Atlantic. I escaped Lucy and my mother and got into the lounge where an orchestra was playing tea-time music. I don't think I set out to amuse; it came upon me. I simply felt like dancing, went into the middle of the room, closed my eyes and danced. This meant turning round and round, quite slowly, with an occasional hop. I became aware that I was being watched and that the watchers were amused. I did not have to open my eyes to see this; I felt it and liked the feeling. I have never lost this liking.

When I was twelve I wished I was an actress. I had no specific thoughts about acting; I did not ache to play Rosalind or in *Bluebell in Fairyland*. I didn't think about words or rehearsals – indeed I didn't want to act. I dreamed, as small boys used to dream of being engine drivers, that I was an actress. I was in love with the idea of actresses because my family had friends who worked in the theatre and their pictures were in the papers. They seemed more interesting than other people and far more glamorous.

At that stage I was in love with both Noël Coward and Ivor Novello at the same time and couldn't decide which most drew out the mother in me. Both came to the house and, because they were fond of my mother, paid some attention to me. Noël had been brought to luncheon by Mrs Patrick Campbell on my tenth birthday and sent me three books by E. Nesbit, thereby adding marks to his score that have never been rubbed out. (All I remember about Mrs Pat on that occasion were her big black velvet picture-hat, piercing black eyes and her searching question to me, spoken in a deep theatrical voice: 'Are you *happy*?' I stored this up and used it years later when I invented an earnest soul-searcher I called Fern Brixton.) Ivor Novello sent my mother a bunch of Parma violets and I told a school friend he had sent them to me. She was amazed, but impressed.

It was about this time that I was fired with the idea of being a ballet dancer, and a more unlikely ballet dancer it would be hard to find. I was still very solid but not yet worried or indeed self-conscious about it (I felt slim in my mind). Square body and legs of the dependable kind; hair tied up in two short paint-brushes. Healthy I was, but lacking in allure. The urge to dance was not for glamorous reasons; I wished to dance for dancing's sake, to be able to leap and spin, full of light and grace. There wasn't a hope.

My architect father was not keen that I should shake the house too much, for it was old and already shuddered when hurried through. But my mother, my fellow-dreamer, understood my dreams and my confidence in them and bought me a pair of blocked black cotton dancing shoes at Gamba's and left me to it, doing her best not to let me realise how pitiful it all was; nor how funny.

We had a hand-wound portable Decca gramophone and I lugged it into the dining-room where it sat on the table playing Schubert's *Unfinished Symphony* while I teetered on my blocked toes, knees bent, holding on to the table with one hand and raising the other high over my head, thumb and middle finger pointing down in what I believed to be the correct way ballet dancers held their hands. The gramophone always ran down before the music was over and I had to come down off my blocks and flat-foot it to the Decca for a rewind. It was also a way of regaining my breath.

A sense of self-preservation made me keep my dancing to myself. It was a secret activity hidden from my little friends. The craze didn't last very long. I never got to the stage where I could let go of the dining-room table long enough to do anything spirited, such as a pirouette; I began to realise that what I had was not what dancing needed, and I gave it up.

CHAPTER SIX

Friends and Relations

PHYLLIS and Rachel Spender Clay were first cousins of my Astor cousins and no relation to me, but I have always felt as close to them as if they were real relations. Their mother, whom I called Aunt Pauline, was Waldorf Astor's sister. She and her husband Bertie Spender Clay included my family as generously as did the Astors, and when we weren't at Cliveden we were probably staying with them at Ford Manor, their house near Lingfield in Surrey. Phyllis and Rachel were older than I was but they tolerated me and I happily tagged along with them. In the last year of the First World War we all went together to Miss Griffiths' small school in the nearby village of Dormansland. At that time they were eleven and nine and I was seven. I didn't yet have a bicycle but they were decent enough to push their bikes and walk uphill with me on our way there and I was glad of their company through a dark and spooky stretch of pinewoods. Coming home downhill Rachel took me on the front of her bicycle and we hurtled over moss-covered stones, bouncing recklessly all the way back without her ever touching the handlebars or brakes. Indeed very little of Rachel touched the machine at all. Once she had got up speed she took her feet off the pedals, stuck her legs out wide, and we roared our way down with wild cries. We usually arrived back first, propelled no doubt by my extra weight. Later, when I had a bicycle of my own, I used the brakes all the way and came home a long time last and was, I expect, looked down upon. The Spender Clays were always intrepid about speed and leaping off haystacks. I was not; but they did not make me feel inferior, as I knew myself to be.

I have never enjoyed speed and I think I may be the only skier who, in the days before ski-lifts, when fur skins were strapped on to skis to help one climb to the top of the slopes, kept her skins on for the journey downhill. I made a slow, upright and stately progress and preferred it that way.

Phyllis and Rachel Spender Clay with me and Bobbie Grant at Ford

All my family loved being at Ford. In the 1914–18 war it was a second home to us. In 1917 the main part of the house was turned into a convalescent home for wounded American soldiers. My father, invalided out of the army, was then doing a war job in Washington, and my mother took us to stay at Ford while she and Aunt Pauline, in becoming organdie veils and pale blue uniforms, had the time of their lives working as V.A.D.s. Uncle Bertie must have been in France. Aunt Pauline and the girls moved into the maids' wing and we went with them. The children ate with the staff in the steward's room and Mrs Jones the housekeeper fell in love with Tommy. He was pretty beguiling at four, pink and white and fair-haired, and a great responder to attentions. Mrs Jones had a dark blue dress that fastened over her upholstered bust in a row of tiny buttons from chin to waist, and when Tommy pressed the right button a sponge cake, almost as delicious as my grandmother's, miraculously appeared from under the table.

In 1918, when the convalescent home was in full swing, my mother met Irene and Vernon Castle and asked them to come and dance for the patients. We were allowed to stay up and watch. The orange velvet-curtained drawing-room was cleared, chairs were arranged at one end of the room and the children sat cross-legged on the floor in front. I think the Castles must have danced to a gramophone because the piano was in another room. Irene Castle was the first grown-up person I had ever seen with bobbed hair and – oh daring! – she wore black satin trousers caught in at the ankle like a French pierrot doll. The picture of her slim figure swinging and dipping is very clear in my mind. I was dazzled by her charm, and something of the rare quality she and her husband brought to their act reached even me, eight years old and solid. That evening may well have been the stimulus that set me wanting to be a dancer.

The house sat on a flagged terrace high in the Surrey hills. It was a place of light and fresh air with views over rolling grass meadows parted by a wide mown path curving towards woods. Over the trees in the pale distance you could see some of the chalk downlands where the Romans had camped. When I first went to Ford as a small child the woods and its ponds were unclaimed, but later Aunt Pauline made the land into a spectacular wild garden where primula, iris and native bluebells spread thickly under the shelter of giant beeches. There were groves of bright azaleas and rhododendrons interspersed with clumps of lilies and blue poppies. In early spring daffodils, narcissi, tulips and forget-me-nots grew in the grass that edged the paths to the woods. Near the house the oval garden, sunk below the terrace, was thick with wallflowers and the biggest polyanthus I have ever seen. Wistaria and laburnum grew there too. It was in the oval garden that garden chairs were set out for the grown-ups, and the rest of us wandered in and out sniffing the heady scents. Lavender grew in fat clumps about the terrace above.

Now when I think of Ford it is always spring and I equate it with the freedom of taking off my winter gaiters and the sounds of the spring chorus. Children there were treated as people with rights of their own. We were not over-organised, neither were we ignored or concentrated on, but it was noticed if children were shy or bewildered, and something was done about it.

I remember Ford most clearly from the time I was fourteen until I married five years later. Breakfast started the day well. A gong went at 8.45 and no one looked critical if we were not dead on time. Hot plates kept the silver-covered dishes warm and the choice was varied – eggs, boiled, poached, scrambled; fish, kidneys, bacon, sausages and fried potatoes; sometimes mushrooms and tomatoes. The long table, covered by a single white damask cloth, could seat twenty-four and often did. We ate breakfast off pink china edged in gold and had our toast and marmalade (or honey or jam) on half-moon salad-plates. Plans for the day were discussed, and in spring and summer tennis began soon after breakfast and went on all day, punctuated by delicious meals of the very best English cooking. There was also a nine-hole golf course, horses for those who rode, and the billiard-room was the scene more of athletic games of 'fives' than of sedate billiards. Indoors life centred around a big main room called the library, although it was not entirely given over to books. It was there we sang with Rachel, or with any one of us who played the piano and got to it first. We also wrote letters there, played Racing Demon and paper games, and after dinner there was Bridge for those who liked it. The atmosphere was not highbrow but it was stimulating, and it challenged one's intelligence in an agreeably undemanding way. To a young observer like me it was not intimidating, nor was the company. Ages and interests widely varied; there was talk of books, painting, the theatre and people but not a great deal about politics, though Uncle Bertie was an M.P. and represented Tunbridge Wells.

In my small world in the middle twenties, country clothes were almost a uniform – for girls, a jersey, skirt and golf-shoes, even if, like me, they didn't play golf. The Gillie golf-shoes came from Fortnum & Mason and were expensive and uncomfortable because they had long leather laces that tied round the ankles and cut. The young men wore grey flannels in summer and plus-fours, with V-necked sweaters, in winter. Their long hand-knitted knee-stockings, made by old nannies, mothers, sisters and aunts, were in camouflage colours of sober browns, greys, greens and blues, and their ties, usually made of foulard in small designs (when they weren't old school or regimental), didn't do much to brighten the general effect. Young men today look a lot more attractive and I prefer their pink shirts and velvet jackets and general air of informality.

It was an era of practical jokes, and being young and carefree it all seemed, as it was, natural, innocent and harmless. No one got hurt, but the kind of life we led didn't include much thinking about a larger world. Soon afterwards that was unavoidable. Meanwhile the girls organised apple-pie beds and once sewed up the trouser-legs of all the pyjamas they found laid out on the beds in the bachelors' wing. As the decorum of the time prevented them from actually witnessing the discovery and discomfort, the exercise seems feeble but it provided a little excitement at breakfast next morning when searching questions about sleeping comfortably and a good night's rest were put to the young men. The sex war was a gentle thing when I was in my teens. Once a large-scale plot was laid to raid another house-party nearby, the adults joined in and it now seems strange that our parents took part and were so enthusiastic. I thought of them as quite old and it is with surprise I discover that, at the time of which I am writing, my mother was in her middle thirties. She was just forty when I got married.

Nowadays the idea of such goings-on, or of a fancy-dress party, fills me with gloom, but then it was exhilarating. We had treasure hunts. (This was before the days of the Bright Young People who played their games in public and understandably raised a lot of hackles.) Our treasure hunts at Ford took place all over the house and out in the gardens and woods and offended no one. Usually my father and Harry Graham, the writer, set the clues and took half a day to lay the trail. We hunted in pairs, a child and a grown-up; each clue led to the next and they had to be found in order. Some were in rhyme, some anticipated *The Times* crossword puzzle and called on our ingenuity. I remember my pride in being the first to guess that 'the chaperons are in rows' led to the gooseberry bushes in the kitchen garden. Such exercises took up the whole afternoon and afterwards we held post-mortems, stretched out to recover on the grass below the terrace, and made sure that everyone else had found *all* the clues.

I wonder whether reading about these childish exercises today rouses the blood? Irresponsibility? The worst killing war in the world was not long over and the next had not yet been sighted. There was an atmosphere of light-hearted relief in those few years; certainly among the young. We stayed young longer then, and that is a luxury gone for ever. The transition from schoolgirl to young woman was abrupt. I wore long black cotton stockings and a pigtail one day, and the next day pale silk stockings, high heels and my hair done up in a precarious bun.

The first time I wore my hair up in public was in Paris. I was at a small finishing establishment at St Germain-en-Laye and we were taken to the Opera. I had used up one-and-a-half packets of strong brown wire hairpins trying to make fast my slippery bun. We heard *Faust* and I never hear the music without remembering an accompaniment of hairpins falling one by one on the marble stairs of the Opera House as we climbed to our box. In the box I stood at the back in the shadows and put it up again. All in vain. Throughout the performance there was a steady drip of pins and by the time we got back to St Germain-en-Laye in the hired taxi my hair was down my back. It took me a long time to master hairpins. The first time I met my husband I played tennis

At sixteen
butter wouldn't melt

with him, my hair in a pigtail, but I got it up after a fashion for dinner in the evening.

It was at Ford, at Easter 1927, that I met Reggie Grenfell. He was there by mistake. Aunt Pauline had pneumonia that year and the house-party was cancelled except for my family and some Bingham cousins of the Spender Clays. No one remembered to tell Reggie that he wasn't expected and he arrived, the only young man to be shared between Phyllis, Rachel, Maggie Bingham and me. Tommy was only thirteen and didn't count.

Reggie's twin uncles, Francis and Rivy Grenfell, had been at school with my father and Rivy remained a great friend until he was killed in the first war. My father was startled by Reggie's likeness to his uncles and amused to find many of the family characteristics in this quiet, tall, dark, rather shy young man. I thought he was pleasant and hoped to see him again when the party was over. He says he decided then and there that I was the girl he was going to marry.

He took a long time to put the decision into words and I had fallen in love with him many months before I was sure he felt as I did. We saw a lot of each other in 1928 at dances and week-end parties, but my parents thought I was too young to be so committed and sent me to

The young man I married

America to visit my godmother, Aunt Irene Gibson. They both liked Reggie very much but felt I should get away for a while and meet other people, though I learned later they both hoped Reggie would be the man I married. He came to see me off on the boat-train at Waterloo and, as he always did when he couldn't speak, hummed tunelessly and I thought and hoped he minded my departure.

I had a good time in America and enjoyed a flattering flirtation with a young American who took me sailing in Maine, and once we stayed out till three in the morning talking under the stars, holding hands. But my heart was already bespoken and I cut short the proposed three months'

Our wedding, 12 December 1929

stay and was home as soon as my parents allowed me back. Reggie and I continued to meet and in the early spring of 1929 he wrote a long letter telling me why he couldn't ask me to marry him. He had no money, did not know when he would be in a position to make any, and didn't feel he should ask me to wait for him. But I was ready to wait for ever and wrote back and said so. We met the next day at the Holborn Empire, a variety house, where we were going with a group of friends to see Max Miller. In the crowded foyer I managed to get next to him.

'Did you get my letter?'

'Yes, I did.'

We were engaged. And only then, after two years, was I allowed to go out alone with him.

It is not easy to describe goodness; it usually comes out smug, unadventurous and without humour or warmth. I have always wanted to write a story or a play about goodness, because, when I meet it, it has always attracted me more than anything else. But it is hard to put on paper. The goodness I mean is a sense of unchanging security, in the widest sense of wholeness; and it is never suspected by those who have it. It is their natural essence; their being expresses it, not in words but in attitudes and behaviour. I have met a lot of it, in a variety of people, but nowhere more consistently than in Reggie. But I don't know how to write about it without outlining, and the point about goodness is that it cannot be confined or described, it can only be sensed and experienced in relationship. It is one of the highest expressions of love – not as A loves B, but as love makes the world go round in a far wider context. I find it interesting that Reggie, who has no formal religious beliefs, never goes to church on his own, doesn't, as far as I know, pray much, yet is at the place most of the rest of us have to strive to reach. His behaviour is instinctively Christian. He is unaware of this and will be surprised to read it. I think he would say he does not believe in an ecclesiastical God but he does believe in Good. As I see it, all good is the manifestation of the only true cause.

Among the good things I remember with particular appreciation is the welcome I was given when I married into the Grenfell family.

Reggie is a member of a large tribe. His father Arthur Morton Grenfell was one of thirteen children and his mother, Victoria, was the eldest of four children of the 4th Earl Grey of Howick in Northumberland. She died when Reggie was five, leaving his elder sister Vera, himself and small brother Harry to be brought up by Arthur's second wife Hilda Lyttelton. Later Arthur and Hilda had four daughters, Mary,

Hilda Grenfell   *Arthur Grenfell*

Katie, Frances and Laura. The three older stepchildren looked upon Hilda as their mother, an achievement wholly to her credit.

Hilda regarded me with some suspicion when Reggie brought me home as his intended. He was the first to look outside the nest and I was partly American, with 'Bohemian' parents, possibly a 'light-weight', and I have an idea she may have had other plans for her elder stepson. But what she got was me, and after some uneasy preliminary manoeuvring in which we both 'boxed clever', neither giving an inch, we found each other's measure and became not only friends but *truly* devoted. Hilda was a beautiful creature, tall and slim with a Botticelli face and a deceptively delicate air that masked a will of iron and fibre of enduring quality. An original, very feminine woman; a getter-of-what-she-wanted by the simple expedient of opening her dreamy blue eyes wider and appealing with an air of totally unmerited helplessness for assistance she did not need but preferred to have. Hilda, like most Lytteltons, had her own way with the English language. Thus, a telephone call to me:

'Darling, it's *such* a heavenly day and I thought if you *happened* to be going anywhere near Bethnal Green between two-thirty and five how perfectly it would fit in with a delicious little plan I have to go and see darling old Anglican Father Wigram and take him some books he is longing to get hold of.'

Me: 'No, darling.'

We knew where we were with each other.

She was loved, cherished and seen through by her daughters, who hoped she would not write too many letters of a 'holy' nature to their husbands, an indulgence she could not resist. I had many 'holy' letters scrawled all over scraps of paper, filled with quotations and references phrased in a mixture of Lytteltonese, baby talk, purpose and affection. She was imaginative over my feelings of missing something when Mary, and soon Katie, began having babies, and I remember an untypically brief note simply stating her awareness of the situation that touched me greatly and drew me closer to her.

She and my mother were faintly wary of each other. Hilda had a proprietary interest in Reggie and watched his growing fondness for my ma with increasingly widened blue eyes. And when I talked too much about the Grenfells and their way of doing things my mother teased me by reproducing Hilda's die-away voice and use of French words in an imitation that secretly amused me but which I did not admit to finding in the least accurate.

What I continue to enjoy about my in-laws is that they like each other and being with them is therefore nourishing and restful. Plenty of family criticism goes on but there is basic loving too; and family gatherings, dreaded by so many in these divided times, are genuinely enjoyed by Grenfells. There is no enclosed we-are-special feeling about Grenfells; they take each other as they are, rejoice over triumphs and are ready supporters in times of need. And they are amused by what the family gets up to; not just nosy, but interested.

My father-in-law was the most generous of men (not excepting Reggie) and one of his happiest occasions down the years was the annual two-day Eton and Harrow cricket match at Lord's for which he hired a coach – not a 'chara', not a bus, but a real old-fashioned four-wheeler coach, *sans* horses, that was somehow hauled to the ground and established on a grassy rise near the pavilion. There the family and its friends congregated throughout the match. 'Meet you at the Grenfells' coach'; and tea and ices were on the go on both days of the match for all comers. When they were small, Reggie's youngest half-sisters, Frances and Laura, were loyally decked out in Eton-blue ribbons and frowned fiercely at any Harrovians wearing cornflowers and des-pised royal blue bows. The match was a fiercely partisan affair and no one felt it more keenly than my pa-in-law who boomed his 'well played' from the top of his coach, his top hat perched over his nose and his deaf aid turned off.

In London during the second war Hilda became an intrepid bicyclist – and survived. She devised a costume to ride in: Mercury-shaped hat

Reggie, Laura and Harry

tied under the chin and a cover-all cape with armholes worn over a skirt fastened by tapes and safety-pins to prevent it rising up when she pedalled. I was on a bus coming home from Piccadilly when I saw her free-wheeling downhill along Park Lane, sweeping half-way round Hyde Park Corner, heading for Chesham Place where she then lived. She looked neither to right nor left but coasted on while strong men driving buses jammed on their brakes and taxi-drivers and others swore and swerved to avoid her as she passed. She was unaware of any perils and got home safely, pink-cheeked and smooth as silk.

From the word go I was accepted in the Grenfell family as one of their own. I believe there was a moment, after I decided to use my married name on the stage, when eyebrows shot up, but nothing was said to me. Reggie is a much loved brother and I am made to feel as welcome as he is when we go to stay with his half-sisters. His own sister Vera is a lynch-pin in the tribe and her home in Berkshire, where she gardens with all the skills of her Grey ancestors, is a meeting place for nieces and nephews, and great-nieces and great-nephews too. There never was a more centrally placed and well-used aunt than V; nor one who responds to calls with greater kindness. Nor is there a more benevolent and imaginative uncle than Reggie's bachelor brother Harry.

Reggie's four half-sisters are very different from each other; all are interesting and attractive and I like being in their company. They write literate and enjoyable letters, and Frances, in particular, has a gift for putting her generous self on paper. She has courage, warmth and wisdom and is perhaps the one to whom I have been closest. I think Laura, the youngest, is the only *entirely* unselfish person I have ever known. She is naturally, instinctively unselfish, without apparently being conscious that there is any other way of behaving. She has much of her father's optimism and her own crystal-clear goodness. She and Reggie between them add up to all that is most admirable and attractive in mankind, and I don't know any people who make life seem more worth the effort than they do – simply by being themselves. It is never what they say – it's the way they are.

I have been blessed with friends who have remained part of my life since we were all growing up in the late 1920s. We don't meet as often as we did and the things that interested us have changed or disappeared, but there is no bond like shared memories of adolescence, and if you have once laughed together at the same kind of jokes this lasts for ever and is very precious. Mary Brassey, Catherine Fordham (Kennedy) and Rose McDonnell (Baring) are three of the close friends who used to share in my cousin Nancy's clothes, and it is them I see standing about in their straight pink *crêpe de Chine* slips up in my mother's bedroom. All of us are now rather different shapes and Catherine is no longer alive, but these are lasting 'special' friends. Their essential values never altered.

To this day my oldest and 'best' friend is Virginia Thesiger. We used to meet staying at Ford. When we first met she was seven and I was nearly a year older and we eyed each other with suspicion, for her parents, Dorothy and Harry Graham, were friends of my parents and this is often reason enough for the children to shy away from each other. But we looked and liked and got on at once; we laughed at the same things and later shared a passion for the movies and the theatre. Virginia was tall even then, very fair with a straight back and long slim legs, and was more grown-up and sophisticated than I was; she was faintly fierce with a cool take-it-or-leave-it air that was intriguing and made me want to know her better. When we 'came out' we went to many of the same parties and wrote to one another when we were apart, a practice that still continues. We did not try to impress each other but felt free to be 'silly', a rare luxury possible only with very special friends. I am blessed with several such friends. The kind of 'silliness' I mean is a bond, a private sharing hard to describe, and Virginia's brand is of the highest order and has a unique element of surprise that is exactly to my taste. Reggie demonstrated active 'silliness' on the morning of our wedding anniversary when he came to breakfast wearing, over his pyjamas, the morning coat he had been married in forty-two years before – and did not mention it.

Virginia and Tony Thesiger

In the early days Virginia and her half-sister Kitty always knew all the latest musical comedy songs and brought copies of them to Ford so that we might sing them together. During the ukulele craze she remembers sitting in the back of the family car with Kitty, the lady's maid wedged between them and her mother and father in front, as they sang and played their 'ukes' all the way from Gloucester Place to Ford, a distance of thirty miles. It took nearly two hours to get there and their parents never complained. Compared with the decibel-count parents have to put up with today the sound of two untrained sopranos and their gut-strung ukuleles must have been quite low. All the same the limitations of such an instrument are hard to take for long and the Grahams must have been remarkably understanding. We will never know what Miss Jameson, the lady's maid, thought about it. Just as well.

Marriage-making is dangerous and doesn't often work well, but when Barbara Bevan, a first cousin of Phyllis and Rachel, who had never been tempted to do such a thing before, met Antony Thesiger (who became one of our most loved friends) on a boat coming home from India, she decided he was just the husband for Virginia; and she was right. The two of them were asked to stay with Barbara and her husband Johnny Bevan in a house they took for the summer holidays near North Berwick. At first they did not appear to notice each other but back in London that autumn of 1938 Tony began to court Virginia and I guessed something was up because Virginia took to going out again after she had come home in the late afternoon – a practice she disliked. She rushed back from whatever she had been doing (usually seeing a movie), hurriedly changed her clothes and was off again, not just once or twice but most evenings of the week. She was not much of a party-goer, but at this time, when I telephoned her around six o'clock to gossip about the day's doings, she was out; and her mother did not know where she had gone. Then there was a charity dance and Virginia invited us to dine before it; she had asked a man called Antony Thesiger to come with us. His name had been occurring, a little over-casually, in her letters and conversation for a few weeks and I was sure he was the reason for her sudden social activity. When I saw them together I knew it was as good as settled and rejoiced. Tony spoke her 'language' in every sense of the word and brought to it a fine 'silliness' of his own. Reggie and I felt he had been part of our lives for ever and the four of us spent good times together in an easy and affectionate relationship that lasted until Tony died.

Virginia has had to contend with some very rough passages. The illnesses and death of her father and, later, of her mother and her half-sister, and then Tony's long and protracted disability, were lived through with shining courage. She is patient and loving and is another remarkable example of selflessness. She has never lost sight of her faith in God; and her buoyant sense of Life as continuity and her undiminished humour sustained all those who loved her and witnessed its support in those dark times.

My mama's second husband, whom she married in 1931, was an Irish-American former football hero (Yale), former movie actor,

My ma and Lefty at Little Orchard, Tryon

Maurice Flynn (nicknamed Lefty because of his left-footed kicking skills), who looked like an illustration to a college story *circa* 1910. Even now I find it difficult to write about Lefty with complete fairness. He came into my life as the villain who broke up my family, and though I know my mother was the strong partner in the relationship and it could never have happened unless she had willed it, it took me time to get over the shock. In the end I did grow fond of him, partly because he made me laugh and partly because he was a likeable creature.

The only writer I've read who describes funny people so that their unique flavour, movements, sounds, gestures and timing live again in one's memory is Kenneth Tynan. In his book *He who Plays the King* he wrote about Beatrice Lillie and Sid Field (and others) and evoked them so clearly that to read him is to relive the delight of their actual performances. I wish he had known Lefty and written about his startling act of the one-armed flute-player; and his understated imitation of an old-time vaudeville star feigning modest reluctance as he milked his curtain calls.

Lefty was not an intellectual but he had natural wit. He admired eggheads, knew when he was out of his depth but thought well of education and brains. He and my mother made friends with a young schoolmaster poet who occasionally read his poems aloud to them. Poetry was unfamiliar to Lefty and he admitted that he didn't always understand it, but he liked the patterns and sounds it made, and he suddenly produced a series of imitation poems that he called 'Plandromes' (don't ask me why; he didn't know either). Unconsciously copying James Joyce he invented words and rhythmic shapes. His Plandromes were meaningless, but in Lefty's deep dramatic voice they sounded like the real thing.

The best memorial to my mother and Lefty is the remembered pleasure and sheer enjoyment they gave their friends wherever they lived and in particular at Little Orchard in Tryon, North Carolina. People still living there tell me that an invitation from the Flynns was a guarantee of a good time. No wine or hard liquor was provided, and it may be that some guests anticipated this, but never noticeably; and there was no need of stimulants to create the right relaxed atmosphere; the hosts naturally generated it without conscious effort. To this day old friends remember the particular enjoyment of summer evenings, on the terrace under the stars, and winter nights when they all sat on long and late round the table while my ma and Lefty played their guitars, sang together, and broke into spontaneous improvisation; and had as much fun as anyone present. Perhaps that was the secret of their relationship – their shared capacity for simple pleasures and enjoyment.

It wasn't only the parties that are remembered; my mother introduced into that small community new ideas ranging from menus, clothes, *décor*, her philosophy and faith, and her own friends from other worlds. One of my regrets is that Reggie never saw Little Orchard in my mother's time. Even for a critical daughter, wary of the new marriage, staying there was enjoyable. The small white house was a place of great sweetness and light.

CHAPTER SEVEN

Mostly about Aunt Nancy

I owe Aunt Nancy a very great deal. Her imaginative generosity to me as a child, as a girl, and to Reggie and myself as a young married couple was unending. She gave me new clothes and I shared a coming-out dance with her daughter Wissie; she gave us our wedding reception and half our first house in St Leonard's Terrace. I was always on the receiving end of her generosity and not only on birthdays and at Christmas.

My Astor cousins have always been part of my life. They lived in enormous houses with regiments of male and female helpers. When Michael and Jakie were young they were reputed not to know that they were rich. They thought *all* their friends at school had a house in London, a house in the country, a house by the sea and a house in Scotland. And many of them did. They may not have expected everyone else to have a house in a parliamentary constituency as their mother had in Plymouth, but all the other houses were taken for granted.

I did not envy them. I wished for nothing better than our way of life; it was friendly and cosy and comfortable. I have never felt completely at ease at the idea of great wealth for myself, because sometimes it seems to blunt the edge of awareness and segregate those who have it in a subtle and indefinable way from the rest of us. I expect the origin of my faintly socialist views came from my pa who was always left of centre in a rosy way that today would not even be thought liberal. In the twenties his views were enough to cause discomfort among his friends in the establishment, because he seemed to herald an era they didn't want to think about.

My cousin Alice Winn said to me: 'You make me so mad. When the revolution comes you won't have any distance to fall!'

My instinct to simplify came from a wish to avoid too much responsibility. It wasn't by any means noble, but did include a suspicion about privilege – a very nice thing so long as it was mine but enraging when it was exclusive to other people. Doors opened easily for the rich, I noticed, and it was fine to tag on behind them as they went through, and I enjoyed it though I didn't think it was fair. But even if I had never experienced privilege for myself I would prefer a society where privilege exists to one where nobody is allowed an advantage, a treat or an escape unless everyone else has it too. That concept limits possibilities and makes for dullness all round. When later we could have afforded it, Reggie asked me if I would like to have a cottage somewhere for holidays and week-ends. I said no, because if we did we would have to go to it. If you have a cottage you plant a bulb and a rose-bush. If you have a bulb and a rose-bush you have to go and see how they are doing. No, I said, I prefer one home that can be left when we are free and can afford to travel and take care-free visits to remote places. Also I have vague worries about the ethics of owning two roofs at a time when so many have none. But this is an arguable point and there are no hard rules.

Nevertheless I must admit I greatly benefited from the riches of my kith and kin. During school holidays Tommy and I were included in everything provided for our cousins. We were expected to ride the ponies, play tennis and enjoy the coaching, use the boats on the river and share in whatever else was going on.

In my early teens I had ambivalent feelings about staying with Aunt Nancy at Cliveden. Half of me loved the big scale of it and the luxury; half resented the tension I sensed between my mother and Aunt Nancy. The rows that happened there were a strain and for years my feelings about the place were coloured by dread. Also I was no good at riding and feared it; and unlike my cousin Wissie I was not popular with my male cousins, who were in the majority, so I tended to avoid group activities and lurk indoors. At that time Aunt Nancy had a way of making me feel that whatever I was doing I ought to be doing something else.

Aunt Nancy: 'Why are you reading in this stuffy room? You must be crazy. You ought to be out in the air.'

Me: 'Well, I was just . . .'

Aunt Nancy: 'Go on out – play tennis – go for a swim in the river. You can read in London.'

Hell. But on the plus side there were white hot-house grapes, peaches and figs. The grapes were as big as your thumb, egg-shaped, pale jade with a bloom on them. The peaches were white inside with dark red markings where the delicious fruit clung to the stone. The

Aunt Nancy

figs were bigger and better than any I have ever eaten anywhere. I enjoyed the French menus and American corn-bread and 'beaten' biscuits. Sometimes there were candies from New York in purple boxes, doled out to us in short rations by my aunt. She kept under lock and key an endless supply of goodies sent to her from the United States.

The company was varied and it was not unusual to meet a duchess, with or without her duke, MPs of all parties, an international banker, a Christian Science lecturer, all mixed up with friends from Uncle Waldorf's English youth and my aunt's American girlhood; and there were younger married couples and, often, a lonely man or woman whom no one seemed to know and whose identity was never discovered throughout the week-end. My mother always believed it would be possible for an adventurer to stay at Cliveden undetected, because Aunt Nancy would expect he'd been asked by Uncle Waldorf or *vice versa*; it could be supposed he was a friend of one of the children's. At week-ends we seldom sat down less than twenty at the table and the young were included at luncheon from a very early age.

I remember Jakie, aged about two, sitting on a high chair with his mouth open for the fork-full Aunt Nancy had ready for him but which, in her interest in the conversation with some visitor, she forgot to deliver. In spite of such attempts at motherhood I don't think she was very good at the job because her interest was always divided; also she rarely listened, she only told.

The larger the house-party at Cliveden the safer I felt; less chance of being noticed and ticked off. Wissie and her brothers managed to disappear between meals and lead their own lives, but I was magnetised to the big hall and I hung about there waiting to see what was going to happen of which I could be part.

The hall at Cliveden was the nerve-centre of the house. It was enormous – stone-flagged floor, with rugs, walls panelled in oak and hung with French tapestries of the eighteenth century. There was a Gainsborough of Mrs Siddons and the Sargent portrait of Aunt Nancy. I once paced the distance from the dining-room at one end of the hall to the corridor leading to the wing at the other and made it to be about eighty feet. You could park at least four double-decker buses in the hall.

The furniture was on the grand scale. A mammoth red sofa, good for bouncing on (forbidden but indulged in) had room for at least twelve children seated in a row; behind it stood a vast desk, piled up

with visitors' books and photograph albums. In season we rode tri-
cycles, pedalled toy cars, walked on stilts, jumped on pogo sticks,
roller-skated and played tag in the hall. The fireplace dominated one
end with an Elizabethan carved stone chimney-piece rising to the
plaster-moulded ceiling. Strong young footmen, wearing wasp-striped
red-and-yellow waistcoats under dark brown tail-coats, staggered in
with logs the size of a stout twelve-year-old boy. The fire generated a
tremendous heat and warmed two naked bronze figures on either side
of the hearth until they were hot enough to burn your hand. Under
the Sargent portrait of my aunt wearing a white dress with a blue sash
stood an enormous table laden with all the daily newspapers, as well as
a week's worth of *The Times*, several weeks' worth of the *Illustrated
London News*, the *Tatler*, the *Sketch*, *Punch* and about a year's supply
of the *National Geographic* magazines.

People staying in the house who didn't know the ropes hovered
by the fire in the hall waiting, as I did, to see what would happen
next. It was not a good place in which to settle to anything. Sooner or
later someone came through – a secretary on her way to my aunt in
her boudoir with a tray full of letters to be signed; domestics on their
way to make up fires or carry bags to bedrooms. Children clattered
down the wide slippery wooden stairs on their way to ride or walk their
dogs.

My aunt would come out of her room, chewing gum, dressed for
golf.

'Where are you all going?'

Too late. The children had got away.

I enjoyed grown up company and didn't mind being told (not asked)
to take visitors to see the gardens and the oak tree where Canning
wrote speeches. Nor did I rebel when told to take them to the war
cemetery cut into the chalk cliffs of Cliveden Woods above the Thames
where soldiers are buried who died in the Canadian Red Cross Hospital
during the First World War. I was proud of it all and glad to show it
off.

The fascination of discovering who was staying in the house also
goes down on the plus side of visits to Cliveden – outsiders were useful
as well as interesting because they drew off attention, and if there
weren't too many relations in the house-party the possibility of rows
was less. When we arrived we went straight to the table facing the
front door to study the room-list, not only to see who else was
coming but where we were to sleep. The printed list of bedrooms began

with the Buckingham Room and dressing-room on the first floor. This was the best suite, facing the splendid view to the south across acres of green lawn below the stone terrace on which the house stood, to the thick wooded cliffs that went down to the river half a mile away. Only once in my life did I sleep in the Buckingham Room and that was when Bill Astor had inherited Cliveden. As a married couple we sometimes rated the next-best bedroom across the passage, the Orange Flower Room with its Chinese wallpaper and northern prospect, but not very often.

In our childhood Tommy and I stayed in the Snowdrop Room on the nursery floor at the top of the stairs with a view north up the wide drive to the Italian marble shell fountain. But sometimes at Christmas as we grew older we were put in the Wing and that was something I did not like at all. The Wing was a separate block of rooms joined to the main house by a curved corridor. I disliked it because it was so far away from the centre of things and at night, sent to bed by 7.30, it felt very isolated indeed. Most of the bedrooms in the Wing faced away from the front door out into a large dark umbrella cedar tree, and the aspect was gloomy. I had a horror of the Wing. It was there we played terrifying games of hide-and-seek in the dark, and a spine-chilling exercise called Iroquois and Cherokees. This took place all over the house and down in the cellars where a railway line ran the length of the building to carry coals and goods from one distant end to the other. We played in teams; one base was set up at the door to the billiard-room in the Wing and the other two hundred yards away in the telephone-room by the butler's pantry. The object was for each player to get to the enemy's base and make his mark in blue pencil on a piece of paper. If the foe saw you *en route* you were taken prisoner. I hated it. There is no doubt about it – I was a coward.

But I enjoyed watching people and there were always plenty of them to watch at Cliveden. I was pleased when the guest-list had names new to me. More discoveries to be made. Sparks flew here, and there was often brilliant talk – and a good many shouting-matches. Before I had sense enough to keep out of them (not easy) I was not always happy at Cliveden, but I can't pretend there were problems all the time. I always found it a restless place and that, coupled with the possibility of being mocked or scolded, made me anxious, but much of the time I enjoyed being there because it was always lively, always a party – if a slightly perilous party.

Aunt Nancy always argued. I thought her interfering and narrow.

My ma and Aunt Nancy electioneering

She was. But occasionally she was right and she was always a fascinating character. She thought me headstrong and self-willed. I was. We came to love each other in the end. As a child I was scared of her sharp tongue. She had an uncanny knack of knowing just where to put the salt in the wound. She teased me for being fat, crying too easily and for my cowardice about riding. I was thin-skinned about myself, easily wounded and I resented Aunt Nancy's criticism of my mother, although, secretly, I knew some of it was justified. But I was fiercely loyal and I also dreaded the rows and the tears and the unhappy atmosphere generated by my powerful aunt. Now I can see her side of the picture and sympathise with her despair over my mother's repeated escapades. She rescued her time and time again and showed much understanding in the last year of my mother's life, when she was living alone in New York, lonely and unwell. Aunt Nancy opened up Little Orchard, the house she had built for my mother, where she was happy for so long, and took her back there to be cared for among her many friends until she died in 1955.

Aunt Nancy had charm, attraction, wit and great family feeling but she demanded priority in her relationships and that may be why she seemed to resent one's other friendships outside the family. The particular crime was to marry into another family. She could never *quite* like her relations-in-law.

'I can't think what you see in them – they're so boring. *Everyone* says so.'

Sometimes I was brave enough to ask her whom she meant by 'everyone'. She side-stepped attacks – 'Oh, you know, everyone – Alice and them.' Alice Winn was a favourite niece and 'Alice-and-them' was a vague but often employed suggestion that Aunt Nancy wasn't to blame for her opinions; she was merely quoting. Usually I was cowardly about counter-attacking, but now and then the injustice of her criticism got me down and I fought for my friends. She collapsed quickly and changed the subject. The small victory was some compensation for the irritation I felt over these unmerited attacks. With all our arguments and disagreements I continued to admire her courage and, as she grew older and gentler and I got braver and more compassionate, I became truly fond of her. I also learned with some amusement that when all in the family was going along peacefully together she didn't *really* like it. Give her a crisis and she rose to it with zest and was practical and effective, a tower of strength to those on whose side she was fighting; you couldn't have a better friend in time of trouble.

After she died a three-inch-thick file was sent back to me with my name stencilled on the cover. In it were letters I had written to her from the time I married in 1929 and carbons of the notes to me she had dictated over a period of about thirty-five years. In almost every one of my letters to her I am thanking her for something. We continued to argue on paper and, from 1939, largely about my job in the theatre. She had a puritanical attitude to the theatre and thought it wicked and, although I think she would have denied this, I believe it lay behind her endless nagging at me to 'get off the stage'.

'I can't think *why* you do it' – and with some truth – 'if your mother had ever decided to go on the stage *you* wouldn't have had a chance.' But she was reputed to say friendly things to other people about my work. I met Robert Donat at a party in 1941 and he told me that Aunt Nancy had said she was proud of me.

Finally all her attacking was forgotten and I was touched to find a letter in the file written to me just after I had opened for the first time on Broadway in October 1955.

I must write to you once more to tell you how delighted I am to think of your great success. I have passed round the notices and I might say someone has kept them, but that doesn't matter. The thing is that it (the first night) is over and you are a success.

After my mother died I wrote regularly to Aunt Nancy.

Admiration and gratitude were always in my feeling for her; so was criticism. I am still critical of her, but she taught me about giving – both how and how not to do it. There can never have been anyone more contradictory. I once made a list of her virtues and what I thought were her faults and they almost exactly cancelled each other out. With the merciful perspective of time it is the good things one remembers best, but I still get mad when I think how she disrupted perfectly harmless times, such as the fireside stories with my mother, simply because she was not part of them. And then I remember how funny she was and all else is forgiven. None of the books written about her has revealed the unique quality of her humour and charm. It is easier to describe her faults, but they were by no means the whole story.

CHAPTER EIGHT

'I Want to be an Actress'

Wʜᴇɴ I left school at seventeen my father insisted I should 'do something'. I was to 'come out' the following year when I was eighteen, but the time between had to be usefully filled. We discussed it a great deal. My father loved and respected the theatre and he wanted to be certain that I was serious about the stage. Did I know that the life of an actress was hard work and required discipline?

While I was still away at boarding school he had written to me:

I have always thought your line of work would be drawing and painting – probably in the poster line or that of theatrical design and *décor*. I still think it may be. At any rate I am not going to push my personal ideas in and say you are to do this or that. All I do know is that I would infinitely sooner see you doing a job of work than doing the ordinary sort of 'season business'. So that's how it is. Even if we don't say 'Hurrah! – jump in – the water's fine' – we certainly don't say 'Certainly ɴᴏᴛ'.

Half of me didn't want to do the 'season business' either. The other half couldn't wait to come out and be a deb. For me 'coming out' meant a milestone passed and a next stage arrived at between childhood and marriage. In my day growing up was a slow process until one came out. Then it was an over-night transformation. This had its advantages as well as its snags. We were allowed a much longer childhood, and more time to develop gently. We had the luxury of sheltered protection and an unhurried emergence into responsibility. Now little girls stop being children at twelve.

Looked at in cold blood it is clear that the idea of doing a 'season' was a way of ensuring that like-background met like-background and intermarried, and thus that class-structure was maintained. This no longer works in the enclosed way it once did. Like-minded is now much more important than like-background, and the class-structure, although a long time a-dying, is frailer and will alter to a healthier condition as it changes. Money will probably continue to separate people, but as we are allowed to own less of it, or the load is more evenly spread, the barriers are coming down and being crossed. I am in favour of this.

I persuaded my parents that I was serious about going into the theatre. I think I meant it, but I have no recollection of imagining what I wanted to do once I got there. The only training I ever had was the weekly elocution lesson with Mrs Alvey at my school, Clear View, in South Norwood on a hill near the Crystal Palace. There my 'best' friend was Vivien Alderson whose home was in Alexandria. In those days South Norwood was still partly country and we had a big sloping garden to play in and there were tennis lawns and a netball pitch behind the house. A public wood adjoined the property and the illusion of being in the country was sustained until a red double-decker bus went by and appeared above the garden wall. The school eventually outgrew its buildings and grounds and moved to Claremont at Esher. But that was after my day. So cramped were conditions at Clear View that Mrs Alvey's lessons on Friday afternoons had to be given in the Science Lab, and the Science Lab was really the conservatory, built on to the side of the house. There, among the Bunsen burners, I breathed and exercised my voice in duet with Mrs Alvey. At first glance she was hardly suited to teach the subject. Not only was she deaf but she was a cockney with adenoids. There she stood, short and thickset, with a blob of a nose and grey hair in an imprisoning Ena Sharples hairnet, teaching me to use my diaphragm as a bellows. She told of gifted pupils whose stomach-muscles were so fully developed that with a single intake and release of breath they could send a grand piano rolling across the room.

We did vocal exercises together. Deep breath; then, starting on a low note, she began: 'Adjels and bidisters of Grace defend us.' She moved up a tone. 'Adjels and bidisters of Grace defend us,' and so on up the scale, teaching us to articulate clearly on the slowly released breath. Mrs Alvey, who didn't wear a corset, invited her pupils to feel the iron discipline of her stomach-muscles by pressing as hard as they could on the beige inserted panel of her long plum-brown princess-line dress. She relied on Shakespeare to develop our vocal technique. 'The quality of bercy is dot strain'd,' she boomed, and I boomed after her. I was allowed to choose my own recitations and overacted in Jean Ingelow's *High Tide on the Coast of Lincolnshire*. I felt worldly and bitter in *The Forsaken Merman*. These recitations were rendered with intensity and not one glimmer of humour.

I had played my first part on any stage as a tinsel fairy in an improvised version of *Hansel and Gretel*, in Aunt Nancy's drawing-room at
Cliveden in the First World War, before an audience of wounded
soldiers. I was five. The role of the fairy was demanding. I had to hold
a wand with a star on it in one hand and a single leaf in the other. The
part called for me to trip on lightly, spot the unfortunate children
sleeping on the ground and drop my leaf as a means of disguising their
presence from the wicked villains who were out to get them. Not only
was this a first time on any stage, it was also a first time of wearing
proper, long, grown-up white stockings – joy, oh joy, the feel of them,
buttoned on to what was inaccurately known as a Liberty bodice by
tapes sewn to their tops. Tape doesn't yield, so after I had knelt to
deliver my leaf and risen jerkily to a standing position there were
sagging knees to the white stockings and quite a lot of wrinkling at the
ankles. It seems I was in no hurry to get off the stage and stood there
smiling in my tinselly sparkle and wobbly wings while my stockings
crept down my legs.

When I was eight I was miscast as a starving Burgher of Calais
in a school play at a church hall behind Peter Jones in Pavilion Road.
Moon-faced Maisie of the Brown Beans, equally miscast, was in
it too, and our portly figures in jagged sateen rags stood about the
dusty stage until we had a line to say; then we stepped forward and
said it. Mine was: 'Bread, bread, give us bread or we shall surely
die.' My particular starving Burgher had naturally pink cheeks, but
my mother, wishing me to appear at my best, topped up the colour
with a touch of powder rouge and a dab of pink lip-salve on my
mouth.

At my next, much grander school, Francis Holland, Graham Street,
(where I met my first 'best' friend Betty) there was a full-scale production of *As You Like It*. The Upper School played the leading parts
but representatives of the lower orders had their roles and mine was a
truncated version of the First Lord. The full part has never given much
opportunity for stealing the show and, cut down to one speech as it
was for me, it was practically invisible.

'Indeed my lord the melancholy Jaques grieves at that and in that
kind swears you do more usurp than doth your brother that hath
banished you.'

It was almost impossible to speak the last part of the speech without lisping, and I couldn't master 'melancholy'. The headmistress
Miss Morrison mocked me for saying 'melon-colly' and told me it

should be 'melan'cly'. As I had no idea what the lines meant and didn't like to ask, I doubt whether my reading amounted to much, though in the privacy of my bedroom I rehearsed it in a variety of voices, inflections and speeds. And because the words were meaningless to me I found the lines difficult to memorise, so the night before the performance I wrote them out very small in Indian ink on the palm of my left hand. They stayed there for days.

At my final and happiest school, Clear View, I was more at home in a cockney one-acter called *The 'At*. By this time I was the tallest girl in the school and except for the part of Miss Pole in *Cranford* I was always cast as a man. So boring. I am one of those women who has never at any time wanted to be anything else but a woman. Lord Dunsany wrote a dull play about Roman soldiers outside a gate and I had to be one of them in a toga and sandals. It was very chilly. I enjoyed *The 'At* because it was a comedy and I had a funny part in it and wore a suit and shoes of my father's and clowned around with a lot of self-satisfaction. I was a slight hit.

When it was decided that I should have a try at acting, my father talked to an old friend from the Lutyens office days, Nicholas Hannen, then a successful actor. He advised me to try and get into the Royal Academy of Dramatic Art where another contemporary of my father's was the Principal. Kenneth Barnes asked me to come and see him in his office and I did a bit of *As You Like It*, as taught me by Mrs Alvey. Somehow I got into RADA and I began in the autumn term of 1927. I had just spent six months in France learning the language and being 'finished', and my father thought it was a good idea to consolidate my French and at the same time find out if I really wanted to be a full-time student at RADA. I was put into Madame Gachet's French class and went up to Gower Street three or four times a week.

I lasted one term at the Academy and played one tiny part in a French play. It was a bucolic piece and I was a dairymaid in a mobcap and sang a pretty little folk-song called '*Quand la bergère vient des champs*' in such a high key that only a dog could have enjoyed it. (Dogs have a far higher sound receptivity range than man; or so I have always liked to believe.) That is about all I remember of my days at RADA except that Celia Johnson was in the play too. She was the only student I met there who gave the impression of total dedication to the theatre. Unlike me, and most of the others, she didn't want to be *thought* to be an actress, she wanted to act. She was very short-sighted and wore steel-rimmed glasses. Even in those early days everything she did showed talent and style. I looked on her with awe and admiration and I still do.

The reason I gave up RADA – or did RADA give me up? – is now forgotten. I had met Reggie and knew I was no longer stage-struck. The fancy had lasted a long time. I think I lost interest in acting in plays because I found it too restrictive. The lines were set and there was no room for spontaneous invention. In a play you had to wait to be spoken to before you could speak. This was not for me. I remember a day-dream to which I can put a date (it was long before James Thurber invented Walter Mitty). The time was 1922. I lay in the bath and thought, wouldn't it be marvellous to be well-known. Well-known for what? Well, being an actress perhaps? I remember, lumpy girl that I was at twelve, bad at gym and games, a longing to shine. I saw myself being recognised in the street and in restaurants. This is what I meant when I said I wanted to be an actress. It is not a good enough reason. I never got as far as dreaming myself inside a theatre or on a stage. I hadn't then realised that responding to an audience was more than a wish to shine.

RADA was the finish of my dreams of being an actress. But I continued to day-dream I was a dancer of infinite grace, moving in slow motion just off the floor, draped in floating chiffon, and I was breathtakingly good at it. This dream took a long time to die; in fact it isn't dead yet. I have only to suspend reason and I'm off, weightless as an astronaut, all fluidity, rising up and over the surface of the room, the street, the countryside. I need no audience, it is quite enough to feel the power and control I have over my exquisite form as it responds to my will. I don't need music. I am the music and the movement.

I Mitty'd all through adolescence about being brave in the face of danger. I saved lives from drowning and fires and stilled panic by my simple rendering of a song. Fortunately I was never called upon to test these heroic dreams.

Apart from singing with my mother I had no party turn. I loved singing with her but cussedly I would not admit it. It was her pride in me that I found irritating. It must be difficult to be a successful mother. It doesn't seem to be easy to find the right balance in encouraging your children. Those mothers who say coldly 'You could have done better' probably do more harm than the mothers like my own who told me I was a success whatever I did. Our mother's line certainly gave us confidence. To her we were remarkable, in her eyes everything we did was special and original, and if you are an honest child, and

I believe I was, you know this is not so. I didn't contradict my mother's view of me but I was irked by it and punished her by being tiresome and unco-operative when she called on me to show off my small talents. Performers who have to be persuaded are a big bore. Now, though I am a professional entertainer and know that it is unseemly to be eager, I have only to sniff the scent of sawdust and like a circus horse I am off at a gallop. But not always. The way to make sure of not turning on the tap is for a hostess to say: 'Oh *do* do one of your funny little skits.' I think my readiness to perform now is not solely a wish to show off. It is sometimes a feeling of wanting to share something I've found funny or sad.

As I wrote earlier, my mother played the guitar in a rudimentary way, but such was her charm and so pleasing her naturally sweet soprano voice, always dead in tune, that she beguiled her listeners, particularly the musical ones. She and I sang the songs of her girlhood. I held the tune and she put in the primitive church harmonies, barbershop style. Occasionally she got adventurous and took liberties with the accompaniment, but mostly we stuck to square harmonies. Later I learned about descants, found I could invent them for our songs, so we changed places, she took the tune and I embroidered. Now and then, the year before I came out, she took me to parties where we sang. I was grumpy about it but secretly enjoyed both the singing and the attention.

Gerald du Maurier was a real star at that time, and my cup was full when he took me down to supper and told me that I looked like his father's drawings. I had never seen one of his father's drawings but hoped it was kindly meant. Some ten years later, looking at an old copy of *Punch*, I saw it had been; and in 1945 I wrote a song with Richard Addinsell about a young du Maurier woman and sang it in Noël Coward's peace-time revue *Sigh no More*.

Apart from school performances I had no experience in amateur entertainment until around 1930 a group of us got up a fund-raising concert at Tunbridge Wells. Someone suggested we should call ourselves The Bright Spots and no one had the courage to say no. When I think of our nerve in putting it on at all, I blush. That is because I have become a pro and my sights have risen. But there is an unkind pleasure in watching bad amateurs, so perhaps the charity supporters at the Pump Room that night had some fun.

One thing the English are not good at is forgetting themselves. I sang a duet with Dick Talbot, holding trembling hands, neither of us daring to look at the other from start to finish, though we sang warmly, 'You are my Lucky Star'. We also sang 'Spread a Little Happiness', backed by a group of friends dressed *à la* Co-Optimists, a famous revue company of the twenties. We did sketches we had seen in London revues. The one about the confused customer trying to buy a dozen double damask dinner napkins went well I remember. Whether we did it from memory or bought the copy and paid a royalty I have conveniently forgotten, but none of us was a thief by nature; it simply didn't occur to us that we owed anyone anything for the use of the material.

The situation today is only a little less blatant. I get letters from eager amateur performers telling me they are working my songs and monologues, taken from long-playing records or taped from radio and television programmes. They write to say they can't quite catch the last line in the second verse and will I please type it out and send it to them by next Friday because that's the day for the rehearsal for the old age pensioners' social. Demands for scripts always follow a television appearance. 'My friends tell me I'm very like you and they love it when I perform your nursery school sketches. Have you any more? Please send me what you can.' Sometimes they send a stamp, but not very often. Is it meant to be flattering? Perhaps I should have a printed form set up saying that my material is the tool I work with and while it is in my repertoire I cannot let it go because it would get frayed at the edges and no longer be mine. Instead I write in longhand, as kindly as I know how, and my advice, which is sincere and practical, is that they should have a go at writing their own sketches. If, as I imagine they believe, they have a talent for performing sketches, then probably they can invent them.

For The Bright Spots I designed and hand-painted the girls' costumes – white Roman furnishing satin sheaths with stiff net Pierrot frills at the neck and around the hem. Bunches of bright flowers appeared all over the place painted in coloured waterproof inks, and we each had a different coloured hair-ribbon and sash. I have a photograph of us standing in a row, out-of-doors somewhere, and none of the four men and only one of the seven girls is sparkling. She was Luise Blackburn, a professional dancer who came to London from America in 1926 with an athletic troupe called The Hoffman Girls. They appeared at the Hippodrome Theatre and climbed up webbing nets that swung them out over the audience; and they did the New Zealand Maori wrist dance, Poi-Poi, in unison sitting on the floor

'*Oh, Mr du Maurier*'

of the stage, and were a big hit. When their tour ended Luise stayed on in London hoping for work. She was 'resting' when we did our concert so was free to join in. Her contribution was a dance incorporating cartwheels and the splits. A dear girl but not very talented. None of us was.

Luise became part of my family in an unlikely way. She was a little older than I was but young enough to continue going to Sunday School, where we met. At that time I was in love with all things American. I had read the St Nicholas magazine since I was small, I devoured American movie magazines, envied American shoes and pined to get over there to visit my relations. So I made friends with this new American Sunday School girl and took her home to lunch. The family responded to her at once. My mother was having a turn-out and gave Luise a pink satin evening dress. Luise liked it so much that she wore it to Sunday School the next Sunday. Times were difficult for

Luise Blackburn with Laura as a little girl

her. The girls she roomed with had abandoned hope of work in London and were going home to New York. My mother asked her to come and stay with us. A bed was put in the old schoolroom behind the dining-room and she had a key and came and went as she wanted. She was never in the way, indeed we hardly knew she was there, but somehow she stayed on for years and left only when the divorce happened and my father sold the house.

She was the most unexpected chorus girl you could imagine – innocent, unspoilt, unworldly, full of zest and hopes. Work was hard to find but she never stopped practising and going to auditions and finally C. B. Cochran gave her a job at the London Pavilion; he was also putting on cabaret shows at the Trocadero and offered Luise a part in a late-night show. She thought the money was not enough and asked to see him about it. She came home and told my father he had stepped up his offer after she had said: 'Mr Cochran, if you want pulchritude with purity you have to pay for it.' All our friends took to her and she came to parties and was much loved by us all.

The cause for which we were raising funds in Tunbridge Wells was one for which I would no longer give tuppence, the Conservative Party. But I wouldn't help raise tuppence for the Lib or the Lab lot either because politically I am non-aligned. I deeply dislike and distrust party politics. I have voted most things in my time. But not Communist. And if I were a Scot or Welsh or Irish I should never vote Nationalist. The world is already too small to break it up into local groups. As I see it we must fight for the rights of individuals, not because they are Scots, Welsh, Irish, English, black or white but because they are the rights of mankind and must be respected.

CHAPTER NINE

Radio Critic into Entertainer

I DO not like a lot of my attitudes in the past, and one of the reasons I have not enjoyed looking back to the early 1930s is the humiliating discovery that I was narrow-minded, prejudiced, self-centred and self-righteous. I think I must have been a very late starter in spite of my apparent sophistication; a false façade as I now realise. No good making excuses but it is the reason why I have not dwelt on those early years.

The late 1930s wasn't an easy time for anyone. I was optimistically sure there would never be a war; Reggie was less certain. We had married in December 1929 on the prospect of a good job for him, but, as happened to so many other people at that difficult time, the job collapsed. We heard about it two days before the wedding. Reggie worked for companies his father managed, but they were precarious and we lived from crisis to crisis; yet somehow we managed, greatly helped by the generosity of my aunts and my cousin Nancy. They gave me presents of clothes and cash, included us in family feasts and festivities as well as week-ends, and for two summers we were lent Greenwood Cottage on the Cliveden estate. Greenwood Cottage had always been used to lend to people. My family had it from 1915 to 1917 after my father was invalided out of the army and went to Washington to work for a Government Department, while my mother, Tommy and I stayed in England. All through the 1920s we had it, off and on, for holidays and the summer. When Aunt Nancy and Uncle Waldorf (her idea and his financial backing) offered to let us live in another cottage on the place until such time as we were better off, we gratefully let our house in London, and in April 1936 we moved to the country.

Parr's Cottage was named after the Astor family butler, an impressive man who lived there until he emigrated to America. Aunt Nancy engaged my architect father to design a staff addition and generally modernise the cottage for us; and from a stuffy dull beige stucco box with a shiny red brick trim he turned it into an attractive, cheerful, welcoming little whitewashed house decked with green paint. Not only did Aunt Nancy have all this done for us but she gave us money to help furnish it – a whole £100. At the time that was real money. For the record: we had made to order from Heal's in Tottenham Court Road four extra-long beds at £10 a pair. Our folding mahogany dining-room table cost £2 10s in the Caledonian Market; unstained oak bookcases from Peter Jones cost £2 10s each; a three-seater sofa and two armchairs were built for us by Vernon & Bromhead in Jubilee Place, Chelsea, for £20 the lot. Until we could run to chintz I bought pink and white checked dress gingham at 1s 11d a yard to do for the living-room curtains. In a sale at Harvey Nichols a grey pile carpet for the dining-room, approximately eight feet by ten, cost £3. Those were the days.

We had no children and at first this was a sadness, partly because all my friends were having babies and I was left out. But we got used to being childless and I am now increasingly grateful that we did not have a family because, although I know Reggie would have been a wonderful father and grandfather, I think I might have been a bossy nagger of a mother. I would quite like to have been a grandmother, but then that's not a difficult thing to be – all the pleasure and little of the responsibility. Looking round at the couples we know who have *remained* consistently happily married I notice that many are childless. Of course it is possible to rationalise anything, and may be that is what I am doing, but I believe there is some truth in what I am saying. Compensating could be a part of it? Perhaps, but it looks to me as if childless couples who are truly devoted find fulfilment without the accepted necessity of dividing allegiance and are not to be pitied.

Because we were very short of money I worried, and now I wonder why it never occurred to me to take over the running of the house myself. I couldn't cook but I could have learned, and the saving in wages and food would have been considerable. (Second thoughts: though the pound was worth a great deal more than it now is, wages were so low that I don't know whether I could have saved much.) We reduced our staff to one – Rene Easden, a quiet, efficient and cheerful local girl who became an important part of our life.

So I had to find a job, but doing what? I drew a little and had been trained for nothing except poster-painting (two terms of night classes at the Westminster Polytechnic). I had designed two posters, one a private commission for gardens open to the public in aid of the Northumberland District Nurses' Association, and the other for a domestic air-line that almost instantly closed down. I had sold a set of Christmas cards to W. H. Smith & Son. This was hardly a full-time occupation for a free-lancer living in the country.

Naïvely I wondered whether I could sing with a band. The few times I had done it at parties, when I visited my mother in America, I had found the microphone easy to use, and listening to the voices we heard on radio and in restaurants I was confident enough to think I could do it too. When we lived in London our idea of a gala evening was to dine and dance to Carroll Gibbons' band at the Savoy. They made a special price for the young, and for £2 10s a couple could eat the table-d'hôte menu and dance till the music stopped. Carroll Gibbons got used to seeing us there and we made friends. I asked his advice. He said I could learn a lot by listening to myself on disc, and offered to make a record with me, and advised me where to book a studio. This was a very kind thing to do because I was only an amateur.

We recorded 'You'd be so easy to love' and when I heard it I wanted to crawl into a hole and vanish. The actual singing wasn't too bad although it was frail; there was no projection and no firm centre to any of the notes and my vowel sounds were a shock. I was forced to accept that it was I who sang 'Yew'd be sow easy to lurve'. I knew nothing about recording nor about covered vowels. I don't remember what Carroll Gibbons said about it but I knew that singing was not then a good way for me to make money. It took a long time for the right job to be found and it happened in a roundabout way.

Ever since crystal sets were available I'd been a radio fan. My brother and I sat in our London schoolroom wearing headphones and squabbled over who was to move the 'cat's whisker' over the crystal to find the programme. We weren't allowed to listen until we had done our homework. After half an hour or so we were told to get something to do; the wireless was considered a waste of time. But years later, when we moved to Parr's Cottage, I found the radio companionable and stimulating. In the evening Reggie and I heard comedy programmes and plays, and by day I listened to a lot of music. One noon a piano recital was broadcast which included Bach's Italian Concerto, a work I particularly like. I was expected up at the big house for one o'clock luncheon but I couldn't bear to leave the radio before the Concerto finished. This meant a hurried bicycle ride up the drive to Cliveden about one and quarter miles away. Some of it is hilly and I arrived breathless and overheated. It was a luncheon party and they had already gone into the dining-room. Pink with rush and guilt I slid into my seat, apologising to my aunt. She ticked me off and went on talking to her neighbour. I found myself sitting next to Mr J. L. Garvin, the editor of the *Observer*, and he asked me why I was late. Until you knew him he seemed to be rather an alarming man, with a fierce face and an eye that wandered. He could be quite chilling, but that only meant he was not aware of one's presence and was thinking about other things. On this occasion he was agreeable and kind. I explained about the Bach and he said he didn't think anyone ever listened to the wireless. I said I did, a lot.

'Do you hear much music by wireless?'

'Oh yes,' I said, astonished that he didn't know about the marvels available. '*Lots* of music. And plays and talks and variety programmes.'

He must have registered my enthusiasm, because some months later when it was decided to start a radio column in the *Observer* he offered me the job. Hilda Matheson had been writing in the paper about radio policy, the international importance of radio, and other erudite aspects of broadcasting, but now they wanted something more immediate, a man-in-the-street review and opinion on what the BBC was pouring out into the air. I had no writing experience except for two years of occasional verses for *Punch*, and it was on the strength of this that Mr Garvin hired me. I needed a job and here it was. Writing was what I wanted to do; by now the idea of going on the stage had long disappeared.

In March 1937 Mr Garvin sent for me to come and see him at Gregories, his house not far from us at Beaconsfield. He told me I was to have six weeks' apprenticeship to learn the radio critic's job for the *Observer*. I could choose what I listened to, write seven hundred and fifty words about it, divided into seven or eight paragraphs, and send this to the paper in London to be set up in print. When the proof reached me I was to bring it back to him and together we would go through my article. He gave me rules to work by, written in his large energetic hand on a big blue sheet of writing paper.

Avoid 'which' and 'and'. Stop and start again.
Facts first – feelings later.
Indicate, don't elaborate.
Short sentences are more telling.

For three weeks I carried out this plan, listened carefully, wrote and rewrote the paragraphs with zeal. Then Mr Garvin said he had cut the apprenticeship: I was ready to go into the next week's *Observer*, and on 11 April my first piece appeared, unsigned. In it I see I praised a Robert Mayer Children's Concert, was critical about a production of *The Cherry Orchard* and otherwise trod carefully, feeling my way. My professional life had begun.

A month later I began to get into my stride. In a week of splendid broadcasts I heard Flora Robson as Cassandra and thought her power-ful, but was not enthusiastic about *The Trojan Women* on radio and boldly wrote that I had found it too slow and too long. But Harold Nicolson reminiscing from Northern Ireland pleased me well. He remembered by sensation – 'tight elastic on a sailor hat, the carved door handle at Clandeboye, and boots loosely laced'. The same evening Compton Mackenzie on the National Programme (later the Home Service and now Radio 4) claimed his memory went back to when he was fifteen months old and watched *A Comedy of Errors* sitting on his nurse's lap. When he was two he fell down a well at Malvern and admired the ferns and patterns of damp on the walls as he was hauled up.

Caroline Lejeune, then the best film critic in the business and one of the *Observer's* brightest stars, told me that when she got a First at Manchester University she decided that if she was clever enough to achieve that she ought to be able to do what she best liked doing and get paid for it; and that is what happened. She was earning her living doing what she most enjoyed – going to the movies. Listening to the radio was hardly the thing I *most* liked doing, but I was a natural radio listener and the job gave me a chance to write, and that was what I most wanted to do. I was having a good time being a radio critic.

We were now settled at Parr's. Another generous aunt, Phyllis Brand, passed on to us her old Wolseley car and we made dignified progress in it until it finally sighed and died, and then our universal provider, Aunt Nancy, gave us a newer and more reliable two-door Ford, dark red and low on petrol consumption.

When we were courting Reggie had given me an occasional driving lesson in his family's high open Austin. This was really an excuse for an escape together to Richmond Park. He bought a little paper bag of green lime-drops for these outings and put them near my seat in the car pocket but was too shy to tell me they were there. I always found them and recognised the signal of his silent overture and loved him increasingly.

I had never really learned to drive until we spent our first summer in Greenwood Cottage, when I was thrown in at the deep end. On Saturday I had never been alone in a car; two days later on Monday morning I drove Reggie to the station, came back to the cottage on my own, and went to fetch him home again, solo, that evening. We had practised a good deal over the week-end. That is, Reggie sat beside me and said: 'Now change gear – look out for the ditch – there's a rather large bus coming . . .' I sweated at the wheel. By Monday morning I had a vague sense of the 'feel' of driving, but we allowed ourselves thirty-five minutes to do the two-mile journey to Taplow Station and needed all of it. With every gear-change I stalled the engine. I stalled it again when I put on the brake at the slightest curve, and again when I saw another vehicle moving in any direction. Reggie was understandably concerned about my solo return to the cottage and wondered whether perhaps it wouldn't be wiser for me to walk home and leave the car for him to collect later that day. But trembling I said I was sure I could do it. The return trip took ten minutes longer than the outward journey because I used up so much time trying to turn the car round in the narrow approach to the station. I thought it politic to wait until all the other cars, chauffeurs and taxi-drivers had left before I dared attempt to reverse. The usual starting and stalling and grinding of gears, and I caused the car to buck in an alarming way. I wept a little, swore a lot and eventually looked up and saw the car was actually facing the way it needed to go. I drove back at a maximum of five miles an hour. After that my confidence increased and I mastered not stalling the engine; but I have always remained a *lento* driver. I don't like speed when I'm driving and I dislike it even more when I'm being driven.

Even before the *Observer* job my days were agreeably full. In a small way I was involved in local activities – an Infant Welfare Centre in Slough Trading Estate, the Women's Institute and choir, and my church. I played a lot of tennis and was on call to Aunt Nancy to help with week-end parties and general odd jobs. This was a small way of trying to pay back some of her generosity. The secretary rang up from London.

'Lady Astor would like you to meet a Japanese princess and her party on Tuesday morning to show them the garden and the house. And she wants a wedding present for a godchild. Please consult with Mrs Ford, the housekeeper, about new lampshades for one of the dressing-rooms; and please will you get Lady Astor some of those biscuits you mentioned.'

I well remember the royal Japanese visitors. We made the tour of the gardens together, sign language and smiles in constant use, and then we fetched up at the house. One of the English-speaking ladies-in-waiting whispered to me that her Royal Highness had left London *very* early that morning. . . . She was too delicate to put it more bluntly. I led the Princess up the red staircase to my aunt's comfortable carpeted dressing-cum-bathroom with its pink camellia-patterned chintz curtains, many built-in cupboards and a dressing-table with pots of cold cream and bottles on it and a pin-cushion spiked with outdated hat pins. The long bath was enclosed at one end by glass screens and had an elaborate arrangement of sprays and a shower and three sets of taps. The W.C., cleverly disguised as a large white wicker-work arm-chair, stood against a wall. I didn't like to point it out to the tiny Princess so I left her to work things out for herself and shepherded the other ladies to other bathrooms in the house. We waited a full half hour before the Princess appeared, inscrutable as ever but, I thought, a little flushed. We had all been getting anxious.

The dogs forced me out for daily walks within the park at Cliveden. Reggie's large black labrador, Nan, with a tail like a windscreen-wiper, swept everything movable off low-lying surfaces. My black spaniel, Gary, came from a pet shop when he was the size of a fur glove and was not like other spaniels: he was born without any sporting or competitive instinct and believed rabbits were provided as playmates for his special pleasure. He looked bewildered and wounded when he lolloped towards them, all eager friendliness, to see them streak away and vanish down holes. He was a pacific dog dear to my heart. I gardened a little, drew and painted a little, wrote verses, played the piano (badly) and sang the songs of our day, as well as (in private) more testing pieces by Fauré, Schubert and Bach.

Now my chief occupation was listening to the radio. The *Observer* bought me a superior new set, a Murphy, and when it first came the novelty of it caused me to sit up into the early hours of the morning, twiddling knobs in the short-wave band, finding snatches of far-away conversations. It didn't matter how dull the talk was – it mostly consisted of radio hams identifying themselves to each other – the miracle of hearing anyone on another remote continent was enough. Once I got on to a famous American programme called The Major Bowes Amateur Hour and this made me feel close to my mother, for she always listened to that programme down in North Carolina. I listened whenever a broadcast promised to amuse, interest or educate me, sometimes in the morning, but mostly in the evening. Meals and chores were fitted in to programme-times. Perhaps portable radios weren't then available; I know I had to be in the living-room to listen to my wireless, plugged in by my armchair.

It was no hardship for either Reggie or me to give up most of our social life to hear programmes. We are sociable but we have never been very social and, though we are no longer gregarious, our friends grow more and more important to us. In London we had gone out a good deal but not to many parties (this was also partly for economy). The demands of my job gave us a ready excuse for avoiding going out when we didn't want to. If a special occasion arose it was usually possible to arrange a hearing of important programmes ahead of transmission. This was a help when broadcasts I wanted to write about were planned for Friday and Saturday, because if I wished to see a proof my copy had to reach the paper by Friday morning. Otherwise additional paragraphs could be dictated over the telephone just in time for printing. Going to Broadcasting House was a new experience, and I felt very special when I announced myself to the girl at the reception desk: Joyce Grenfell of the *Observer*.

I have been going to Broadcasting House ever since, wearing a variety of hats. From radio critic I went as performer; I was a member of the Pilkington Committee on Broadcasting (1960–62) and later, for six years, I was on the B.B.C. Advisory Council. In between and to this day I go as performer or talker.

Mr Garvin continued to keep a friendly eye on me and sent me encouraging notes:

You have got the flick of the wrist in writing. Stick to the terse rhythm, but never let it become irksome. The moment *you* feel that staccato is cramping you, go legato a bit if you like.

The *Observer* paid £10 a week for the job. This was real money and we needed it. Two young men friends of ours, then rising well up the ladder of the diplomatic corps (both became ambassadors, one a peer and the other a knight) were justifiably surprised to learn I was earning exactly the same as they were. They had had to pass exams to get their money. I knew it wasn't fair and felt guilty. Reggie said people might not be paid enough but were rarely paid more than they were worth. In my case I wasn't sure this was true but it didn't keep me awake at night.

I found it difficult to concentrate for long, listening to the wireless, unless I had something to do with my hands, so I drew or sewed and made notes about what I heard. In season I made Christmas cards and presents and all through the year I sewed fine seams, making petticoats and camiknickers and nightgowns for myself and special friends. It was worth putting handwork into real silk *crêpe-de-chine* and sheer handkerchief linen lawn. I took to making blouses from sales remnants but never managed to set the sleeves in the right way round at the first try. I prided myself on my tiny stitches and learned to make tucks and roll hems and do *appliqué*.

Some of the listening was done from a sense of duty rather than pleasure. There was a distinction between radio plays and radio dramas. It was the dramas I didn't fancy. I thought they were conceived on a scale too grand for the medium, with crowd scenes and sound-effects, fanfares and specially commissioned music. They were 'costume plays' for the most part, sometimes written in verse. I imagined the actors in tweed suits (both sexes) moving quickly from far corners of the studio toward the microphone and away again, murmuring 'rhubarb, rhubarb' in a variety of moods – menacing rising to rage; enthusiastic-loyal, disapproving-disloyal; bucolic-cheerful; socially merry with high laughter. They played in the market-place as country-folk, on castle ramparts and in forums as conflicting partisans. They gave us confronting parties in places of government – the House, the mill and the pit head – and none of it was my favourite kind of radio. In modern plays and features the cliché sound-effects grew tiresome. I began to wonder whether the sound-effects department had only one recording of a creaking door, only one car-engine revving up, one screech of brakes and up-fling of drive-gravel. These became very familiar to the regular listener; and so did the crying of gulls, a shorthand sign-post to tell us the scene was set at or by the sea. The birds became a joke.

I had been writing the column for sixteen months when I was surprised by a feature programme with a difference. It was called 'Guide to the Thames'. As I listened I noticed the players did not address the microphone head-on every time they spoke, as I had grown to expect they would (in the manner of old-school actors trained to speak directly outwards across the footlights). In the crowd scenes they spoke to each other, sideways-on as it were, putting the listener in the position of eavesdropper, the third side of a triangle. The dialogue gave the impression of being improvised. Sentences, as in real life, were left unfinished and gave the effect of the microphone moving amongst people instead of people coming up to speak into the microphone. It made a vivid picture.

I wrote about 'Guide to the Thames' on 14 August 1938, and noted it had pace, humour and style and was not built-to-order but 'written with enthusiasm and given with freshness'. The *Radio Times* said it was written and produced by Stephen Potter. Phyllis Spender Clay, now married to Philip Nichols, was a friend of Stephen Potter and his wife Mary and, after reading my piece in the *Observer*, she thought we should meet. It took time to arrange a date and it wasn't until early in November that Reggie and I came up from Parr's to dine and stay the night with the Nicholses at their corner house in Chester Square near Victoria. It was an unexpectedly country-like house to find in London, and Phyllis kept it simple with pale linen covers and curtains, and I remember pretty Italian pottery she had brought back from Rome where Phil was First Secretary at the British Embassy.

Stephen Potter, who had been a lecturer at the University of London and written a book about Coleridge, was at that time working in the BBC features department under Laurence Gilliam. It was Gilliam who revolutionised that department and chose Stephen to join his staff. Stephen was tall and rangy with rough fair hair on end. His tie never sat right underneath his collar and he smoked dangerously. Carpets and chair-covers in the houses of his friends were scarred with little black holes where his ash had burned. You could push an ashtray toward him but he never saw it until too late. He told me his worst burning was an entire sofa.

His wife Mary was called Att by those who had known her as Mary Attenborough at the Slade School. She is a very distinguished painter and when we first met her she was already well known and highly regarded. The impression she made on me that night at the Nicholses' has lasted – a woman of quiet charm, country feeling, warm, with a pleasing wide cat-smile. She still dresses in her own dateless fashion, in the colours of her own individual palette that she uses in her paintings – chalky terracottas, pale turquoise, faded blues, whites, creams, grey and stone colours, sharp yellows, pale sage greens, soft browns and reds. Att 'fixes' flowers (my mother's phrase) so that they don't look as if they had been organised. Three yellow roses in a milk jug 'fixed' by Att satisfy my eye better than any specialist's arrangement. (I have a prejudice against flower arrangements unless they are superlatively handled, as they were by Constance Spry. It is the lesser talents I deplore, the anglicised Japanese type of horror – two vertical bulrushes with an iris emerging from a bit of old drift-wood, sitting on a brass Benares tray. In New Zealand I saw an exhibition of flower arrangements set to a theme, 'Spring in Paris'. One had a little metal Eiffel Tower, a rose and a lady's garter . . .)

At dinner with the Nicholses and Potters I found myself describing a talk our Women's Institute had heard at the monthly meeting in the Recreation Hall at Cliveden a few days earlier. The visiting speaker told us about Useful and Acceptable Gifts and how to make something from nothing. She had an unlocalised accent of great daintiness and spoke carefully, every consonant sharply finished and smartly delivered with all her vowels aslant. Her lecture was a collector's item and I collected it. It wasn't only what she said that was worth garnering but also the way she said it. My audience was responsive and I made the most of being the centre of attention. We sat on at the candle-lit table while I got 'possessed' as I used to do in the dormitory at boarding-school. There was no need to invent any of it. The stuff was rich grist and I simply milled it. Considering what a lot I got out of that talk I suppose I should have discovered the lecturer's name and sent her a royalty, but at the time I didn't know about such things.

After the dinner-party we all said we must meet again, but Reggie and I were living in Bucks and the Potters at Chiswick, and the Nicholses went back to Rome. Then about Christmas time the Potters wrote to say they were having a little party on Friday 13 January 1939, and hoped we would come. On that cold and frosty night I met Herbert Farjeon and the direction of my life was changed.

Bertie Farjeon was the author of the revue *Nine Sharp*, then just finishing a sell-out run at the Little Theatre in the Adelphi. He was also theatre critic on the *Tatler* and had edited the Nonesuch Shakespeare. He had a face I always wanted to draw because it was unorthodox and fascinating; an El Greco face, slightly crooked, long, pale and bony. He had El Greco-like hands, too, with fine wrist-bones. His eyes, behind glasses, were very dark and when he laughed he did it silently but shook his head and shoulders.

I came to know him as the perfect listener to whom to read new material. He wasn't easy to please but when he liked something he showed it generously. We were on the same wave-length in a great many ways, but I didn't agree with him when he said as long as there was emotion the world would survive. I would have said in spite of emotion, and because of love, life is indestructible. Apart from Reggie and my father, Bertie was the man whose opinion of my work mattered

Stephen Potter and I working in my kitchen

most. I am grateful that it was he who started me off in the career that has been such a passport and door-opener.

B.B.C. friends of Stephen's, a Swedish diplomat and Francis Meynell are some of the people I remember at the Potters' party. The room was full and friendly. We felt welcome. The atmosphere was sympathetic, and I was there as a fellow professional among artists and writers and actors. Delicious cold foods – long French loaves of bread, a board covered with cheeses, a big block of butter on a dish and plates of Austrian *apfelstrudel* – were laid on top of the piano, among other places, and most of us ate sitting on the floor. I had just finished eating when Stephen came over to where I was, next to the Swedish diplomat, and said: 'Will you please do that Women's Institute lecture for us.'

Except for school plays and the momentary lapse as a Bright Spot I had never been a party entertainer. Getting 'possessed' was different and did not happen to order. I had not thought of the Women's Institute talk since the evening at the Nicholses' two months before and I said as much, but Stephen said: 'Please do it,' and clapped his hands for silence.

'Joyce Grenfell is going to give us a lecture.'

Years ago I had played hard to get when my mother wanted me to sing with her, but I had grown up since then and, though I protested a little at Stephen's startling announcement, there was an expectant silence and I knew it was up to me to fill it. It seemed less alarming to speak from where I sat on the floor. I explained about the Women's Institute occasion and told the party about the gifts we could all make, including a *boutonnière* from empty beech-nut-husk clusters to cheer up the lapel of a tired winter suit. I said that all the gifts I would tell about were not only easy to *make* but ever so easy to dispose of. I reproduced the manner of the lecturer, click-finished my consonants and slid my vowels as she had. I also remembered her way of pointing to the imaginary lapel with her little finger, the hand, palm up, against her chest.

I told of modernistic waste-paper-baskets made from disused biscuit tins, obtained by making love to our grocer and wheedling him into giving them to us; of candlesticks built from empty wooden cotton-reels, and decorative daisies for the mantelshelf or window-sill contrived by marrying pipe-cleaners to white linen pillow-slip buttons and fixing them firmly into blobs of our kiddies' plasticine at the bottom of wee honey-pots or fish-paste containers. And finally I gave them the lecturer's 'comic turn' – Dicky Calendars. 'Dicky is made from two indiarubbers or, as I called them when I went to school – BUNJIES.'

What I didn't remember I made up, and it went well. I stood up after this and someone brought me a glass of lemonade. I had noticed (I was already aware of the audience) a quiet man sitting on a chair against the wall at the back of the room. He had laughed appreciatively and was still amused when he arrived at my side.

'May I ask who wrote that piece you just did?'

'No one wrote it,' I said. 'It was mostly a *real* talk to our Women's Institute meeting in the country, and I embroidered on it.'

'Do you think you could write it down? I'd like to use it in my new revue.'

He said his name was Herbert Farjeon. And I was even more flattered, because we had been twice to see *Nine Sharp* and thought it splendid.

Driving home with Reggie through frosty fog, the evening whirled through my head – the pretty little house with its upstairs drawing-room, white walls, white sofa, white-covered divan and one scarlet-

Herbert Farjeon

patterned armchair; Mary Potter's pictures framed in light wood hanging on the walls; soft lighting, the fire bright and early spring flowers around. The evening had been a success and I was on fire with the excitement of it all and Bertie's invitation to me to write the sketch. We discussed it as we nosed our way along the old Great West Road towards Parr's.

It is therefore a surprise to find how coolly I played it in my weekly letter to my mother written two days later, on Sunday, 15 January. (Shortly before she died she sent me a parcel of all the letters I had written to her through the middle 1930s.) The first three and a half pages are full of the news of Virginia and Tony Thesiger's engagement. At the bottom of the fourth page I wrote on a separate line:

'I don't remember what else happened.'

But then the Potters' party must have come zooming back to me. 'There were about twelve of us for supper,' (so much for my impression of twice that number) 'and we sat and talked.' I described my performance and what Bertie had said to me. 'So on Wednesday I'm toiling up to St John's Wood' (toiling! I couldn't wait to get there) 'to lunch with him and his wife. . . . Rather fun even if it doesn't come off.'

A week later I wrote that I had been to St John's Wood and met Charlotte Leigh for whom I thought the sketch was intended. I had got it down on paper and after we had had lunch I read it aloud and Bertie said yes, he did want it for the new revue in March. He and his wife Joan were relieved to find it was as funny as they hoped it was; because the day after the Potters' party they had begun to wonder whether perhaps they had dreamed it; or had it simply been a very good party? Charlotte Leigh thought I ought to come into the revue and do the lecture myself. I took that to be politeness. But Bertie agreed with her.

I forgot to tell you that Mr Farjeon actually wanted me to come into the revue but I don't think I'd be good on a stage – I may do all right in a small room but the stage is quite different. Anyway he wrote to me and said that if I ever did want to I must let him know at once, whether tomorrow or in five years time! Nice that.

At first I didn't seriously entertain this crazy idea, nor did Reggie, but Bertie wrote and asked me to think again about his offer. He seemed convinced I'd succeed on the stage and said he thought I should try it and see. It seemed foolish not to take the risk but, as I wrote to my mother, I didn't particularly want to go on the stage.

This oddly enough was true. I was contented with the quiet life in the country and my enjoyable radio jobs, and here was an invitation, unexpected and unsought, decidedly flattering but disruptive. Of course I played with the idea and imagined the first night, but I did not expect or want stardom. The role I was offered was an 'extra', a guest appearance in a revue. I would not be part of the cast and this lessened the weight of responsibility. Not for a moment, even then, did I think of the theatre as a career. Writing was what I wanted to do and if I went into the revue it would be a once-only experience, certainly an adventure, but not important in the way the critic's job was important to me. Perhaps that is why I wasn't nervous about trying something different. I didn't expect to fail or I would not have said I would do it; but nor did I dream dreams of show-stopping success. It was not modesty that kept me from Mittying. The point was that the theatre job did not matter one way or the other. Being *asked* to do it was the thing; how it was going to work out did not yet concern me.

As the idea of going into the revue grew in my mind I asked the three most important men in my life what they thought about it. Mr Garvin felt that whatever widened my horizon made me more valuable to the paper. My father thought I might as well have a try –

why not? And my husband, who is a very wise man and realised he would have to go on living with me whatever I decided, said: 'You had better do it because you'll always think you *could* have done it if you don't.' With these encouragements I told Bertie I would come into his new show.

There was a slight stir in the family. Had my mother been given the same chance she would not have hesitated to accept it and said so. Aunt Nancy, as I have said, was horrified but loyal. She came to the opening night bringing a large party of my kith and kin, most of whom were surprised. They had never noticed any signs of talent but were civil and, I suspect, nervous. Virginia wondered.

As the time drew near for rehearsals to begin my chief worry was whether I would remember my lines. At school I so lacked concentration that I seldom managed to memorise anything.

Lewis Casson once told me that until an actor could speak whole pages at a time, automatically, without stopping to make any sense of them, he did not know his lines. I could never have done that. I had no technique for learning. I had to think, line by line, what I had written and where it came on the page. I still memorise visually. I know exactly at what part of a page certain key nouns or important phrases are placed, and it was seeing in this way that helped me to nail down the objects I was talking about in that first monologue – the beech-nut-husk cluster, biscuit tins, Dicky calendars.

I tidied up the first version of 'Useful and Acceptable Gifts' I had written down for Bertie and said it over and over again, wherever I happened to be, in the bath, on my bicycle, weeding, or walking the dogs. I practised it under my breath in the train, in the bus and at the hairdresser. I had it by heart by the time rehearsals began at the end of March. The evening before the read-through, Bertie and Joan invited the company to a party at Loudoun Road, St John's Wood. The cast of the last revue, *Nine Sharp*, eyed the newcomers to *The Little Revue* with some suspicion. For three of us it was to be our first West End appearance; for one of us it was a first appearance on any professional stage anywhere. Vida Hope had done pantomime at the Unity Theatre, Bernard Miles was a regular at the late night Players' Club under Charing Cross arches. I was the only complete novice.

Someone asked me if I had ever played at the Little before. I noticed his silence when I explained my position but did not then realise it meant he was dumbfounded. The stars of our revue were Hermione Baddeley and Cyril Ritchard. George Benson and Betty Anne Davies, with Charlotte Leigh, were the featured players. Cyril and Hermione were polite to the newcomers. Only Charlotte was really friendly; but I was so innocent that I didn't realise the feelings pros have about amateurs, and I wasn't even that.

After we had been running for some time, and I was established and accepted by the company, Cyril confessed to me that he had grown more and more depressed as I rehearsed, and had told Bertie he had better get rid of me before we opened, because if he didn't I would wreck the show and they would all be out of work in the first week. Bertie had admitted he was disappointed that I had not shown again the spark he had seen in me that first time at Stephen's house. But I knew nothing of these gloomy views and plodded on. The fact was I was a bad rehearser, with no technique to fall back on. I needed laughs to get the thing moving, and after the first few times I had done the sketches there were no more laughs from the other actors sitting about in the stalls waiting to rehearse their own numbers.

By now I had two monologues in the programme. Bertie had telephoned me to say I must have two appearances, one in each half. Could I produce a second sketch? The very next day I rang him from Parr's to tell him I had done a three-part piece about three different kinds of mothers – would that do? Writing material came easily to me then.

The first night was on Friday, 19 April, at 7.30, to be followed by a second performance at 11.30 for the profession after their own shows had finished. There was also to be a charity dress rehearsal on Wednesday night, two days before the opening, and a stop-and-starting dress rehearsal the following evening to tidy up what went wrong at the charity show. My mind was fixed on the importance of Friday, *the* first night when critics were coming. I wasn't bothered about the charity show. I knew my words by now and I thought my dress was lovely – pale grey chiffon over pale blue chiffon, a peasant dress with a laced-up bodice, low round neck, short sleeves and a very wide circular skirt. Over it, for my first appearance, I wore a geranium-pink wool jacket, with a lot of silver sequin embroidery round the neck and shoulders, sent to me by mother (prettier than it now sounds). The rest of the company were edgy; they said charity audiences were hell and wouldn't laugh. I didn't see why not. They were just people who might have paid double but that need not prevent them from responding, need it? Just you wait, they said.

Our compère was Ronnie Waters, six foot three with flaming red

Publicity photograph for my first revue

hair. I suppose, like the rest of the company, he dreaded my appearance, fearing the worst, and to help the situation he announced me with tremendous zest.

'And *now* . . . *direct* from the Women's Institute . . . Miss . . . Joyce . . . GRENFELL.'

It was the sort of introduction that leads the audience to expect an entrance, naked, on an elephant. Instead it got me in my grey chiffon and little pinky red jacket. They applauded quite warmly and I later discovered the place was full of friends, supporters of the good cause, who had come for that reason and for the remembered joys of Bertie's previous revue. They were, I think, surprised to see me on the stage and clapped to encourage me.

But then something happened. I began, as all real Women's Institute lecturers begin:

'Madam President – Fellow Institute members – good evening.'

I spoke in the dainty way of the original speaker and I suppose the audience recognised the authenticity of what I said and how I said it. We were off. I said a line. They laughed. I said another. They laughed. It was a sort of game, with me holding back the next line till the very last moment and then letting them have it. An audience, a responsive audience, was what I had missed in all those dull rehearsals. Now the thing worked, now I could experiment with it, certain of the way I wanted it to go. I felt as if I were riding a marvellous great white flying horse in perfect rhythm, with perfect control; I felt as if I were playing superlative tennis with a challenging opponent – long, even rallies and then a sharp change of pace – and my point.

I have never again had quite such an astonishing and thrilling experience with an audience. It was a first time so good that it gave me confidence, enough to know that such a relationship between performer and audience was possible. I walked off to prolonged applause. Ronnie Waters, waiting to announce the next item, said: 'What about that!' and smiled. The other three girls in the dressing-room had heard the laughs and looked at me in a new way. Charlotte said something friendly like 'I *knew* you'd do it,' and I sat down at the dressing-table and stared at my made-up face in a daze. The same miracle happened in part two when I took off my red jacket and appeared in the grey to do 'Mothers'.

Bertie came backstage and said 'Well done'. Some friends came up the stairs to the Sarah Siddons dressing-room and congratulated me. I cleaned my face as Charlotte had taught me with liquefying cold cream, and wiped it all off on a rough towel, and went home alone in a taxi. I had forbidden Reggie or my father to come near the theatre till Friday, the real first night. Now, sitting on the edge of my seat in the cab as we drove through Trafalgar Square, I thought to myself – but it's *easy* and it's fun. It's marvellous fun. I *can* do it.

We were staying in London with Aunt Pauline Spender Clay in her big flat in Kingston House South in Ennismore Gardens. Reggie was waiting up for me and I told him how relieved I was. In fact I was not a little puffed up; I *could* do it. Performing on a stage, I said, is no more difficult than playing in a room.

But it is, and in the stop-and-starting rehearsal, without a proper audience, the most salutary thing that could happen to me happened. I dried. That is to say I forgot my words, lost my way and just stood there, humiliated and appalled. Partly tiredness, partly too much confidence and the cold empty house after a willing and warm audience. I had relied on the come-back of laughter and it wasn't there. I had no technique to cover up unexpected silences where laughs were supposed to be. Instead I panicked.

Virginia and Tony Thesiger sat suffering for me at the back of the hollow auditorium, and when it was over they took me off to a dim little restaurant we found nearby. Reggie had joined us at the theatre, still forbidden by me to see the show till the first night, and they all did their best to cheer me up, but I was low. Even the pretty amethyst brooch the Thesigers gave me seemed a mockery. Well, I thought, I'll do the opening night tomorrow as best I can and then on Saturday I'll tell Bertie I had better bow out. It won't hurt the show. I'm an extra anyway and not involved in the ensemble. Back at Ennismore Gardens Reggie made comforting noises, but I was beyond reach.

We had a rehearsal call at 11.30 next morning. A beautiful spring day. I had risen up again and my natural optimism had begun to take over. We were dismissed at one o'clock and Charlotte Leigh and I went with John Pritchard to eat food we didn't in the least want. I only craved long iced drinks of lemon, rather sour, but I did eat some lamb and cabbage.

Charlotte had been my guide and mentor all through rehearsals. She told me what make-up to buy and where to buy it, she showed me how to use it. We had some time to kill and decided to have our hair and nails done in honour of the first night. Madness! I have since learned never to have my hair washed on the day I need it to look its best. Mine, slippery still, tended to come down as it had done at the opera in Paris. (Thanks to hair-spray this is no longer the hazard it once was, but hair that has to recover from the shampoo and settle down, as mine does, needs time, and now I always have mine done at least two days before special occasions.) I slept peacefully under the dryer at Selfridge's where my hairdresser friend, Miss White, sensing the importance of the day, cared for me with kindness. Then Charlotte and I sent telegrams to the rest of the company and had a large tea in Selfridge's restaurant where I drank three breakfast cupfuls and ate a toasted bun and some layer cake.

We were too early to go straight to the theatre, instead we sat in deck-chairs below the Adelphi in the Embankment Gardens. It was warm and sunny. People passing by didn't know what a momentous evening was unfolding. *Not* important, I told myself, but excitement was rising in me and I couldn't sit still. The stage door man was surrounded with flowers. He had them arranged all along the passage. Twenty-seven telegrams for me, and a note from Cyril saying 'Welcome to this strange profession and may you have a personal success.' Considering he was so doubtful about my appearance it was generous of him. Bertie's telegram read: 'I know how you are feeling but you needn't,' and my father's said 'All goes well.'

After it was over I wrote six pages to my mother describing the eventful week and included a list of all the family and friends who were at the opening and came backstage to see me afterwards. It was impossible to get them past the crowds on the stairs trying to see Hermione and Cyril, so I went down to meet them in the alley-way outside. I think the prevailing emotion was one of relief. My pa said he now knew the full meaning of the words 'strained relations'.

Reggie came to both performances and understandably had an easier time at the second; the critics had gone home and the pros were relaxed and appeared to be easily amused. Ivor Novello came backstage and said: 'I wish Nora could have been here.' (I remembered the Parma violets I pretended he had sent me.) More warm kisses and congratulations from Dorothy Dickson. It was heady stuff.

We bundled all my flowers and ourselves into a taxi and as it was about to start a young man ran over to the window and said how much he admired my 'controlled understatement'. I didn't know how to respond to this so I said 'Thanks awfully' and drove away. We got to bed at four-thirty in the morning.

Oh, salutary bad run-through that black Thursday. When I came to the first night I was chastened, humble – but hopeful, because I suspected an audience might help. I was on my toes, ready to fly again, if possible; and I flew.

The press notices next day were enthusiastic about the revue, so were the three evening papers; so were all the Sundays. And I was very warmly welcomed. James Agate of the *Sunday Times* gave me the best of all the generous notices: unlike some entertainers, he said, I was never too long. But he only saw my first number by the skin of his teeth. Bertie anxiously watched him loiter in the foyer as the first numbers played on stage and still he didn't go in to take his seat. Finally he wandered slowly down to his front stall as I was announced. And he was well amused and, later, said so in print.

My original salary, fixed for the run of the revue, was £10 a week, the same sum as I earned on the *Observer*. After we opened Bertie Farjeon did a very unusual thing. He said my success merited a rise, and he put up my salary to £12.10s. Such things did not often happen in the commercial theatre; but Bertie was an unusual man.

CHAPTER TEN

The War Begins

OUR new life at Parr's fell into a pattern. I still drove Reggie to his morning train and in the evening, when I went to take the 6.22 to London for the theatre, I left the car for his return. He fetched me home from Taplow at the lowering hour of half-past midnight and never complained. At first I stayed with Virginia on the nights before matinée days, but much later, when she went to Bristol, Aunt Pauline Spender Clay let me go to her flat in Ennismore Gardens whenever I wanted to, and if Reggie was in London there was a bed for him, too. Now and then we went away for week-ends, and, wherever I was I continued listening to radio programmes for the *Observer*.

It was a gay summer. Early in May Aunt Nancy gave a ball at 4 St James's Square, and I wore the pleated white net crinoline she had given me the year before. Her turquoise-and-diamond bandeau tiara was often lent to her female relations, and it was my turn to wear it that year.

The ballroom with its tall windows facing the square was decorated with whole cherry trees. Earlier in the day gardeners from Cliveden brought a load of flowers from the hothouses and set the cherry trees in a mixture of potted primula and brilliantly coloured cineraria. They appeared to be growing in a bank of moss and grasses. In the smaller green drawing-room bowls and bushes of gardenia scented the air. Half the fun of parties in St James's Square was looking at people and flowers. I have always enjoyed people-watching.

It was a year of 'firsts' for me: the revue, my first professional gramophone record (the two monologues from the revue), a first broadcast for the BBC – a gramophone record recital – and my first visit to the Theatrical Garden Party as a pro. The Little Theatre Company ran a penny-rolling game and made £23. (Noël Coward appeared in the Grand Giggle Tent and 'Ivor Novello was a picture in full Tyrolean costume, knees and all'). In July I accepted my first private engagement, at the house of Lord and Lady Halifax to entertain the King and Queen after dinner.

With part of the cheque for fifteen guineas that Lady Halifax sent me I bought a coat in Harrods summer sale, black with a flared skirt and a Persian lamb fur collar, and I wore it all through the war as my 'best'. Then it went to my youngest sister-in-law Laura, who wore it for a further four or five years as her 'best'. It cost eleven guineas.

In the middle of August I wrote to tell my mother that life was going on as usual with a few European rumblings added. Old people pulled gloomy faces and forecast war, but I did not believe it would come. Just to be on the safe side I invested in a box of drawing-pins in case I had to put up a black-out.

The day after war was declared, torn between a wish to allay her fears for us and yet tell her about the excitement of events, I wrote her an account of the days leading up to the declaration:

4 September 1939.

Well, well, so it's war.

So far it doesn't look or feel like one, but I daresay by the time this reaches you we'll have had a taste.

Everyone goes about with gas-masks tied by strings over one shoulder. Sugar is unobtainable in Maidenhead, but that is only because its transport was delayed while evacuation of children, pregnant mothers and the blind took place. Fortunately we have enough to go on with.

We've been playing all week to tiny audiences and on Thursday evening Charlotte and I, after eating our supper, came out of Lyons to find posters saying that A.R.P. wardens were ordered to report at once. This shook us a bit and we turned up at the theatre half expecting there would be no evening performance. But there was. Luise Blackburn was coming down to Parr's for the night and the following day and we met at Paddington to get the last train. Reggie met us and said cheerfully that Hitler's sixteen-point plan had been broadcast, and we all went to bed full of hope. And slept like logs. Reggie went off on his early train as usual (given a lift to the station). I slept till nearly 10.30 and woke up just in time to hear the news bulletin. 'We regret to announce,' said the speaker as if he was speaking of the tiresome wet weather 'that the international situation took a grave turn during the night.' Such coolness is the greatest help, preceded as it always is with the chattiest 'Good morning everybody'.

Luise and I were sort of pooped by the news and spent a shiftless morning in our wrappers, only bathing and dressing in time for a lunch we didn't want. All the time we were quite un-depressed.

I rang Reggie to ask him to find out if the revue was playing that night. We were, but he couldn't get through to tell me by telephone and his tele-

Weekly letter to my mother

gram didn't arrive until 5.30. The train to London left at 6.40. Rene Easden had begun her three weeks' holiday the day before and her understudy went home as soon as she had given us lunch.

Luise and I had to shut up the house, leave some food for Reggie and get down to the station. I was sure we wouldn't be playing, so I hadn't changed from my skirt and shirt. A scramble followed, we closed all the windows and drew the curtains, lured Gary in from the garden to do watchman duty in our absence, and we were just going to get into the car when the back door bell rang. I rushed to answer it and there was an evacuation officer with a small girl in school clothes. 'Here's your child', he said, told me her name and was just going when I had intelligence enough to say I had room for two children, so he went back to his car and returned with a second child. Situation! Here was I with two small girls of twelve, a cold tongue and some uncooked potatoes in the house, no one to look after them, and a train to catch. Thinking swiftly and deciding that it didn't matter if I missed the show in times like these, I ran up to Mrs Jeffries's house (she was the wife of one of the Cliveden chauffeurs) to see if she would oblige by minding the children for the evening, but I found her door shut and her other neighbour said she was down the road looking after Bert's mother, old Mrs Jeffries. So I decided to go up to Rene's, tell her all and beg her to come back from her holiday. (I knew she wasn't going away and she lived only two hundred yards up the road.) She was out, but her mother said she would certainly come back and not to worry; she was shopping in Burnham and would go to Parr's as soon as she returned.

By this time our train was due but, as trains were said to be running late owing to the vast evacuation scheme, we gambled on catching it and went to the station, leaving the children to settle themselves in. I drove via Burnham in case we should meet Rene on her return and we did. I told her what had happened and, angel that she is, she said she didn't mind a bit missing her holiday and would pop up the hill to look after the children right away. So we left in high relief. Luise was coming to London with me to collect her passport, money and steamship ticket (home to America) and as I didn't want her to stay alone in London she was coming back with me after the show. Our train was an hour and three-quarters late at Taplow. We crawled into Paddington with only just time to tear along the crowded and almost totally dark platform, go out into the street, find a rare taxi and arrive at the theatre at 9.15. I am on at 9.30. The black-out in London was complete and I had never realised how dark a lightless town could be. We crept along at about five miles an hour. I may add it was pouring with rain.

Luise came with me in the taxi and took it on to Bloomsbury where she has been lodging. At the theatre I threw my clothes on and just had time to collect myself before I was called. The house was minute; about forty. They behaved grandly and made as much noise as they could; in fact they worked harder than we did. Bea Lillie (sixth visit) and Phyllis Monkman were in front. So was Reggie.

After the theatre Luise, Reggie and I got the same taxi we had taken from Paddington. They were impossible to get that night and Luise very sensibly made the driver wait for us. We got to Paddington about 11.20 and caught the 10.45 that had not yet left. There wasn't a light anywhere and we had some difficulty in finding room in the crowded carriages. We found places and as we got accustomed to the gloom could see our fellow-passengers. There was a young mother in the corner nursing a tiny baby. Her husband sat opposite with a two-year-old boy asleep in his arms. I thought she looked pretty tired, so I offered to hold the baby and discovered it was born only three weeks ago. I suggested she should lie down, for there was room, and she got some rest that way during a very tedious journey in a train that stopped at every single station all the way down. . . . They had left Rochester – danger zone – earlier that evening and were aiming for some relations at

Lent Rise near Burnham. They planned to get out at Burnham and walk, but we discouraged this – two babies, a wet night and a suitcase for a mile and a half walk didn't seem a good idea. When we got to Taplow I drove them and Luise to Lent Rise, dropped them and returned for Reggie who had started to walk, carrying Luise's case. Bed certainly felt good that night.

Next morning I drove Reggie to the station and reminded him to carry his gas-mask. Luise and I went on to Maidenhead to buy black-out material (and some tinned food) and spent the rest of the day sitting in the sunny garden cobbling the stuff up into curtains. When I telephoned the theatre no one knew whether there would be a perform-ance that evening and I was advised not to try and get in to London. The evacuees, Margaret Wallis and Gwen Cooke, both scholarship girls from the Godolphin and Latymer School at Hammersmith, did not have to report to the village school until Monday and asked per-mission to go into Burnham for 'a look at the shops'. They were al-ready homesick for pavements, but I doubted whether the delights of the short High Street would cheer them up. In those days there was only a butcher, greengrocer, baker, newsagent-confectioner, the post office and a sparsely equipped draper with a dull side-line in fancy goods. It was better not to discourage enterprise and off they went skipping down the long hill that I feared was going to be rather less fun to walk up. But they seemed rewarded by their outing and came back with comics, sweets and healthy appetites for tea.

Immediately war was declared the Astors offered to have a Canadian Red Cross Hospital at Cliveden. Aunt Nancy said there was going to be a great deal of work for me to do when the hospital was established and she decided with typical generosity this was the time to give us a new car. She also thought bicycles were going to be in short supply and told me to go and buy three new ones, for herself, Alice and me. I told Virginia I'd keep beds for her and Tony, but they decided to stay in London for the moment. Virginia was already driving for Lady Reading's Women's Voluntary Service. My pa was staying with friends in Berkshire and would await events.

Alice Winn's house, Taplow Lodge, became a home for eighty-one children under five, most of them born out of wedlock. Their numbers rose to eighty-two when Aunt Nancy came back from a visit to Kentish Town with a small boy whose mother was pregnant with her eighth child and in need of temporary relief. I was one of the local helpers who worked at settling in the children and the inadequate staff in a house not well suited for such an invasion. We all wore identity labels and carried our gas-masks but, so far, it did not feel like war. Radio programmes were made up of news bulletins and gramophone record recitals, and I wondered what I would find to write about in next week's *Observer*; and how long my job on the paper would last.

I ended the seven-page letter to my mother with news of the family's immediate war efforts. Reggie had applied to join the 9th Lancers but there had been no reply to his letter. Reggie Winn was in the Grenadier Guards reserve and had been told to wait for orders. Michael and Jakie Astor had joined the Territorials earlier and were already in khaki. (Aunt Nancy said Jakie looked like an *hors d'oeuvre* in his uniform.) Bill Astor was in Egypt and hoped to join the Navy; David Astor was doing something hush-hush for the time being. He later became a Royal Marine.

We are extremely well, happy and busy. I never seem to stop. Now don't worry about us. If we're blown up we're blown up and Life being what we know it is (spiritual and therefore eternal) it doesn't matter. Anyway we shan't be. This is said to be a safe area.

The authorities changed their minds about that and Gwen and Margaret and their school moved on to Newbury, further away from the danger of bombs aimed at London. I was sad when they left. They were only at Parr's for a few weeks but long enough for us to like having them in the house. They were easy visitors; thoughtful for their age, tidy and not unduly noisy. Agreeable sounds of laughter came from Rene's sitting-room where they elected to do their homework and spend their free time. We never saw the girls again, but thirty-three years later, after one of my television programmes, I had a letter from Gwen, the quiet one with red hair. She said she didn't suppose I'd remember her, but I did, with affection.

After two weeks of wondering how the war was going to develop, *The Little Revue* re-opened on 20 September and I went back into it on a three-month contract. At first we played it as a non-stop entertainment. This meant we did three shortened shows between 1.15 and 6 p.m., and the audience, as they did at the cinema, came into the theatre when they pleased and left when the programme came round again to the number they had first seen. A new financial arrangement was arrived at. All of us were paid £5 a week and then different percentages were awarded to individuals out of any profits that might be made. I wrote to my mother that my expenses were:

Season ticket to London and back to Taplow	10s
Underground season Paddington–Charing Cross	3s
Theatre tips	10s
Income tax	£1 10s

That left a balance of £2 7s – that's something these days.

Petrol-rationing came in at once and we were allocated five gallons a month, exactly the amount needed to get to and from the station – and no more. I laid in six pairs of silk stockings, two new sweaters, a black skirt (from Marks & Spencer, 4s 11d), six large-sized boxes of Kleenex tissues and some sanitary towels. Virginia asked her cook to order some Bromo lavatory paper. How much? 'Oh,' said Virginia, 'a case or two.' It took strong men to deliver the enormous order that arrived, and throughout the war Virginia gave her friends packets of the precious stuff at Christmas and for birthdays.

Letters to my mother at this time were full of my pleasure at the National Gallery concerts. They were the inspired idea of Myra Hess and were held at luncheon-time in the bare-walled rooms of the National Gallery. All the pictures had been taken to places of safety. I am one of thousands who were nourished by these concerts. I went to work in the canteen that provided sandwiches and excellent coffee before the music began at 1.10 p.m. We made delicious sandwiches, new to me, with fillings of honey and raisins in brown bread, chutney and cream cheese, dates with cream cheese, chopped celery, fish and cress; and now and then home-made pâtés. We buttered and filled from 10.30 a.m. (one day we made seventeen hundred sandwiches and would have made more but the bread ran out). It was a very popular canteen and Irene Gater, who organised it, gave me the enjoyable job of carrying the artists' food to the green room. Myra Hess was an old friend and I often sat with her at the concerts behind the platform curtain, hidden from the rest of the audience. Unless it was one of the big occasions when all the rooms opening off the central gallery were in use, a curtain was drawn behind the performers and that room remained empty, and we sat there in privacy – Myra, her niece Beryl Davis and Howard Ferguson, when he could get away from his R.A.F. duties to help her organise the programmes.

I went to the Gallery whenever I could and on New Year's Day 1941 Myra invited me to be a nightingale on a water-whistle in a performance of Haydn's Toy Symphony. The Isolde Menges Strings were the orchestra and our conductor was Kenneth Clark (then Director of the National Gallery) who had never done such a thing before. Myra

Howard Ferguson and
Myra Hess at Parr's

and Irene Scharrer were cuckoos, Moiseiwitsch took the triangle and Elena Gerhardt beat a small toy drum. My contribution was straight-forward, with one exacting passage of six bars continual bubbling to be done on a single breath. Also in the programme was a unique perform-ance of Schumann's *Carnaval*, played in turn by all the pianists present, and as well as Myra, Irene and Moiseiwitsch they included Clifford Curzon, Eileen Joyce, Denise Lassimone, Kathleen Long and Cyril Smith.

Since I have appeared on the television quiz 'Face the Music' I am often asked where I studied music. The answer is nowhere. I learned to play the piano as a child but never practised. I learned about music out of loving it. From the time I was a baby I heard music and I sang nursery rhymes with my mother before I was two and a half (or so I am told). I went to concerts from an early age and played the gramo-phone as soon as we had one. Ragtime, musical comedy, the Unfinished Symphony, Kreisler playing his violin solos, some Brandenburg Con-certos and *L'Après-midi d'un Faune* stood side by side in a rack. But my experience of chamber music was limited until this great chance of hearing so much of the repertoire came my way at the National Gallery; and I made the most of it. In the months I was at the Gallery concerts I heard all the Beethoven quartets performed in two separate series. It was there I discovered late, but never too late, the marvels of Mozart.

146

Myra Hess at the National Gallery

Music was particularly important in the terrible (beautiful) spring of 1940 – continuing days of cloudless blue skies and more and more tragic news. Lilacs flowered and the London parks shimmered in a dozen different greens. Day after day we came out of the Gallery, dreading to look at the evening posters. On the day Holland fell I heard Mozart's clarinet quintet (K 581). I was behind the platform curtain with my shoes off and my feet up on a chair. As I listened I had an intuitive feeling of hearing beyond the music to some sense of infinity. It was 'evidence of things not seen' – or heard. I cannot put it more plainly but I believe anyone who has had this experience will know what I mean. It was first a recognition and then an acknowledgement. There were no pictures in my mind, nor were there any words; but I had a glimpse of unchanging limitless life, of spiritual being, that no war or misery of uncertainty and fear could ever touch. Some years later in New York I went to hear the Budapest Quartet play Haydn. The players were not young and they had been together since their student days. I had the impression that they no longer needed instruments to make music. Their understanding of it transcended instruments and performance. It was as if they no longer needed know-how, wood, cat-gut or muscle; no medium for them and no auditory nerve for us. We both included the music. Again a sense of recognition and acknowledgement. These momentary experiences were metaphysical but not psychic.

The day after Holland fell Myra played Bach's Brandenburg Concerto No 5 'with a motley assembly of strings'. She was hard hit by the news; her career had begun in Holland and many of her friends were Dutch. She was very low but she had that quality of greatness that disregards self. When she died an American critic wrote: 'You don't go to a Myra Hess concert to hear Myra Hess, you go to hear music.'

The rest of 1940 was a mixture of activity. I worked in a troop canteen in Maidenhead as well as at the National Gallery. After *The Little Revue* closed in March, Reggie and I stayed on at Ennismore Gardens and went home to Parr's at the week-end. At first he had been refused by the army because of varicose veins and came to work in London at the Ministry of Economic Warfare while his legs were treated. I met Harold Lindo, an architect who, like Reggie, was awaiting his call-up. He played the piano and had a collection of original and amusing songs and when we were both available we did troop concerts together. We taught each other new numbers and went to hospitals, gun-sites, barracks and the inevitable canteens all round our part of Buckinghamshire – and as far as Wiltshire and Oxfordshire.

In June Reggie was passed by the doctors and went to join his new regiment, the King's Royal Rifle Corps (the 60th) in Wiltshire. The night before he put on his uniform we had our first night-time air-raid warning and were glad to be together. Parting was hell. I wrote to my mother:

He is very relieved in his mind to be doing something. I can't say I feel the same. However I do appreciate his sentiments and realise that if this island is to be a battle-ground he is better off with a gun in his hand. I've no other plans than to work at Cliveden [at the Canadian Red Cross Hospital now nearly built]. But Alice [Winn] and I are toying fairly seriously with the idea of working in a munitions factory. . . . Don't worry about us, women aren't allowed to make the explosive part! [We didn't go into a factory.] The stories of heroism in the great evacuation from Dunkirk still seep through. And there are cosy little stories, too, like the one about the man who swam two miles, when his ship was torpedoed, with his pet black rabbit on his shoulder and his pet pigeon on his head.

Many of our friends were tortured by the question of whether to send their children to Canada and America before the invasion we were

Reggie joins the K.R.R.C.

told to expect. Aunt Pauline Spender Clay took five grandchildren to Canada. Reggie's sister Mary Waldegrave and a cousin Molly Baring, between them shepherded thirteen children under eleven to a French Canadian village in Quebec. Mary was pregnant, and after five daughters, gave birth to a son on the other side of the Atlantic. Alice Winn's little girls, protesting loudly, went to cousins of ours in Ohio. It was a time of upheavals and family farewells. I was glad I didn't have to make that difficult choice.

The hospital, built and given by the Canadian Red Cross, opened on the old polo-field at Cliveden in July. It covered a wide area. Offices, store-rooms and the officers' mess surrounded an open, grassed square; the wards, like teeth in a giant comb, led off a single continuing spine-corridor. All the buildings were low and cheerful, airy and light. The wards had pale green walls and floors of shiny red composition; and the tables and chairs, sent from Canada, were made of light maplewood. Garden doors at the far end of each ward opened on to what remained of the polo-field, edged by the beech-woods. None of us who went to work there had ever seen such a luxurious hospital. Distances were considerable as we soon learned when we had to carry goods from the Red Cross store-rooms all the way to patients in their far-away beds.

Alice Winn's house, Taplow Lodge, where the eighty-one orphans had arrived to stay when war broke out, was turned over to the nursing sisters for their home (I don't know what happened to the orphans). The nurses wore the same becoming bright-blue poplin uniforms with gold buttons, stiff white collars and cuffs and floating organdie veils as Canadian sisters had done in the 1914–18 war. Before the hospital opened Aunt Nancy asked me to help entertain the unit when it arrived, and I put on a concert for them in Alice's old drawing-room, now the sisters' mess. Elsie Suddaby, at the height of her singing career, came over from Bracknell to play and sing for them, and I did my repertoire – still very small but beginning to grow. At first it was hard going. The audience appeared to be stunned more than delighted, but they warmed up as they got used to us, and afterwards when we were having good Canadian coffee and cakes I was told that for some of them this was the first professional entertainment they had ever seen. The unit had been recruited in Winnipeg and many came from surrounding prairie country where there was not much music and no live theatre.

Before the patients arrived it was decided to organise sight-seeing tours to Windsor and Oxford, and I led the parties. Aunt Nancy had run into four homeless young Polish sailors in Plymouth who were about to join the British navy, and invited them to spend their leave at Cliveden. They came with some of the nurses on the trip to Oxford, and we ate our picnic lunch in Christ Church Meadows. All of a sudden one of them said something in Polish and they burst into a four-part folk-song of some sort; it was very moving. I don't believe any of them had sung it since they had left home and they were obviously stirred. One of them picked grass throughout, another kept his eyes shut. We were quite silent after they had sung, and soon they sang another. The whole scene was touching and so pretty. Four young men from Poland sprawling in the grass by the river with Christ Church behind them, the day sunny with big rushing clouds; and the Canadian girls beside them, their jackets off, in bright butcher's blue shirts – all of them in England to help win the war. Sentimental, and true.

In August Harold Lindo's papers came and he went to India, so he was no longer available for concerts. Friends introduced me to Eve Clarke. My heart sank at the idea of singing to an accordion, but it was the answer to the demand for concerts at small gun-sites and in places where there were no pianos. Eve was the wife of a doctor, mother of two small children, and very musical. We were instantly compatible. She was even taller than I was, inclined to vagueness, but fun to work with. She was free to do concerts and as eager as I was to get to the places not yet served with entertainment. She could play most songs requested by our audiences, from current favourites and folk-songs to Viennese waltzes and Italian pieces. Informal sing-songs, in which we did a short programme of rehearsed numbers and then had a free-for-all with the troops, were our forte. Eve travelled with a knapsack on her back and carried her accordion.

Patients began to arrive at the hospital in August. As a Red Cross welfare worker I was allocated two wards of twenty-four beds to cherish. One was a short-term ward for ear, nose and throat cases; the other, ward eleven, was for chests. Here patients stayed in for much longer periods and were in greater need of attention. I spent much more of my time with them. Anna Millar and Edna Leishman were the nurses with whom I became friends. Ben Schoemperlen was the doctor and our orderlies were Crawford and Dobson. It was a particularly happy team. (Years later when I did concert tours of Canada we always had re-unions. Friends I had made at the hospital from Winnipeg, Toronto, Ottawa, Vancouver and Calgary all turned out to meet me.)

My job was a mixture of welfare – handing out gifts from the Red Cross, writing letters for those who couldn't – and endless shopping. When petrol allowed (we had coupons from the Red Cross) I took up-patients to the movies and home to large teas at Parr's. Eve and I sang and played in all the wards in turn. The shopping had to be done by bicycle in Burnham village and at first it was not too demanding. Razor-blades, soap, Brylcreem, writing paper that wasn't Red Cross issue, tobacco that the P.B.X. didn't supply, and birthday cards and the sending of cables. One February I was asked if I would kindly 'purchase a "Valenstein" ' for a French Canadian patient to send to his girl. As the war went on it became more difficult to find the goods for which I was asked, but after October, when I had gone back into the theatre, I had a wider range of shops to explore and went almost daily to Selfridge's and the Oxford Street Woolworth's for the 'boys'.

We heard the blitz on London and saw the searchlights and shell-bursts, but our twenty-five-mile distance kept us out of the action. There were a few isolated bombs dropped in the neighbourhood, but nothing serious and no casualties. I found it a temptation to stay up late leaning on the window-sill of my bedroom at Parr's watching search-lights comb the skies over Slough. Now and then we saw a plane, a miniature white cross in the beam, and a few seconds later shell-bursts exploding like flowers all round it. There were cows in the field where racehorses used to run and they coughed and were restless when they heard the guns. I knew my mother was worried about me and I tried to convince her I had no need to go to the city until things calmed down; nor did I want to. I had not been to London since the blitz began. My father spent seven hours sitting in a deck-chair in his cellar with his tiny elderly housekeeper, Alicia, sitting on another directly behind him. He said they really could not go on like that, and moved his bed down to the ground floor and hers to the basement.

At first theatres stayed open and, obedient to air-raid wardens' commands, audiences stayed put until the all-clear sounded. A Prom concert audience had to stay at the Queen's Hall for six or more hours and held an impromptu session with solos and community singing until four in the morning.

The National Gallery concerts now took place in a big lower room. I was no longer free to go to the canteen and only rarely managed to hear a concert. Myra Hess was determined to keep them going as long as she was allowed to, and went to the Gallery every day, ready to play herself in case other artists failed to arrive. She came to stay for two nights in September to get away from the bombs and the deafening noise of AA guns and offered to play for the staff and patients while she was with me. I was anxious about this because, when I asked any of them if they liked music, they all said 'sure' and went on to mention *Rose Marie* and songs they knew from movie musicals. Early in the week I typed out a notice and put one in each ward, the officers' mess, the sisters' home and the orderlies' mess:

It is probable that Miss Myra Hess may be coming down to stay with Mrs Grenfell in the near future and she has kindly offered to play for those interested. If you like *serious* music, please sign below. Details later.

I expected and hoped that the underlined 'serious' would discourage all but those really interested and that we would have a handful of real enthusiasts at Parr's. But I had underestimated Canada's love of serious music, and at least forty signed on. So with Aunt Nancy's permission we had the concert at Cliveden.

As we sat in the Long Drawing-room the brilliant evening light was low and the sky went pale greeny-blue after earlier rains. The view from the windows across the lawns to the woods, the river and the fields beyond was striped with long blue shadows. It didn't feel like war-time. Alice and I had arranged sofas and chairs and cushions on the floor at either end of the room; the piano was in the middle, lit by a single standard lamp, and as the daylight faded Myra was islanded in a warm pool of light; an intimate setting, and a change from the wards and public rooms the men and nurses lived in. I watched their faces as they listened to the music; for an hour or so they were in another world. She played a Bach gigue and the *Appassionata* of Beethoven and, in answer to a request, the *Moonlight*, before finishing with her own arrangement of 'Jesu Joy of Man's Desiring'. Alice and I were very late for our shift at the canteen and left Myra surrounded by appreciative Canadians. One of the doctors told me next day it had been the happiest hour he had ever spent.

All theatres, except the Windmill, closed when the blitz began, but after a while it was felt that entertainment should go on, and Bertie Farjeon collected an unusual company of players for a programme called *Diversion*. This was a familiar word at that time; wherever bombs had dropped the streets were closed and yellow signs saying 'diversion' appeared. Edith Evans and Dorothy Dickson shared the number one dressing-room at Wyndham's Theatre, Irene Eisinger, the Mozart singer, and I were up in number two. George Benson, Walter Crisham, Peter Ustinov and Joan Sterndale Bennett were in the company and a very young man called Dirk Bogarde played small parts in sketches. Edith read some poems and did a cockney monologue about a bombed-out hop-picker; Dorothy burlesqued 'A Nightingale Sang in Berkeley Square' and danced with Wally Crisham; Irene sang Mozart; Peter Ustinov did impressions of five producers directing a Shakespeare play; and George, dressed in Norfolk jacket and tweed hat, sang of the joys of clean living, home-made bread and ale. My new sketch was called 'Canteen' and grew out of experience, and I repeated 'The Three Mothers' from *The Little Revue*.

At first Edith Evans and Dorothy Dickson seemed unlikely stable-mates, but their dressing-room sharing worked. Dorothy advised Edith about make-up and clothes, Edith talked to Dorothy about books and poetry, and they complemented each other in a friendly way. One day I went into their room before a performance and found them deep in a discussion about the story of Elisha and the Shunamite woman.

I was still able to work at the hospital and do the show. But there was little time for social visiting except on Sundays. My days went like this:

Breakfast at 9 a.m.

Train to London about 10 a.m.

Shopping for patients

Picnic lunch at Wyndham's Theatre

Matinée at 2 p.m.

Back to Taplow on the 4.22 p.m., taking off the heaviest part of my make-up in a taxi to Paddington Station. Straight from train to hospital for about an hour and a half.

Home for bath, supper on a tray, and bed by 10 p.m. A full life.

I had no more time for bicycling, but I got plenty of exercise one way and another.

Christmas 1940 was not a time for celebrations. Reggie didn't get leave. Nor did Virginia and Tony. Laura Grenfell came down to Parr's with me after the Christmas Eve performance and we spent the next day lunching at the big house and visiting the hospital wards. There was no time to feel sad.

CHAPTER ELEVEN

Odd Jobs

FRIENDS, and I include kith and kin, are a most important part of a happy life. In a perfect world we would not only love one another but, equally important, like one another. I always hope my friends will like each other; when they do there is a special grace at work. But my ring of friends includes individuals who remain precious to me alone; non-blenders, special contributors. I have learned to settle for these one-to-one relationships and treasure them as such. Discussing this with Virginia, with whom I share most tastes (among the exceptions are her love of football on television and her preference for man-made objects against mine for those of nature) we agreed that the marvel is the supply of friends 'for all seasons'. One loves them for a mixture of reasons and not always because of matching tastes and rhythms. I have friends dear to me with whom I have very little in common except affection; with others it is our shared interests and discoveries that bind us – coming to the end of museum-visits and sight-seeing at the same moment is a great bond; so is sharing the same wave-length of humour. But friendship is more than a meeting of minds, it includes heart, and the ways to it are numberless.

On the whole I have found it best not to lift weights off my chest and put them down on the chests of those I love. There has never been anyone in the world to whom I tell everything, but I know I could tell anything to Reggie, and to Virginia, and they would 'alter not'. As I see it friendship, like a good marriage, is sharing, but with rights of privacy. Respecting each other's individuality and idiosyncrasies allows for the right to differ and remain fond. Above all in important relationships it is *liking* that matters. The practical teaching of the New Testament commands us to love one another; to like everyone is not possible. When loving and liking happen at the same time it is having the best of all possible worlds. I have found it in my marriage.

Dr Thomas Jones, C.H., a Permanent Secretary to the Cabinet through several regimes, was a special friend and had been since he first came to stay at Cliveden when I was a child. I knew he was a power behind thrones, but it was as a friend that I knew and loved him. He was years older than I was, older even than my father, but it never mattered; there is never an age-gap in such friendships. T.J. was short, sturdy, with thick white hair and eyes that went up in the corners when he was amused; he was Welsh first and British quite a long way later; although a part of him disapproved of nationalism it was strong in him. He usually wore very dark suits and boots and a black Foreign Office homburg hat. Among his many talents was the successful pulling of strings, not only in the interest of those in whom he had faith but also in the interest of Wales, and sometimes of the whole United Kingdom. He was a great introducer of the right persons at the right moment – a sort of people's impresario – and he had a gift for friendship. I am one of dozens who had a 'special relationship' with him, and somehow he had time for us all. Apart from my father he was the only adult who took my early writing efforts seriously enough to read them as if they were important. He gave me the honour of his total concentration and when he asked questions he appeared to be genuinely interested in the answers.

Through him I met Sir Walford Davies and his wife Margaret and learned more about music. We all went to Gregynog to stay with the Davies sisters, Miss Gwen and Miss Daisy, and T.J., who had arranged for me to be invited, told me that when new staff were needed for the house, garden or farm, the sisters advertised for a contralto-housemaid, a bass-undergardener or a tenor-cowman to take part in the Gregynog choir. All through the winter months the choir, under a professional master, worked on programmes for the summer festival, when musicians like Sir Adrian Boult and Sir Walford came, with their wives, to lead the music. I was there when Elsie Suddaby, Mary Jarred and Keith Falkner sang Bach's St Matthew Passion in the big white music-room hung with a series of Monet's water-lily paintings. When there was religious music a great El Greco was put on a stand to conceal the choir and the conductor. It didn't do more than hide a few of the performers and I always wanted to move it to the side because, as it stood, it was more of a disturbance than an inspiration. Staying at Gregynog was a mixed blessing. The music was unalloyed pleasure but the atmosphere in the house was cool, correct and daunting. Even T.J. was subdued by it and we sometimes escaped to go and see his old friend Dora, Mrs Hugh-Jones, who lived in a cottage in the grounds,

Dr Thomas Jones

where it was possible to forget one's ps and qs for a while. But he was devoted to the two maiden ladies and had a missionary zeal to try and persuade them to enjoy their bounty and use it more widely; and I think it was he who persuaded them to do great things for the National Library of Wales bequeathing it their pictures and books. T.J. was very good at spending other people's money for the benefit of the community and could get money out of unexpected stones for causes he thought important. Until he died I reported regularly to him, sent him what I wrote and told him about any new developments in my life and work. He was a very dear friend.

Soon after the second edition of *Diversion* settled in at Wyndham's Theatre, Edith Evans drove down to spend the night with me at Parr's. I asked T.J. to luncheon to meet her. It was rather like watching two puppies sniffing round each other. The great are like that at first meetings, I've noticed. They look and sniff and question and probe and retire. Edith was just T.J.'s drop I thought, but there was no time for him to discover this. Next morning we walked up to Cliveden. T.J. was there and later we compared notes on watching Aunt Nancy doing her stuff for the great actress. There was a good deal of authority about my aunt that morning. Neat mauve outfit. Pink in the cheek and a light in the eye as she talked of nursery schools and children's rights. They both knew Bernard Shaw. He was half shared between them for a while. T. E. Lawrence was introduced into the conversation. It was all very well done and Edith was left with a clear impression of a dynamic little woman with a way-with-her, which, after all, was just about right.

I had met the Shaws on and off since I was fifteen, and one Christmas he had given me an envelope with seven signed postcard-sized photographs of himself and said: 'One for every day in the week and all out on Sunday. And don't sell them till I'm dead.' I gave an American admirer one of them, unsuitably inscribed 'to Joyce Phipps', and the other six have vanished. When I was sixteen G.B.S. saw a Christmas card I had drawn and told me I should become a commercial artist. I liked the idea. McKnight Kauffer's posters were being talked about and for a while I dreamed dreams of painting posters as brilliant as his.

'What you need,' said G.B.S. 'is a Jewish great-grandmother. All creative people should have a Jewish great-grandmother and then they would know how to set about selling their work. As it is, don't do it yourself – get an agent.'

I knew very little about my ancestry, and after my father died in 1954 *Burke's Landed Gentry* wrote to me as the eldest child of the eldest Phipps to correct the proof of an entry about the family for the next edition. I was amused to discover that a Phipps great-great-grandfather had married the daughter of Moses Benson of Liverpool. Maybe I did not need an agent after all. But when I began to do films I knew it was essential to have one, and Celia Johnson introduced me to Aubrey Blackburn, and he looked after me until his retirement; a very happy relationship – no contract, simply an understanding. He never expected me to take work I did not fancy. Not always the way with agents.

Mrs Shaw wore light colours with touches of sage-green and she had a necklace of green stones that exactly matched her eyes. I remember her at Cliveden, long before the war, sitting at one end of the Long Drawing-room knitting socks, while G.B.S. at the other end was telling a group of us about Mrs Patrick Campbell's beauty, folly and passion for him. Throughout the account Mrs Shaw kept up a tolerant murmur: 'Nonsense, G.B.S., you're talking absolute nonsense.' After thirty or more years she still cared enough to protest.

Bernard Shaw at Parr's

Writing to my mother in the spring of 1941 I kept up a relentless barrage of criticism of America's continuing isolationism. My poor mother. She loved England, she loved me, and she must have had a vile time of it. Alice Winn told me to tell her that when anything awful happened in the war we didn't say 'Poor Holland' or 'Poor Belgium', we just said 'Poor Nora!' I realised how much she was suffering on our behalf. Nevertheless, I continued to nag and bully her as if she were responsible for America's refusal to be drawn into the fighting.

Reggie was promoted to Captain in March, and the increased pay was a help. *Diversion* came off in April. Another pattern of days began to emerge. I went back to Parr's, took to a bicycle again and added a third ward to my care. It was possible to do more concerts and I began to broadcast fairly regularly, sometimes to America in the middle of the night from the deep recesses of the Criterion Theatre in Piccadilly, now a BBC studio. On these occasions, because of air raids, performers were allowed to stay on after the broadcast. Bunks were set up at the back of the dress and upper circles. I was once in a quiz programme with Bea Lillie and Harriet Cohen, among others, and after we came off the air an elderly male studio attendant in an overall showed Harriet Cohen and me to our beds and looked after us like a mother. 'You'll be quite safe and cosy here,' he said. I undressed and put on a nightdress and was intrigued to see that Harriet Cohen put her nightdress on *over* her red velvet evening dress before getting into her bunk. Beatrice Lillie preferred to risk the bombs and went home.

In the summer Bea came down to the Canadian hospital and did a show for the patients. Organising the event was a big responsibility. I rounded up local talent from among the staff and patients for the first half of the programme, ordered the microphone, arranged for a piano to be moved and tuned, and just hoped all would be well. We gambled on it being a fine afternoon for it was to be held out of doors; it was a beauty, warm and still with a cloudless blue sky. Beds were rolled on their little wheels from the distant wards and up-patients sat on the grass on grey army blankets. The supporting talent was better than I dared hope. A lieutenant whistled sad tunes and made bird noises; various nurses and orderlies sang – 'The Mountains of Mourne', 'Lazybones', 'The Sunshine of Your Smile' – and a hit was scored by a patient making sparks fly when he tap-danced in his huge boots on the shallow concrete steps we used as a stage. Then it was Bea's turn and, mercifully, she arrived on time, wearing a long purple dress with silver embroidery and carrying her familiar white ostrich feather fan with which she made great play. I had wondered whether her sophisticated performance would go down with that audience. There was no doubt about it. All her neatness, economy and controlled clowning, and the joy of her unexpectedness, made instant communication. The audience roared its approval the minute she stepped out on to the stage. They relished every move, raised eyebrow, trip-up and vocal understatement. She is an artist and, for my money, the funniest woman there has ever been.

In August the Bernard Shaws came to Cliveden for two weeks, bringing with them their Jaeger sheets and vegetarian foods. I was told by Aunt Nancy to keep an eye on them, take him for walks and see that she was kept happy. Aunt Nancy herself was having a short break up on the Island of Jura on the west coast of Scotland. Stephen Potter, who had asked me whether I could arrange for him to meet G.B.S. because he had an idea for a radio programme he wanted to do with him, came down to see me on the day G.B.S. had invited himself to tea at Parr's. I reported to my mother:

G.B.S. won't do the programme because he says he is too old, which, being translated, means his teeth don't fit and make rude noises that would be particularly exaggerated on the air and his vanity won't stand for such a thing. And I think he is right. He *is* older but he is incredible for eighty-five. Looks wonderfully pink and white and fresh and beautifully dandified. I do like attractive old people. Both the Shaws take trouble over their appearance. The more I see of them the more I like them and find their company stimulating. When he isn't putting on his act, is not being the contradictory small boy who must take the opposite view – then he is a charmer and what he has to say is worth hearing. I've had several quiet meals with them and we have talked of books, of Barrie, of music, of Elgar; of the stage and Mrs Pat, of the English, eugenics and food. Mrs Shaw is very deaf, which means that conversation takes time and must be executed *fortissimo* and that can make almost anything one says sound worthless! We left most of the talking to G.B.S.

Later that summer Eve Clarke and I, taking with us our rations of butter and marmalade, went to stay in Wiltshire while we did a series of concerts in the Salisbury Plain area. Our hostess, still living in the grand manner, welcomed us but feared we had arrived at a moment when things were not going too smoothly. The boiler had burst; her footman, graded C3 (and therefore not eligible for the services), was subject to brain-storms – had one – and vanished in her car. Her cook, supposed to have recovered from concussion caused by a fall from her bicycle, hadn't; a house-trained dog had made a vast and unexplained pool in the middle of the drawing-room carpet, and another guest staying in the house arrived back somewhat late after dinner to find herself locked out until, after she had bayed like a wolf on the front lawn, someone had woken up and let her in. We hoped we would not add to the troubles, and made ourselves scarce until it was time to go and sing at an army camp. But before we set off we were summoned to hear the radio news – Attlee telling of the historic meeting between Churchill and Roosevelt. We were thrilled with the drama of it.

Reggie's leaves flew by too quickly. When he was at home we returned to our old life of gardening, taking the dogs out, doing *The Times* crossword puzzle, sitting contentedly by our own fireside. I had to go on looking after my hospital wards but skimped the visits a little while he was there. In September he had a two-day leave and we went foraging for food. He got a rabbit. Nan (the black retriever) got another, and I picked about three pounds of blackberries. A lovely afternoon, almost like peace-time, except that we knew he had to go back to his camp the next day. But we were fortunate in being in the same island. My cousin Ann Holmes had not seen her sailor husband Johnnie for a year; and then, in August, unannounced, he arrived on her doorstep with the happy news of a shore job, miraculously only three miles from the cottage she had rented in Hampshire.

In September Rene was called up to go into the A.T.S. It was a blow. She was housekeeper, secretary and friend, and my heart sank to my knees when I thought of being without her. I was very spoiled. I had never had to think about details and had never done much for myself about the house because Rene did it all for me. She dealt intelligently with everything, and I could not think of a single thing I would alter in her. She told me in her inexpressive little voice and with a completely blank face that she felt Parr's was her second home, and I knew, when she said it, that she was as unhappy about the parting as I was.

Mrs Proctor, with two little girls, came to look after me. Her mother's home was at Windsor and she went there for week-ends. She was gentle, kind and a good cook and we got on happily together. She asked me about our pictures. My father had sent the Sargent portrait of his mother and the Healey of his great-grandfather for me to house until the war was over. The Healey shows a young man in a white linen suit standing on a bluff above the Hudson River near New York. It was painted in the early 1800s. Mrs Proctor said:

'Might I ask who that portrait might be of?'

'My great-great-grandfather.'

'Tst. Tst. He doesn't look old enough.'

With some difficulty I managed to get tickets for her to go to a broadcast of *Itma* with Tommy Handley. The nation laughed regularly at this programme and I hoped Mrs Proctor had enjoyed it. Putting her hand over her mouth as if to apologise she said: 'I couldn't help smiling.'

I did my first 'big' solo twenty minutes' broadcast at the end of October, seven sketches produced by Stephen Potter. He gave me dinner first at the Café Royal. It was a bitter night and I was wearing every form of wool. Inside the Café Royal I peeled off a few layers and enjoyed a delicious war-time meal. The studio was an underground news-movie theatre. We got there about 8 p.m. and I slogged solidly – timing, balancing, cutting and trying out effects such as stepping to the side of the mike and calling out, to give the perspective of distance. There was a lot to do in such a programme. I went on the air at 10.40 after a break at 10 when Stephen left to go to his club to fetch Eric Linklater, the writer, who wanted to hear the broadcast, and who sat in a stall seat and laughed so loudly at the balance test that we decided he had better go in the control-room with Stephen so as not to put me off.

Rene Easden looked after us at Parr's

Even so, the two of them laughed with such abandon behind their glass panel that the sound came through and actually went out over the air through my mike, some forty feet away. As usual just before the red light went on I got a turn-over in the pit of the stomach, but the whole thing went smoothly and with no sense of rush, for which I was glad. Two days later I got mail. One postcard said: 'Dear Madam, thank you very much indeed.'

When Mrs Proctor went home to her mother for Saturday night I was alone in the house. Here was a chance to prove I could manage on my own. I wondered if I'd mind the solitude. I didn't; in fact it was pleasant. I had Nan for company, and Mrs Proctor had left my supper ready. I kept the boiler in, stoked the Aga and generally housewifed; a tiny triumph (and high time too) that liberated me from that time forward. But I was not alone very often. Sylvia Skimming, a child-hood friend who lived less than two miles away, was glad to get away from her family from time to time. We worked together at the hospital. She was a restful companion; we sat in amicable silence at the end of the day, had the same taste in reading, radio and food, and got hungry at the same moment. Our paths have not crossed often since those days but when we meet we pick up the threads where we last left them with a smooth feeling of continuity.

Cynthia Wedderburn came down to escape noisy London nights. She has always been the friend to whom I show work in progress, because I find she knows what I am trying to say and meets my intention half-way; she is usefully critical at the stage when ideas are still tentative and I need encouragement of a confident, constructive kind. This is a moment when destructive criticism withers the original idea before it has grown its own legs. I respect Cynthia's judgment and very much appreciate her quick response to certain of the characters I have created. We share a great many tastes, and she is one of the first friends with whom I exchange books and ideas about faith.

The khaki scarf begun for Reggie in 1939 was still on the knitting needles at Christmas 1941. He didn't get Christmas leave, but Virginia and Tony did and spent three days with me at Parr's. Mrs Proctor and her children went home to Windsor and I coped. I had begun to understand the boiler better, could cook cauliflower and chops. Progress. Full stop. I sent off a hundred and seventy-five cables to Canada from patients in the hospital.

CHAPTER TWELVE

Songs with Dick

EARLY in 1942 Clemence Dane introduced me to Richard Addinsell on the steps of the National Gallery in Trafalgar Square after one of the lunch-time concerts. At the time I did not know how important this was to be. I had come to know her in 1940 when her war-time 'postscript' broadcasts for the BBC were widely listened to, and the London office of the *Christian Science Monitor* asked me to interview her for the paper. On the strength of one meeting at Aunt Nancy's house I telephoned her and asked if she would allow me to come and see her and, with her usual warmth of heart, she gave me an appointment and I came up from Buckinghamshire with a pencil and pad ready to do the job.

She was born Winifred Ashton and took Clemence Dane as her pen-name; all her friends called her Winifred. Everything about her was on a generous scale. She was a beautiful woman, splendidly large, with a noble head and a presence. She sailed into a room, her back straight as a dancer's, her full flowing dresses sweeping the ground. The dresses were made of soft materials always in the same shape: scooped neck, long sleeves and voluminous skirt. Outsize sprays of great silk roses, poppies or chrysanthemums were pinned to one shoulder. She wore her soft thick dark hair brushed straight back and put up into a precarious knot at the back of her head; a classic style exactly right for her uncontemporary looks. She had a deep musical speaking voice and an uninhibited laugh.

Until I knew her better I found her intimidating. She would have been surprised to know this for it was far from her intention. She had much energy and an expansive heart; both swept her on, and the result left one a little breathless until one got used to it. One of her most endearing characteristics was the flattering assumption (she was never patronising) that the rest of us were as informed and well-read as she was, but this was not always the case. At first I felt overwhelmed

Richard Addinsell

and out of my depth, but I realised it was a compliment to be expected to know all about St Sophia, the Luddites or Charles Williams's books. When I went to interview her she soon saw I had no idea how to set about it, so she showed me. Once I had recovered from the surprise of being taken over I was truly grateful for her help because she knew what she was talking about and I learned a lot from her.

In February Winifred invited me to a small supper party. I had got into the habit of not going out much, and I didn't often go to London. It was difficult to find a bed, and parties without Reggie weren't much fun. But I remember the excitement of getting this particular invitation and deciding to wear my favourite dress – a handed-on moss-green velveteen sent by a friend in New York and quite the most glamorous I had ever worn. It had its own rustling taffeta petticoat ending in a box-pleated frill, and I was particularly happy in it because it was warm as well as becoming. (Comfort is of first importance to me. Heaven knows I have my share of vanity but increasingly I put warmth and ease before discomfort and elegance.) Winifred lived over a wholesale

Clemence Dane

florist in Tavistock Street, Covent Garden, in rooms hung with her vivid paintings of people and flowers; and that night I met Lilian Braithwaite and her daughter Joyce Carey, Fay Compton and, for the second time, Richard Addinsell. Of course, his name was well known to me from his film scores. He had written the music for *Fire Over England* and *Goodbye Mr Chips* among others, and now his 'Warsaw Concerto' from the film *Dangerous Moonlight* was famous and had become a favourite with the troops and in particular the RAF. It is romantic music with clear, strong tunes. The theme was played by concert pianists, dance-band pianists, and by ear on lamentable canteen uprights through the length and breadth of Great Britain and it was continually broadcast. I heard it in every form and, like the rest of the listening public, I whistled it, hummed it and loved it. There were others at the party but I no longer remember who they were.

After supper Richard Addinsell played the piano. He knew all the songs I best liked – songs by Kern, Gershwin, Rodgers – and he played them in his own very individual way. I moved over to the piano as if drawn by a magnet, and he invited me to sit beside him on the long piano stool. 'Do you know this?' he said, and played 'The Most

Beautiful Girl in the World' from *Jumbo*. I sang it with him. Then he played 'Where or When' and I sang that. At first I was tentative but gradually I grew more confident. He said, 'Let's do it again.' We did it again and this time I took risks with the improvised bits, and it got better and better (or so it felt). I had the time of my life. My voice has never been big and in those days it was frail and amateurish; if I pressed too hard I went flat. Singing small with Dick made my singing seem better than it was. Musically we felt together; there was no effort to find a blend, we simply blended.

Years afterwards Dick told me he had noticed a certain boredom among the rest of the party at the other side of the room as we went on and on from song to song with increasing enjoyment. I hadn't noticed any of this. I was having far too much self-indulgent fun. I had no need for an audience; no need to be listened to. It was taking part that was so satisfying. Some people get a lift from strong drink; I get it from singing. There is no pleasure for me that can compare with singing, quietly and freely, with a sympathetic pianist; and when singing with a pianist of Richard Addinsell's calibre the intoxication is without measure. That evening at Tavistock Street was one of the very special times and never forgotten.

Good tunes don't need filling in. Displays of arpeggios and meaningless runs up and down the keyboard usually mean poverty of imagination. I think Kern, Gershwin, Rodgers, etc., should be allowed to be themselves; I do not like pianists who try to make Gershwin sound like Chopin, and Kern like Rachmaninov. But all tunes can stand imaginative arrangement and that is what Dick gave them. He played the songs in the best contemporary manner, full of his own invention, but he never embellished for filling-in purposes. Whatever he played was musical and rhythmic. When he played the piano it never seemed to be a percussive instrument. And he never drowned the singer.

In June Dick gave a supper party at 25 Mortimer Street, and we performed to a glamorous company of theatre friends, as well as to Winifred, Victor Stiebel the dress designer, then in the army, an Admiral and a General. Noël Coward paid us compliments. But as I wrote to my mother: 'The big thing of the evening was when Dick told me he had written a new song for me. It is quite lovely and I've written – or am writing – the words! It is probably to be called "That's All for Today" and it is a letter song.'

Among the other jobs I had never thought of doing was writing lyrics for songs; nor had I ever collaborated with anyone, and I did

Reggie   *I like to think I once looked like this*

not know how songs were written. In this case Dick wrote the tune and sent me the top line. I fitted words to it and rang him from Parr's, twice daily, with new versions. In London he carried the telephone to the piano and played his alterations to me. I sang my new words to his accompaniment and thus the song got finished. In the end our first song was called 'Nothing New to Tell You' – a letter to a parted love and, in wartime, very topical; I gave the first performance of it with Geraldo and his orchestra later in the year. This was the beginning of a happy collaboration, and I owe Dick a great deal not only for the music he wrote for me but for his growing friendship.

A prime test of friendship is when a friend has enough affection to criticise another, not for critical reasons, but from a sense of caring. If Winifred's energy and largeness of heart carried her on, my blinding egotism propelled me. It didn't prevent me being interested in other people and caring for their welfare; but egotism is blunting and never attractive and I had it a-plenty. My parents had done their best to point out that bossiness alienates people, but it took me for ever to find this out and I'm still having to learn. I was quick to notice overpowering characteristics in other people. Aunt Nancy, all five foot of her, was an astonishing force, and I reeled back from her attacks, but, even when they were justified, the only lesson I learned was how not to do it her way. Years later B.B.C.'s Woman's Hour had a series called 'A Letter to Someone Else's Daughter'. I based my piece on the ineffectiveness of being bossy – except as a repellent. It was written out of experience. Dick did me real service in pulling me up when I bulldozed on. Of course I didn't enjoy it at the time, but I knew what he said was right, and I was glad he had the courage to speak. It cemented my friendship with him.

Writing songs with Dick has been very important to me. He composed the music for almost all my lyrics until ill-health forced him to retire. In the 'ballad' songs he wrote the music first and I fitted words to his tunes. In 'idea' songs with stories we reversed the process. We adjusted to each other's work until we both felt it was right. There always has to be give and take in the marriage of music and lyric and we used the telephone a great deal. Of course we fought for what was important in our own work, but on the whole the collaboration was a close and easy one, for we did not differ over essentials. I think we are both instinctive writers and this can lead to a clash of wills, and occasionally it did, but somehow our mutual respect resolved problems and the end-product, well honed, was a true collaboration.

In the summer Bertie Farjeon was planning a new revue to be called *Light and Shade* and he invited me to come into it. Since the revue was an evening one it would not be possible to commute from Taplow, for there were no longer late night trains. After much heart-searching I decided I should stick to the hospital job. At the end of July I went to the opening night and was saddened by the sentimental nostalgia and the absence of Bertie's usually astringent comment. He was a conscientious objector and so hated war that he couldn't satirise the current social scene. The revue was too gentle. Bertie's sister, Eleanor Farjeon, who wrote books of great charm, had a hand in several of the numbers and her sweetness knocked the edge off Bertie's wit. We didn't laugh much, and there seemed to me too much 'beauty'. The party I went with, and the audience in general, left the theatre with a feeling of disappointment and mild depression. The critics were not enthusiastic.

Two days later I got in from the hospital to find that Bertie had been

Richard Addinsell

trying to get hold of me since early morning. He rang again and it was to ask me to help him: would I come into the show and try to salvage it? I felt miserable at saying 'No', but on top of my own wards I had taken on Sylvia Skimming's work while she had some leave. And my engagement book for August was full of troop-concerts. I wasn't all that modest but I did not honestly feel capable of saving the revue. I cannot now remember what made me change my mind nor how I got out of the promised concerts, but on 17 August I slipped, unnoticed, into *Light and Shade* with some new material written in a few days and instantly memorised. (At that time new material appeared to write itself on command.) In spite of a kind notice in the *Observer* from Ivor Brown my return to the stage after an absence of fifteen months did not save the show and, at the end of three weeks' struggle to survive, it quietly came off.

Dick wrote another tune, a waltz, and wondered whether it was a show number on a bigger scale than our first song, but I thought it was a natural follow-on from 'Nothing New to Tell You'. After the letter-song the new one would celebrate the reunion of two people. 'Leave' was very important in those days, and Dick's opening phrases clearly said to me, 'I'm going to see you today – all's well with my world.' He liked the idea and I went to work on the lyric. When I wrote it I had not realised that it could have a wider application than the meeting of parted lovers; but a letter from a woman who heard the song broadcast on the day her baby was to be released from hospital, after many months, told me she felt the song was meant particularly for her. It became my signature tune and I use it in all my programmes. We recorded 'I'm Going to See You Today', with 'Nothing New' on the reverse side, at the old H.M.V. studios in Abbey Road. Those were the days of recording on wax, long before the blessed invention of tape. It was nerve-racking to wait for the red light to go on in the studio, knowing that in the recording room a big wax 'master' disc was revolving on the turntable and if one made the slightest mistake the whole thing had to begin again with another great wax 'master'. Dick and I, tense as fiddle-strings, had to make three separate visits to Abbey Road before we achieved our first professional gramophone record together.

Walter Legge, who had produced our record, was organising concerts for Ensa (Entertainments National Services Association) of 'straight' music for the troops stationed in Northern Ireland and he offered me an eight week tour as compère to a mixed company of singers and instrumentalists, with a spot of my own at the end of the programme. Since Aunt Nancy did not approve of my return to the theatre and had made threatening noises about taking back Parr's Cottage (and using it to house someone who would agree to stay and work full time at the hospital), this seemed a timely invitation, and I felt it was a good moment to get away. Also by now I had been called up to do 'entertaining' as my war job.

Reggie was in favour of the tour. Aunt Nancy rang me one morning at 8 a.m. and gave me hell for not being in the A.T.S. I took it calmly and made my decision to go to Northern Ireland. T.J. was comforting and understanding and said I must do what I believed to be right. He thought entertaining was going to be more and more important; it was my job and I ought to do it.

I went to London to prepare for the tour, and to broadcast for the first time 'Nothing New to Tell You' with Dick playing, accompanied by Geraldo and his concert orchestra. Afterwards I telephoned everyone I could get hold of whom I hoped had heard us, but I could not get on to Reggie who by now was in a camp near York. I stayed with Virginia and, instead of giving her flowers to say thank you for my visit, I went in search of bulb-fibre – a rarer and more precious token of my appreciation. While I was out I unexpectedly spent my broadcasting fee on a black wool suit for myself. I have found that the best shopping is done when it is unpremeditated. (After the war Virginia and Tony went out one Saturday morning to buy a reel of cotton and came home with a Bentley.)

Aunt Nancy was away when I decided to accept the tour and I telegraphed her to ask what she wanted me to do about Parr's. This time she said: 'Well, it's your house. You must do what you want with it.' Mrs Proctor stayed on to caretake and forward letters. I was not sure about it but I half-expected to come back and take up the hospital job again at the end of the tour. Farewells at the hospital were touching; I had made real friends among the staff and the long-term patients in ward eleven. Reggie rang me from Yorkshire and Aunt Nancy called from Plymouth on the morning I left Parr's. It was pouring with rain and Reggie's retriever, black Nan, went into a corner of the living-room and looked pathetic. I did not like going away and wished I had not said I would do the tour.

Leaving England was complicated. I had not noticed, until the morning of my departure for Northern Ireland, the printed slip in my passport that told me that all books, photographs and papers (my songs and copies of lyrics) had to be censored before I left. I took a taxi to an office in Kingsway with a suitcase laden with all the papers, and left it there while Dick and I made a hurried private recording of two more songs we were working on; back to Kingsway, lunch with Dick and then I caught the three o'clock train from Euston where I joined 'The Music You Love' company.

Travelling with an Ensa company was a new experience. Diana Menuhin said that Ensa headquarters in Drury Lane should have 'Abandon Hope All Ye Who Enter Here' written over the door, and I came to know what she meant. I think part of the trouble was the inexperience of some of the organisers, who did not always realise that different callings needed different handling. Thus it was not a good idea to send as manager of a 'straight' music company a man who did not like music and whose working life had been spent running variety tours, and not variety tours that played No 1 dates – or even No 2 dates. I have long forgotten his name but not his manners nor his aversion to music and, unfortunately, to musicians. At first I was as enraged as they were, and then it seemed more intelligent to try and make the relationship work. But it was not made easier when I heard him telephone to the entertainment officer of the next camp at which we were to play to say that he knew the boys wouldn't like the show he was bringing because it was 'all gloomy serious stuff'. Complaints went back to Walter Legge in London with appeals begging for more mercy in the planning of an itinerary that sometimes took us fifty miles each way over bad country roads in a battered bus to do two shows in one evening. We knew there was a war on but we felt we weren't helping to win it under those circumstances. The manager was reprimanded and somehow we jogged on through the eight weeks, and it was not all unpleasant.

On the first day Gwen Byrne, who was our solo pianist, and I found we were expected to share a room and though we made friends each preferred to be on her own. We opted out from the Ensa hostels and managed to find ourselves inexpensive rooms nearby. We ate at the hostels at least once a day and I remember being brave about a black beetle in some heavy porridge and not mentioning it to anyone except Gwen.

The 'gloomy serious stuff' was a hotch-potch of well-known classics, such as 'One Fine Day' (soprano), 'On With the Motley' (baritone), 'None but the Weary Heart' (contralto). Plenty of Chopin on the piano, Kreisler pieces on the fiddle, and 'The Swan' on the cello. The tenor had a wider selection of 'gems' from which to choose. There was a regular argument between him, the contralto and the cellist about whose turn it was to perform the guaranteed show-stopper – Handel's 'Largo'. Originally it was a tenor aria, but arrangements have been made for contralto and cellist, and the artists took it in turn to make certain of success with it.

The original idea for the concerts came from a small minority of troops asking for some 'real' music. I think Ensa, or else the artists, showed cowardice in not giving the deprived minority the nourishment it sought; instead they went for easier popularity and the genuinely musical audiences remained starved. In spite of the manager's low opinion the concerts went well. Audiences, particularly the more discriminating R.A.F. were enthusiastic and wolf-whistled after particular favourites like the Gounod–Bach 'Ave Maria'.

By this time American troops had arrived in Northern Ireland and we went to their camps. These men were there principally to clear land

and build airfields and had come from north-western States. Most were country boys, unsophisticated and musically fairly illiterate. Like many of the Canadians at the Cliveden hospital they understood class-ical music to mean Victor Herbert and songs from musicals. We had to be very patient with the slowness of these American audiences and their amazement at the sight of a cello. If the cello was a puzzle, so were my monologues. Many of the audience did not find them either funny or interesting. Perhaps they found my satire of canteen ladies and vil-lage mothers so like life that they felt no need to respond? Sometimes the sketches were heard in silence, broken only by coughs. Whatever the reason was, I had to make do with fragments of appreciation, and the going was rough. But I had a number of short 'silly' songs written for me by Virginia and some collected from my mother and Harold Lindo, and these went well and restored my confidence. In letters to my mother I reported that audiences got better as the tour went on. Perhaps I had begun to learn how to cope with the challenge of un-responsive listeners.

Northern Ireland grew on me and the week we spent in Five Mile Town near the border was a happy one. In those days the place con-sisted of a single street of houses with a few general stores where heavy boots hung from the ceiling and there were dried grasses on the floor. I had my hair done in the sweet-shop-cum-coiffeuse where the owner locked the door because – 'as it was Fair Day the cows might come in'. Unspoilt country with small white farms seething with chickens, ducks and mud rolled on either side of the long street. I enjoyed listening in to Irish conversations. There was a mild dog-fight in a café where I went for a cup of coffee. After one owner had extracted her dog she looked at him and said with severity: 'Now conduct yourself.' When the sun was out it was 'a brave day'; when the rains came it was 'attacking weather'.

Local people were hospitable and the whole company was bidden to tea at a house nearby. I am a large woman but our two women singers were a good deal larger. At one moment Gwen Byrne found herself the only member of our group in the room. She asked a Belgian pilot who was mysteriously at the tea party: 'Where are the others?' 'The big pieces,' he said, 'have gone on in advance.'

Walter Legge asked Dick Addinsell to come over and join the tour in mid-November, as our guest artist, to play the piano arrangement of 'Warsaw Concerto' and to accompany me in a group of our songs and some current hit-songs that would please the Americans – and a large section of our British audiences too. I half dreaded his arrival because of company jealousies and pettiness. We worked to make our contribution well rehearsed and professionally skilled. Our welcome was a shock to the 'straight' musicians and our success made it worse. But soon, after some moments of silent disapproval, we were grudgingly accepted and the atmosphere cleared. Dick, who is a shy man, but not when playing the piano, was included and I was readmitted to the group. Answer to prayer.

At the end of the tour Dick went to Dublin, and I visited my godmother in County Antrim and then joined him in the Republic for two eye-widening days. No black-out, plenty of food, Germans mingling with the Irish, and John Betjeman, in a flat cap, representing Great Britain doing a diplomatic job that enabled him to report back on the social comings and goings of the enemy. He showed us eighteenth-century Dublin and the enchanting Chapel of the Lying-in-Hospital painted with cherubs. Part of me could not help enjoying the creature-comforts of a country not at war, but the other half resented every blazing light, helping of cream and the sight of those Teutons walking free. We left Ireland in a thick fog and came by way of Strabane and Glasgow to spend a night in Edinburgh in order to see Noël Coward and Joyce Carey who were on tour with two of Noël's plays. The night we were there they gave *Present Laughter* and we were bowled over by the splendour of the playing, the production and Noël's talent, craftsmanship and wit. Next day, full of happiness, I joined Reggie in York before returning to Parr's. It was very good to be together again and we told each other the war couldn't last much longer. We were wrong.

I was to play a part in a film called *The Lamp Still Burns* at Denham and had a diary full of troop-concert dates in the New Year. Reggie was expecting to be posted to the War Office. We decided, sadly, to leave Parr's and look for a flat in London. Reggie's Christmas leave was spent in turning out and packing up the cottage. His sister Laura was with us and we had a Christmas dinner treat of eggs and bacon and tinned fruit salad in our warm kitchen. We went to tea with Aunt Nancy that afternoon, and the next day Virginia and Tony joined us for some of his leave. Early in 1943 I went to stay with them in Cambridge Square until I could find a place of our own.

Aunt Pauline Spender Clay was still living in a roomy flat in Ennismore Gardens, quiet and comfortable, and we went back to stay with her. She would only let us pay a token rent to cover meals and laundry.

Virginia Thesiger

Self with snail

We moved in on St Valentine's Day 1943 and were very content. For me the whole of that year was filled with troop-concerts in camps and hospitals and canteens up and down the land. I did bits in films and wrote more songs with Dick, and there was endless rehearsing with a series of accompanists, and long train-journeys, often standing in the corridor.

CHAPTER THIRTEEN

Viola and I Work our Way through the Middle East

It was the hospital concerts that interested me most, and in August 1943 Ensa asked me to act as compère to a five-handed concert-party doing ward-shows in service hospitals in Lancashire and Cheshire. I joined them for four weeks and had my own 'spot' for monologues and songs. The unit did not prove to be very lively. The leading figure, our pianist, was handicapped by not being much of a sight-reader, nor could she cope with accompaniments of any complication. I gave her my music a week before I joined the company but she never quite mastered the notes of my songs and our performances were undeniably perilous. I sympathised with her – up to a point; I, too, was that kind of piano-player; but I was not a professional accompanist. We had a husband-and-wife team with an accordion-concertina act that ended with him playing 'The Bluebells of Scotland' on two concertinas at the same time, one in each hand pressed against his chest, and cymbals tied to his knees. His wife rang hand-bells. Our singer, a statuesque blonde like a Staffordshire china Ceres, Goddess of Plenty, wore three evening dresses for the programme, one for each appearance, and had a swooping soprano voice that plummily sang a trifle under the higher notes.

The standard was so low it was funny – but not quite funny enough. Certainly not funny enough for the audiences. But there were remarks made, on and off stage, that I stored away and some of them came in useful years later when I was writing material for radio and for my own stage shows. The concertina-wife looked over my shoulder at a reproduction in *Life* magazine of an Italian picture of the Virgin with the baby Jesus standing on her hand. 'Well,' she said, 'you can see it's a little boy, can't you?' In the bus on the way to a concert I heard her explaining to Ceres why she wasn't much of a reader, not of *books*, that is. 'You see, I can't stop thinking, I'm thinking all the time, that's why I can't read a book. I'm thinking all the time; I'm a *terrible* thinker.'

The comedian played the violin a little, conjured well and did unrecognisable impressions. He had been a street musician, in velvet jacket and beret, with a pet monkey on his shoulder. (He still wore the clothes but had left the monkey behind.) His best beat had been near Broadcasting House where he had a coin-in-the-hat relationship with 'all the stars' and once spoke to Bernard Shaw. 'I know all the aristocrats – Sir Duff and Lady Diana and little Johnny; Binnie Ale and Eric Mashwish – good old Eric!' At each hospital we visited he asked for 'the loan of a broom or brush' and made his entrance with it, backwards, threw the broom off-stage and said: 'Give that to the R.A.F. and tell them to make a clean sweep over Germany.' This never raised a reaction of any kind beyond stunned silence, but he kept on saying it, night after night, day after day. But he was a very good conjurer, particularly after the performance when he did small tricks at close range with an impressive skill.

One day he told me he had decided to write a monologue for me. The scene, he said, is Buckingham Palace when the King is presenting posthumous medals to the families of lost heroes. 'There's this little lad comes up to get his dead dad's medal – you'll like this bit – "He left behind his self-same mould" – that's the little lad, see, the spit of his dad – "his self-same mould".' I was inspired to say I thought the piece should be spoken by a man; it would lose something if it was done by a woman and I wondered whether he had thought of sending it to a music-hall entertainer of the day who specialised in heart-wringing material – Izzy Bonn? '*Marvellous* idea,' said our comedian, delighted as if he had thought of it himself. 'That's it! Izzy Bonn!'

My position was a tricky one because I was ashamed of the poverty of the programmes we provided, and there was not much I could do about it. I knew, from playing in the wards at Cliveden hospital with Eve Clarke, that it was possible to create an intimate atmosphere far more successfully than we had managed to do with this five-handed group stuck at one end of the room, or patients' lounge, with no chance of improvising the programme or involving the audience as we had been able to do on our own.

At the end of October Noël Coward got back from a tour of the Middle East where he had been playing in hospitals and told me there was a lot of work to be done there and I ought to go out and do it. He said all he had needed was a pianist and a piano; and it would be the same for me. I would be mobile, as the two of us, an accompanist and myself, could be easily transported and sent to places where it was not practical for Ensa to send larger parties. As well as North Africa Noël was particularly interested in troops stationed in Paiforce (Persia and Iraq) whose task was to police the Aid-to-Russia route from the Indian Ocean northwards and maintain communication and R.A.F. bases throughout the area, and who felt forgotten while they served in non-combatant zones. He said there were not many large centres but plenty of small units in isolated places, and hospitals, often in tents. He recommended me to Ensa and they suggested a six-month tour. 'Nonsense,' said Noël when I told him. 'You can't keep fresh to do the job properly for so long. Go for eight weeks.' I settled for ten and Ensa agreed. Reggie thought it was long enough and encouraged me when I quailed a little; my father said the enterprise was well worth doing, and Aunt Pauline, enthusiastic at such an opportunity, opened up old trunks and produced a pair of fur-lined boots and an inflatable air-cushion; both invaluable.

At first Dick Addinsell hoped to go overseas with me, but his doctor said he mustn't; the bad back that had kept him out of the army could not stand up to the rigours of such a tour. It was a blow to both of us. At that time I worked with whoever was free to play for me when engagements turned up; I had several good players on the list but none of them was available to leave England, nor did I think any one of them was quite flexible enough to fit in with work that I knew would demand a degree of improvisation and easy adjustment to strange situations and conditions, both in and out of working hours. For my own sake I hoped to find someone congenial, with the same ideas about the purpose and demands of such an assignment. As I saw it we were being sent to provide a useful service, and to do it well we should need a sense of proportion and the spirit to enjoy adventure. This last was not my strong point but I hoped to improve it. I wasn't afraid of the task ahead; I was grateful to be doing it; and though I was squeamish about some of the possible hazards we might have to face, I decided I could trust my usual expectancy of good. I asked everyone I met if they knew of a pianist to fit the requirements of the job; talent and ability to play all kinds of music on any kind of piano, and health and strength enough to endure the long hours. Mr Faraday, who ran the Star Studio, where Dick and I usually recorded the songs we had written, said he knew exactly the right person to go with me, a girl called Viola Tunnard. Before I had time to telephone her I heard her name again from Sylvia Bruce Lockhart, who ran a mobile concert-van servicing searchlight and gun sites round London. She agreed with Mr Faraday that Viola

Viola Tunnard

Tunnard was the answer to my problem and put her in touch with me.

We arranged to meet at my mother-in-law's flat where there was a piano, and on a cold grey morning in late November Viola arrived wearing a black fur coat with a stand-up collar and no hat. I registered a pale drawable face, with good bones, dark hair, wide-apart brown eyes and a beguiling, shy smile. In repose her mouth went up at the corners. She was diffident about playing my kind of songs. She said she didn't suppose she'd do them the way I wanted them done. We ran through some of the numbers, and I noticed she played 'ballads', such as 'Can't Help Lovin' Dat Man' and 'The Way You Look Tonight', as well as Dick's songs, rather better than she did the jazzier ones. I sang them better, too.

'Would you like to do the tour?'

'Do you think I'd be good enough?'

'Yes, I do – I'm sure of it.'

'Well, if you're sure . . . I'd like to go.'

'That's fine then.'

We had to be ready to leave any time after 23 December. There were endless visits to Drury Lane for briefings and inoculations. (We waited till we arrived in Cairo to get our khaki drill uniforms. These were useful for journeys but we never wore them otherwise, because we soon learned the troops preferred to see us out of uniform; and the informality of our shows was helped by our civilian appearance.) A great deal of muddle went on at Drury Lane, and my letters to Reggie and my mother and entries in my journal were full of rage at the general inefficiency and wasting of time. Doubtless Ensa had its problems, but from our point of view it was exasperating trying to get information and decisions from H.Q.

The departure date came and went. Our passports had not been given back to us by Christmas Eve, so we were pretty certain not to be summoned until after the holiday. Aunt Nancy asked Reggie and me to come to Cliveden for Christmas but I was on a stand-by call and it seemed wiser to remain on the spot in case the call came at short notice.

Reggie and I went to a Christmas party at Winifred's. She had collected Lynn Fontanne and Alfred Lunt, then appearing in Sherwood's play *There Shall Be No Night*, as well as her close circle of Dick, Gladys Calthrop, Victor Stiebel and Joyce Carey. (After the war, I went to supper with the Lunts in New York. Alfred cooked us a Lucullan feast, and Lynn showed me how to achieve a fold at the back of my up-swept hair that I have used ever since and for which I am constantly grateful.) We knew there would not be many taxis on the streets that night, so Joyce Carey, Gladys Calthrop and I had brought our heavy shoes in bags, as we used to carry our slippers to dancing-classes when we were little, and we put them on to walk back home at midnight. The silence in the Mall was broken only by our feet as we strode down the middle of the empty road under a starless sky. We seemed to be the only people out at that hour and it didn't take us very long to get to Chesham Place, where Joyce lived, nor to Cadogan Place, where Gladys had a flat, but the last lap to Ennismore Gardens seemed to take for ever. The party had been worth the long walk. That year Winifred wrapped her Christmas presents in bright yellow paper and had a candle for each of us bearing our names. The parcels were piled up on the piano. She and Olwen Bowen-Davies who lived with her at Tavistock Street had prepared a splendid un-warlike feast for us all.

Viola and I were supposed to go by air to North Africa but we only rated as second lieutenants and that was not a commanding position. There were no priorities available for Ensa. We couldn't make plans beyond each day and it was difficult to settle to anything, but I spent two mornings sitting to Winifred. She had begun a picture of me earlier in the year and our delayed departure was a chance to get on with it; but not in peace. A new production of *Hamlet* was in rehearsal and Pamela Brown had to learn Ophelia's songs. For some reason it was here she came to do it. Winifred was an expansive worker and liked plenty of space to step back into in order to see what she had put on the canvas, but that week she and I were confined to a small corner while a friend of hers gave singing lessons to Pamela Brown. Such was Winifred's concentration that she was oblivious of the sounds from the piano area, and never touched the cups of tea Olwen brought in to us except to rock her cup a little as she manoeuvred her position to and from the easel. At the same time as the singing and painting, another friend sat reading in an armchair by the gas-fire. The portrait was never finished.

Reggie and I kept telling each other that ten weeks would soon fly but the continued delays of my departure made going away harder. He was about to rise to the rank of major and that was going to be another help to our finances. I was cared for by Ensa who paid me £10 a week and all found. Eventually word came from Drury Lane to say we were going to North Africa by sea, and on the morning of 13 January 1944 our train left Euston for an unnamed western seaport.

We recognised Liverpool, where a harassed padre asked me if I had seen his 'Communion tackle'. Standing about on the docks on a frosty day we eyed our fellow-passengers, got into a Royal Army Service Corps lorry marked 'Civs.' and sat there for forty minutes while more and more troops arrived in army vehicles. One truck had the names of Maureen Higginson and Lilian Hackenbush scrawled in chalk in childish writing on the door panel. We ate flannel-vest meat-paste sandwiches bought at Euston and awaited orders. On board we were each given a large cabin on C deck. The ship was a former P. & O. liner and our steward, a hardened veteran from a lifetime of carrying passengers to and from Cape Town, said he hoped this trip would be better than the last one. They'd been dive-bombed. After this we paid attention to boat drill and did as we were told, putting ready a little pile of *absolute necessities* in a pillow-slip to be grabbed in an emergency. There was one during the trip and we each went to our cabin as instructed and stood there clutching our pillow-slip, heart thudding, but the danger passed before we were ordered to the lifeboats that we had made sure we could locate in a rush. The captain of the ship (S.S. *Strathmore* disguised as D 19) gave us a pep-talk soon after we had settled in and told us not to keep diaries. I decided that a journal written in an exercise book was not a diary, and throughout the tour I wrote every few days in a series of such books an account of our doings and of the people we met.

Viola and I were not the only women, nor the only civilians, on board. There were the wives of diplomats; Red Cross, W.V.S. and Y.W.C.A. workers and Free French women on their way to join General de Gaulle, as well as British service personnel, and nurses. Our particular friends were a young Irishman, Denis Baggallay, and John Ambler, with whom we walked and talked, played deck tennis and discussed the lives we hoped to lead when the war was over. Denis had flaming red hair and a rider's stoop. When she first saw him Viola said she wondered what it was she missed as she looked at him, and then realised it was a horse. He was twenty-five and married for a year to his lovely Betsy. He and John Ambler looked after us and helped to make the twelve-day journey a pleasant time. 'Once a Girl Guide always a Girl Guide', so I knew when our convoy turned left, as it were, instead of continuing westward into the Atlantic. The weather got warmer and warmer and we saw Gibraltar. I felt guilty at having such a good trip and wished Reggie was with me. With us on board were 'The Two Leslies', a music-hall act well-known on radio, and together we did some concerts for the troops, the ship's crew and the officers and civilians. The Leslies' material was broad and went very well. My offerings at the first show had a quieter response – to put it mildly. I was not a total failure but my confidence was temporarily shaken. I too had some broader material and, for the next concert, I added the (innocent) version of 'The Tattooed Lady' taught me by an American soldier in World War One, which in those days I had been forbidden to sing. It went well.

I have always known that my 'act' does not fit in with a variety bill. It works successfully only when I am on my own and can create my own climate. This is not because I am snooty, exclusive or can't take competition; it is because the way I work and the material I write is in another key. I need a quiet atmosphere and a gentler tempo. When my programmes come off it is because the audience has contributed its imagination as well as its attention. The shows we did on board gave me no time to establish that kind of relationship, so I learned which numbers in my repertoire served variety, and dropped the rest. Happily I was not called upon to be in many variety bills.

Viola played the piano for church parades and, every afternoon, eightsome reels, as well as responding to invitations to play in the lounge. The pianos throughout our tours were almost without exception bad; the ship's pianos were brutes. Had we known it this was a foretaste of pianos to come. I doubt whether we ever found such a whited sepulchre as the instrument in the Main Lounge of D 19. It had no middle C, no notes *at all* in the last two octaves of the treble, and C sharp above the non-existent middle C played a chord-combination of C sharp and A flat. It was heart-breaking for Viola. She was hardly ever able to produce really beautiful sounds. Most of the instruments were mini-pianos and it took her a while to get used to them being short of notes; she found her fingers running up on to the wood. She brought a metal tuning key with her and used it everywhere we went. Somewhere along the oil pipe-line in Iraq she lost it, but a huge Texan engineer at one of the 'stations' made her a new one and saved the day.

I have a picture of Viola plumbing pianos all over the map. She did wonders and managed to make even the most miserably inadequate instrument sound better than it deserved. It was a real pain for her to work on such pitiful pianos. Some barked harshly, some appeared to be strung with wool. Pedals varied from the almost efficient to the permanently loud, with hum. But she gallantly played what was asked for – 'Clair de Lune', the theme from the 'Warsaw Concerto', Chopin waltzes, Rachmaninov preludes, and added Scarlatti, Bach, Mozart and Brahms when they were likely to be enjoyed. She deserved a decoration for the way she managed those damnable pianos.

Algiers revealed itself to us very early one morning, a white cliff of a city rising through a mist out of a calm pale sea. We were met by a French woman welfare officer who drove us five miles along the coast road to the Ensa hostel at Point Pescade. It was a *maison particulière* in all senses of the phrase. Meals were taken in a suntrap with bright yellow, blue and orange glass and hung with orange crêpe-paper curtains. Marble floors throughout, no rugs, no running hot water and cot-beds just six inches off the ground. It was a particularly cold January. A variety unit called 'This and That' and the 'Two Leslies' arrived soon after we did and demanded tea. We settled for coffee and tangerines and took ourselves out for a walk up the steep lane behind the villa. Through an iron gate we saw our first lemon tree, a Della Robbia against the clear blue sky. We began to feel better. Geranium hedges spilled over in guardsman's scarlet, pink and white; almond trees were out everywhere, and as we climbed higher up to fields the ditches were full of wild iris, tiny yellow marigolds, a giant stitchwort and a plant new to us that we were to see everywhere on both sides of the Mediterranean, locally called *vinaigrette* or *la fleur anglaise*, an exquisite lemon-yellow weed with furled buds that opened to look rather like freesia flowers and was a menace to farmers. We also noted an Arab youth wearing a hairnet. A fruitful walk.

Roger Makins was number two to Harold Macmillan, our Minister Resident at Allied H.Q. in Algiers. He was an old friend of Reggie's and when he heard I was in North Africa he invited me to bring Viola and stay at the requisitioned Villa Desjoyeux that he was sharing with Harold Macmillan and his P.A. John Wyndham. The villa was large and comfortable. It was carpeted, had hot water, was run by Grenadier Guardsmen in sandshoes and stood high up in the residential area, just above a villa where General de Gaulle had his H.Q., with views over the city to the harbour.

When we arrived we found John Perry of H. M. Tennent, the theatrical management company, staying in the house on his way from Gibraltar to Italy. He was A.D.C. to General Mason-MacFarlane and awaited an air priority to take Pluto, the General's great dane, to Naples where the General had gone in advance. A hundred and fifty pounds of great dane takes a lot of transporting and, as we knew only too well, air priorities were not easily come by. John Perry and I agreed that it would simplify matters if Pluto were lost. That evening he disappeared. When we got back from dining out, at 11.30 p.m., John was still in the garden calling and whistling and, probably, cursing. At 4 a.m. an Arab guard sleeping in his tent by the front door was scared to screaming point by an affectionate great dane licking his face. Much relief all round and a priority came through later that day.

We soon began our hospital shows. Throughout our time in North Africa, Malta, Sicily and Italy, we visited on an average three, sometimes four, wards a day. (On the next tour in India we eventually had to cut down to two a day because of the heat.) We went to the first ward in the morning some time after 11 o'clock. I found it difficult to decide whether it was better to make an occasion of our visit and herald it in advance by posters, and then make an entrance; or to walk in unannounced and make ourselves known first to the patients in beds near the door, and then quietly walk up the ward, each taking a side, and having a word with the rest of the men. Viola liked the second way better but I knew that an 'occasion' looked forward to and made something of added to the value of the visit and was not an excuse to boost our egos. Every hospital was different, so was each ward. Surgicals and medicals were usually much iller than 'orthopaedics' and in these wards we found it wiser to leave it to those in charge to present us as they thought best. But we always did the walk up the ward (while the piano was being man-handled by an unnecessarily large group of vocal Italian prisoners-of-war) and I memorised where in Great Britain each patient came from, and then, when we had a free-for-all singing session at the end of our thirty-five-minutes set programme, I tried to sing a song appropriate for the swede-bashers from Lincolnshire, the Cockneys, Scots, Yorkshire-men, Taffies and so on, in which they could all join. We usually spent about an hour and twenty minutes in each ward.

Our idea was to be as undemanding as possible and to make the visit informal. There were sure to be some men who did not want to be entertained and we did not want to embarrass them. It seemed to me unfair to take advantage of an audience that could not get up and walk out if it wanted to. I made it plain that no one was expected to look, listen or applaud. So often they couldn't anyway.

I was glad I wasn't very young; at thirty-five I could represent mum, auntie, the wife or the girl-friend, and I didn't need, though I got, wolf-whistles and other signs acknowledging my sex. Viola also had a full share of the whistles. We didn't work for them, nor did we under-estimate their friendly significance.

From time to time in the hospital wards we met an unco-operative type. The first indications were witticisms mumbled under his breath to his near-by cronies; obviously personal and unflattering witticisms. He was a challenge and my heart quailed when I marked him as I came in. I had to learn not to show that I had noticed him. It was a help, and of course salutary, to remind myself why we were there; not to be buttered up for one thing. We were there to try and engage the patient's interest (to entertain in the real meaning of the word) and lead him out of him-self and his worries into the outside world, still going on, still there, in spite of the horrors of the war; and to try to help take down self-isolating barriers. That was the point of the job – not just to 'cheer-up-the-boys' and fill in time (though that had its uses), but to help in linking up again with a continuing life with changeless values in it.

Sometimes the unco-operative bully-boy would affect to read a newspaper to show he wasn't going to be bothered to listen. Now and then he might sneak a look over the top of his paper to see what we were doing, and when he did I felt a little spurt of hope. If this happened again and, later, he put down the paper and, later still, he turned fully towards where we were performing and joined in the singing, then I knew the barrier had come down. He had stopped thinking inwardly and, unselfconsciously, had come out of himself and joined the rest of us. We had met. I came to know that his sort of resistance was often a kind of anxious embarrassment and not antipathy. Being trapped and sung at must be discomfiting; I realised it, and learned to get rid of my own fear and selfconsciousness. Then a relationship was established. I found it fascinating to watch shy and introverted patients relaxing into acceptance, and counted it a real blessing when we were all in the circle – very rewarding.

We tried to work in every ward of each hospital and stayed until the visits were completed. At first we were in danger of being overwhelmed by the sights we saw. Then compassion took the place of personal distress, and it was the presence of love, practical and supporting, that impressed me most and helped me to continue our work.

After doing shows all day Viola and I longed for quiet evenings, but social life seemed to be part of the job. We supped in messes, went to parties and were bidden to dine with the Duff Coopers in another requisitioned villa, of Moorish style, on the heights above the Villa Desjoyeux. They had come to take over from Harold Macmillan, soon to be transferred to Naples. Their chef was an Italian prisoner-of-war and I remember a splendid fish arranged in a life-like curve on a bed of greenery with its mouth full of pink geraniums. It seemed a pity to disturb it, but I was on Duff Cooper's right and was served first and had to do so. Lady Diana, dressed in pale blue Greek draperies, looked like a goddess. Opposite me sat Martha Gellhorn, then married to Ernest Hemingway, and I heard her say: 'He wears a beard because of his work and it is snow white. He is a literate who can't stand the company of other literates.' Duff Cooper said he quite agreed with him.

One of our extra-curricular jobs was to go to dances. This was hard work at the end of a day in the hospitals, but there was such a shortage of women that it was difficult to refuse invitations without seeming unfriendly. Viola went on her own to a 12th Lancers occasion near

Algiers and got back at 2.30 a.m., her arms full of mimosa and her knees shaking after non-stop whirling and a wild drive back in an open jeep. The young men of the unit were enthusiastic and tireless and there had been only twelve girls for them to dance with. 'Not nearly enough,' said Viola. Later, in India, we found ourselves at Poona (not, after all, a particularly funny place) and bidden to the Forces Club dance where we were made to feel irresistible – lines formed to await our favours on the dance floor. It was known that we were on a hospital tour but we were a little surprised to hear ourselves announced as 'two well-known artistes who have been flown out from home to entertain men in bed'. A man standing behind Viola said: 'Cor, so they've laid that on now,' but on the whole the introduction, though fully registered, was tactfully ignored and we thought it best to pretend we hadn't heard it.

I have a fatal attraction for small men, and in Dacca I had a tiny persistent partner with a grip of iron and a fine Palais de Danse style, who led me through some dashing routines involving spins and swoops and gave me a lot of enjoyable exercise. When the evening was over he took his black Tank Corps beret from under his shoulder flap, put it on the back of his head and saluted me: 'Ta,' he said. 'I enjoyed it.' Me too.

Sunday was our free day and Roger took Viola and me to see the Roman ruins at Tipaza. Usually 'special' days are good for some private reason – the company or the circumstances. This particular Sunday was a day on its own, out of time, and for none of the usual reasons. The luminous light was gentle. I thought it must be like the light that people rejoice over when they find it in Greece. We drove along the coast-road in pale sunshine between verges thick with wild flowers – great candelabra-like asphodel, gorse and broom; giant green and white stripe-leaved thistles as well as all the small ditch-flowers. Before exploring the ruins we sat on a grassy bank by a field of new wheat, shimmering green through the red earth, and ate our picnic lunch. Goldfinches flashed in and out of olive trees. Below us two naked boys, white against the gold-red rocks of a tiny curved bay, sunned themselves after a swim in the sparkling aquamarine sea. Between the rocks and where we sat two smaller Arab children in long grey gowns moved slowly through sparse scrub collecting firewood. Apart from the goldfinches the only other sound came from the children singing a repetitive falling tune as they worked.

After our picnic we explored the ruins set on the very edge of the little cliffs, and walked on low-growing aromatic plants that scented the fresh, still air. A shepherd came through with a flock of bleating, multi-coloured sheep, brown and white, black and grey, black and brown, white and beige, all with long swinging petal ears.

I had not been prepared for Tipaza and the impact of the deserted ruins in this setting was powerful. I wished I were educated and knew some history. Even without knowledge I was filled with wonder; with it I knew the experience must be even more thrilling.

Harold Macmillan and I share the same birthday and that year it fell on a Monday, so we celebrated the day before with another picnic, this time in the Forêt de Bainen, pine-scented with views of the Mediterranean through the trees.

Harold in a flat 1910 cap worn centrally was far off in a ministerial trance for a while, but as he meandered through the forest he was very companionable and friendly. He has a way of pouring out but appearing not to absorb; but he does absorb. Coming back we stopped the car and all got out to pick wild flowers. The Minister and Roger bent down to pick yellow jonquils growing in drifts. Viola and I went further off the road and found several kinds of wild orchis, a purple valerian and lots of scratchy blue anchusa growing among iris stylosa.

CHAPTER FOURTEEN

Hospital Wards and Isolated Units

BETWEEN January 1944 and the end of March 1945 Viola and I went to
fourteen countries on two separate tours. The first ten-week trip expan-
ded into fifteen weeks; the second took us away for five months. Reggie
expected to be posted to Belgium in August, and that is why I agreed
to do the second tour. In the end he did not go until much later and I
had to leave him in London. It was a strange war in which wives went
overseas while their husbands, in greater danger, served at home.

Looking back on those tours I now see them (although I did not
realise it then) as the time of my life. I was learning how to do my job
under the most demanding conditions I was ever likely to meet; I was
seeing the world, and getting an opportunity as never before or since
of doing what seemed to be useful work that stretched me to the full.
The warmth of the welcome and the affectionate farewells when we
left each new place might have turned our heads, but, in all honesty,
Viola and I were both so grateful to be allowed to do the job that we
were slightly awed by it and that kept us humble. Very seldom is one
called upon to do more than one thinks possible. We did get tired, but
I knew that the spiritual source of energy was available to be drawn on,
and because there was so little time to think about ourselves, we were
able to carry on working for longer than we might have done under
less challenging circumstances. We grew working muscles and learned
techniques that allowed us to be spontaneous and ready to improvise.
Noël had been wrong about not staying fresh for more than eight weeks.
The rewards were more than enough to keep us going.

When we left Algiers in the middle of February we began to face up
to tougher living conditions. Spring had already arrived in the low-
lands by the Mediterranean, but as we climbed up to the table-lands,
going east, it was still a much colder winter than I had imagined possible in that part of the world. Ensa provided us with a station-wagon
type of car driven by a young French-Algerian whom we named Joli

Garçon because, in his beret and grey suede gloves, he reminded us of a number in one of Bertie Farjeon's revues. Joli Garçon was not communicative. He used a Gallic shrug of the shoulders to answer most questions and didn't appear to have much faith in himself, human nature or his car. A few days before we set off he had taken us up a steep, unfenced mountain road, and in negotiating the top hairpin bend he put the gears into drive instead of reverse and stepped on the accelerator. Mercifully the engine stalled. Up on the plateau it began to snow and the car, overheated by its struggle to the heights, stuttered and stopped. Joli Garçon tried to start it again but it wouldn't go. The snow turned into a blizzard. He shrugged his shoulders, said nothing and settled down in his seat to await events. We did not know what to suggest so we settled down too. Suddenly there was the thud of pounding hooves and out of the swirling snows raced a line of black Arab ponies, manes flying, heads tossing, heels kicking up – a black-and-white frieze design of startling beauty as they moved across our path. Joli Garçon sat up and said '*Tiens*', tried the key in the now cooled engine and it started. 'One never knows,' he said with another shrug, and on we went. He was not my favourite kind of driver.

After the snows it rained and sleeted and was very cold for most of our time in North Africa and, later, in Italy. Viola and I were sometimes billeted in the nurses' quarters and had first-hand experience of the tough conditions with which the sisters had to contend for long stretches at a time. Service hospitals in the Mediterranean zone were housed in schools, monasteries, sanatoriums, and in tents and Nissen huts set in thick glutinous grey mud. The nursing-sisters wore battledress and gumboots. When we commiserated with them over the depressing inconvenience of mud they said that after months of wet weather they'd got used to it. We admired them and only complained quietly to each other as it got on to our clothes and into our luggage. I lost the King's Royal Rifle Corps brooch Reggie had given me. Misery.

Lavatories were seldom close to sleeping quarters – any distance up to a hundred yards away – not very handy when one was compelled to pay a visit in the middle of a winter's night, boots on bare feet, coat over nightdress, head down into the sleet through mud. Plumbing, or rather the absence of plumbing, became a subject of keen interest. On our second tour in warmer places we met the usual eastern hole-in-the-floor with raised non-slip places for our feet. Both of us were put off by the absence of sitting equipment. We far preferred quite long walks across the desert to canvas-walled privies, open to the skies.

These were usually arranged companionably in separate pairs, and we journeyed together from our tent with our torches and sat gazing up at the unaccustomed placement of the stars, talking of the day's doings.

I have always been one for a bath a day and in warm weather possibly two. We did not always find baths, but there was always hot water in jugs or buckets, and I became skilled at all-over washes, even in unheated, uncarpeted rooms in icy weather, standing in a couple of inches of water in a bucket while I washed myself in a tin basin. Two bath memories have stayed with me. In Sorrento we were billeted in a charming Edwardian hotel by the sea, taken over by the British Red Cross as a convalescent home. We arrived late and I was faced with a tub full of scalding water and not a drop in the cold tap. I hadn't had a proper bath for days and pined for a good soak, but time was short. I was soon due to give a show and could not wait for the water to cool. I soaped myself all over, standing on the mat, and then plunged. I came out bright red all over, thudding. It was worth it. The other bath memory is of a tin tub, Victorian model, at nine thousand feet in Darjeeling, filled with water carried in by our bearer and assistants, in disused petrol tins. I had it in front of a roaring log fire.

Our arrival in Naples in the middle of March coincided with Vesuvius erupting in the grand manner. I went with Harold Caccia and his American opposite number Sam Reber to look at the lava coming down the mountain-side. Our driver, Private Tchaikovsky of the US Army, told us he was only distantly related to the composer. He drove his jeep across country, by-passing an endless line of cars, nose to tail, chugging slowly up the rough track that passed for a road, and brought us to within a quarter of a mile of the high red wall of lava visibly moving, and hissing as it came down. Our faces glowed in the hot air blown off the flow. Small particles of red lava thrown up into the sky made a firework display of star fountains.

After weeks of anxiety Viola at last heard that her younger brother, Peter, whom she knew was in the battle of Anzio, was safe. His regiment had suffered heavy losses, and several of his friends had been killed. He was on leave and we took him with us when we drove to Sorrento to do a concert. Vesuvius went on erupting and a luminous smoke-fog came off the molten lava and made all the colours of spring vegetation on the lower slopes appear startlingly brilliant green in its strange light. Next day we had transport troubles (no novelty). Peter somehow produced an unpromising and battered open desert-car that soon broke down on our way to an R.A.F. hospital. We stood about in sticky mud; by this time great belched-out clouds from the volcano were flung up in a menacing pall below the clear blue sky ahead of us. Each thrust threw up tightly curled grey cauliflower clouds, sometimes pink in the sun that came out after the heavy rains. Presently an Army truck, with three Guardsmen in it wearing their down-the-nose peaked caps, came along and gave us a lift as far as the local Guards' H.Q., where we learned that the R.A.F. hospital was being evacuated because of encroaching lava. We were told not to proceed and went back to Sorrento for an unexpected bonus – a day of rest.

There was plenty of social life in Naples. Roger Makins flew in from Cairo, and Harold Caccia asked Harold Macmillan and us to luncheon in his ice-cold requisitioned modern villa, built on a promontory with panoramic views of the Bay, the city, and Vesuvius still blowing grey cauliflowers. John Wyndham was there too; he had lately been in London and gave us an account of the bomb that fell in St James's – 'the street near Wilton's Oyster Bar and Spink was littered with a confusion of medals and shellfish'. Harold Macmillan read aloud to us from Boswell's *Life of Johnson* particulars about Papists, because, he said, Latin countries awakened all John Wyndham's Protestant feelings, and Harold wanted him to hear Johnson's views on the subject. After luncheon some of us went to Herculaneum. 'Chester Terrace, Regent's Park,' said John, looking at the décor of urns, swags and fluted columns, so familiar in English Regency houses. A guide in spats pointed out the plumbing arrangements. 'Look at de bart,' he commanded. 'Look at de cake on de table, slize iz off-cut. Look at de lavatrine in de kitchen.' A curious arrangement we decided.

One of the temptations on the hospital tours was the lure of historic sites. We were often near treasures – Leptis Magna, for instance, and Deir-ez-Zor on the edge of the Euphrates – but neither was on the direct route to where we had to go, and we decided, feeling noble, that unless there was a legitimate reason – i.e. troops to be entertained – we must not go out of our way to sight-see. There were a good many ancient sites on our direct routes and we never missed a chance of visiting what was legitimately available. I went on wishing I was better educated. Viola's father had brought her up on the classics, and I relied on her to tell me about the places we saw, for there were no books to hand and we did not often find ourselves in the company of informed guides. She mocked my ignorance of the ancient Greeks and Romans but allowed that I knew more music than she did. I had had seven years longer for listening, but none of the insight into structure and musical logic that she had already acquired. When we went to concerts together after the war I learned to listen and hear in a new way, and I continue to be grateful to her for that. And for introducing me to bird-watching. Her father was also a botanist and ornithologist, and she grew up in Norfolk with a natural interest in both. I caught some of this from her and when I got home Reggie and I began to watch birds together. He soon outstripped both Viola and me in observation and knowledge and has become a dedicated 'birder'.

We were given only six days in Sicily, and on a cold clear spring evening after our day's work we managed to get to the amphitheatre in Syracuse which Plato is supposed to have visited. The place was deserted. Wild flowers grew in cracks between the almost white stones. We stood in silence, stirred by history and the splendour of the theatre. Viola, following a tiny green lizard, climbed to the top of the tiered seats, and I stood below on the stage and declaimed to her, to prove what we had been told about the perfect acoustics. All I could think of to say was 'Mary had a little lamb', and every familiar syllable reached her intact. Inspiration always deserts me in amphitheatres. When at last in 1972 Reggie and I went to Greece with my brother Tommy and his wife Mary, the high spot of all we saw was Delphi. Up in the shallow theatre against the mountain, with a dramatic back-cloth of gorge and rocky cliffs before us and the April air loud with goat-bells, cuckoos and nightingales, I went and stood in the middle of the paved stage while the others clambered to the back row of the auditorium, so that, once again, I could try out the acoustics. Did I think of something appropriate, by Gluck perhaps or Purcell? No. Instead I heard myself singing, 'And when I tell them how beautiful you are, They'll never believe me.' Irving Berlin has his rightful place, but it isn't, I think, in the flower-edged theatre at Delphi. A group of bewildered French tourists heard me out and then tendered a round of applause I did not deserve.

In the Middle East we kept hearing about Isfahan; a place not to be missed. The name was familiar to me but I couldn't think why, and then I remembered. The year after we were married Philip Connard, the painter, asked me to sit for him, and twice a week for two months I went to his studio. While I sat there with our character pekinese, George, on my lap, I sang every song I knew – nursery rhymes, Negro songs my mother had grown up with, musical comedy and music-hall songs, hymns, folk-songs and songs of the day, with a little Bach and Handel thrown in. As a reward for this questionable contribution Mr

Connard gave me six singing-lessons from his friend Mark Raphael, and so much did I enjoy them that I arranged to have more at my own expense. It was the first time I had paid to learn anything and because of this I took the trouble to practise. Mark introduced me to Fauré and I sang 'Les Roses d'Isfahan'. I liked the word 'Isfahan', but in my ignorance I had not realised it was a real place in Persia. At H.Q. in Baghdad I asked if we were to be sent there. The officer in charge said it was not on our itinerary, but there was a small unit stationed in Isfahan made up of Signal and Meteorological Corps and Military Police, seven men in all, and he agreed to let us go and entertain them. They certainly qualified as an 'isolated unit', and this made the detour legitimate.

We arrived at night. General impression of flatness, straight streets, straight poplar trees, spaciousness and peace. No view from the hotel bedroom, but in the morning I jumped up to look out of the high bathroom window and caught a glimpse of shining domes. Archdeacon Richards, Welsh and enthusiastic, took Viola and me out in a two-horse droshky and we clip-clopped round the town in a sight-seeing drive. My journal records intense delight in the delicate sixteenth-century wall-paintings of flowers and birds in the Ali Kapu pavilion, where a Shah of the day and his court had watched polo from the open verandah on the first floor. The game began on the Maidan in Isfahan, and the original stone goal-posts (surely a nasty hazard to run into) still stood there. We went to the top of a six-storey building, the highest in the place, and looked down on the flat roofs below. Domes winked in the sun, and all around, beyond the city limits, was an edging of mountains; fairy-tale mountains like an illustration by Edmund Dulac, with sharp peaks and blue shadows, and an outer range capped with snow.

After the long black clothes of the women in Egypt and Baghdad the pale pastel-coloured, voluminous top-to-toe capes worn in Isfahan were pleasing to me. A bell-flowered crowd of women, only their eyes showing through slits, moved as if they were on little wheels. We went to the underground bazaar and saw a giant oil-press, a Heath Robinson contrivance made from whole tree-trunks, with pulleys worked by a blindfolded camel trudging round and round on big spaniel-like feet. Cobwebs the texture of tweed appeared to have been made by a property-man for a spooky Hollywood movie. We came out into the light on to a flat roof, where craftsmen, each in his own small eight-foot-square space, sat cross-legged making 'antique' playing cards for the tourist trade. I preferred the sight of men and boys block-stamping with traditional

Arriving in Baghdad (Note Aunt Pauline's useful boots)

Persian designs twenty-yard lengths of cotton spread on the ground. The 'sensible' shoes I bought in Cairo turned out to be too short in the toe, and once again I was grateful for Aunt Pauline's fur-lined boots, though they were decidedly cosy on those mild autumn days.

In a moment of panic the isolated unit decided its mess was not big enough for our concert and borrowed the larger room of the Anglo-Polish Club. The club secretary invited 'a few Poles' to come too. These turned out to be about a hundred and fifty refugees from Russia, mostly old men and women, but there was also a contingent of school-girls. The Britons sat in the front. I tried to explain to a kindly but humourless interpreter what I was about to do, item by item. 'This is just a little silly song about security' (Virginia's parody of 'My bonnie lies over the ocean', 'My bonnie is stationed at . . . . . .'). What followed was always a long spiel that could not possibly have been a translation of what I had told him, and I wondered what he was talking about. The unit and their friends appeared not to mind the boring pauses while the interpreter droned on; but it was tough going, probably for the Poles as well as for me. Even so the experience was less arduous than our performance at a convalescent home at the northern end of Malta, given in a disused chapel with a very high platform. There the audience, men and women all in battledress, sat on backless benches a long way below me. I sang and they applauded. I did a monologue to total silence except for coughs. I sang again and the house cheered up; another monologue and down went the temperature. Puzzled, I whispered to Viola that we had better stick to songs, and thus the strange monotonous afternoon came to an end. Back-stage the padre in charge hoped I had enjoyed the audience. I hesitated. He slapped his knee in sudden recollection: 'I forgot to tell you – they were all Yugoslavs.'

The atmosphere in hospitals, wherever we went, was set by the matron, even more than by the commanding officer. When she was good her influence was felt in all departments. When both had the qualities of leadership (not dictatorship), authority, a sense of proportion (humour and justice), compassion and concern, the place had an affirmative and healing climate. When these were lacking the hospital failed to fulfil its potential. We went to very few unhappy hospitals.

Matrons in all shapes and sizes have stayed in my memory: Irish eccentrics; Scottish comforters who provided shortbread and drop-scones for tea; Welsh dreamers with fey ways but organisational powers; English mother/nanny figures. In one of the hospitals in Italy, at Bari, which had been blitzed and was bare and draughty, Matron kept her budgies in adjoining cages with communicating doors; she had a plaster statuette of a stout child, all pout and pinafore, where the birds could see it for company. Also in Italy we met a small matron with a large green thumb for growing African violets. Her bathroom was crowded with successful plants blooming profusely, and good enough to win prizes at the Chelsea Flower Show. She had them ranged along the edge of her bath, in the sponge-rack, on the window-sill, on top of the lavatory cistern and on the floor. Moving about was hazardous. 'You see they love the *steam*,' she told me. In India a matron – expecting the answer No – said to me: 'You don't mind smallpox, do you?' We played in the doorway of an isolation tent to three surprised soldiers.

The entertainment and welfare officers we had to work with were a rum lot. Rum is the right word. I am not in sympathy with drunks, and rarely in my experience does liquor bring out the best in people. Coping with those who had taken enough to slow up their thinking and blur their speech brought out intolerance in me. There is no boredom like the boredom of trying to get through to a sozzled entertainment officer who was not interested in what he was supposed to be doing in the way of organising our shows, and only wanted to be left undisturbed by a big bossy outsider like me who demanded action. I don't get angry very easily, but when there was plenty of time to plan for us, and (recurring worry) our piano, and nothing had been done, I did get tetchy.

Viola said I was worth watching when I became what she called 'altesian'. This was a word she made up from the French *altesse*. It seems that I got more and more dignified, taller and more distant. I never entirely lost my cool, but I made it clear that I was not pleased. It usually worked. But only after a great deal of emphasising and the use of plain language.

In places where it was really difficult to lay things on for us we almost always found efficiency and imaginative kindness. Most of the officials who looked after us were helpful. Three weeks of constant company (we spent that amount of time in most areas) established a relationship and we grew fond of our managers. At first, until they knew us, there was sometimes an assumption that we were only in the business for 'a good time'; this meant parties in the officers' mess after the shows. We were a disappointment to them because that was not our line. Another difficulty lay in the mistaken assumption that we preferred officers to other ranks. Finding the right balance when bestowing the gracious pleasure of our company was tricky. If we went exclusively to OR canteens it suggested we spurned the bosses. And *vice versa*. We tried to combine all ranks in after-show gatherings. In small units it was possible and worked well, in bigger camps there had to be a choice or a long evening of visits to all the separate messes. Hard work.

We arrived at one of the many isolated Signal Corps posts and were greeted by a Cockney with a fog-horn voice who asked, as we got out of the car: 'Is it true you turned down an invite to have dinner with the Brig so's you could meet the boys?' It so happened we had, and the brigadier thought it a good idea and was pleased about it. 'The boys heard you had and they're all tickled.' I asked him how on earth they knew about it. 'We're Signal Corps,' he said. 'We hear *everything*.' I was amused; but afterwards wished I had said, what both Viola and I felt, that this notion that officers snatched everything and that I'd socked them in the eye by refusing the brigadier's invitation was nonsense. Part of the reason for us being out in those far-off places was to combat homesickness, and we knew that a captain could feel just as far from home as a private, and there was nothing to choose between them when it came to deciding where we should go after the concerts were over. But, if the truth be known, it was generally easier for us in the other ranks canteen.

There were many agreeable characters – skilful drivers, sergeants-in-charge, as well as entertainment officers – who looked after us; but of them all Corporal Sid Weatherill of Leeds, who drove us in Iran on our second tour of Paiforce, is the one I shall always remember with special affection. He had a pale, long-boned face, dead straight dust-coloured fair hair and a world-weary look that was wholly deceptive. He was a sharp, terrier-like man with Yorkshire doggedness and humour; and he took to us as warmly as we took to him. Unlike Joli Garçon, Sid was my favourite kind of driver – confident, rhythmic and care-taking. (I've noticed that musical people drive the way I like being driven – Sid liked to sing.) His wife, whom he married shortly before coming out to Paiforce, was a Maltese girl in the A.T.S. He showed us their wedding picture, both in uniform and Mrs Weatherill in glasses. At that time perhaps the Ecumenical Movement had not begun. 'At our wedding,' Sid said, 'we couldn't have no pomp or confetti or music because she were a Roman Catholic and I am a Christian.' They had been allowed a few flowers. 'Before she joined up she were a bakeress.'

Driving down a narrow road (miles of it) above a deep gorge, we met Aid-to-Russia convoys, coming at us at speed, driven by opium-high drivers risking all in their zeal to keep together. There were forty vehicles in a convoy and we were told that never more than thirty-nine reached base; but no one stopped to see who had gone over the side of the mountain. It was a testing road for anyone; but Sid, the back of his neck bristling with concentration and his fine-boned hands gripping the steering wheel, gave me some confidence, though I sat tense when we came to corners and the oncoming trucks roared toward us. 'I'd shut your eyes if I was you.' In the middle of an enormous stretch of barren country on the way from Tehran to Isfahan we took a wrong road. Without a smile Sid told us in his flat Leeds voice, 'Ah thought we orter turned at the last round-about by the post office.'

In 1944 the highways in Iran, not yet tarred, were deeply ridged and corrugated and there was no way of avoiding a rough ride. Sid apolo-gised for the road, as if it was his fault that we were so shaken about and had to hang on to the seat in front to prevent ourselves bouncing up and hitting our heads on the roof. He said he thought we'd better take it smartly, and 'get it over with'. Night had fallen and, as we rattled and bumped on our way, one of the back wheels came off, rolled past us, turned left across the path of headlights and disappeared into the dark. We skidded, out of control, and came to a stop in a ditch on the edge of the desert. None of us was hurt but we were all a little extra alive. An escorting jeep, just ahead of us, driven by an Indian in a grey knitted cap and goggles, with an armed military policeman beside him (there had been hold-ups by bandits on that road), came hurrying back to see if we were all right. Sid took the jeep and drove it in circles, combing the gritty desert with his headlights, looking for the wheel. It was eventually found some way from where we had stopped on the *right*-hand side of the road. It had rolled in a complete circle round the staff car.

One day we visited nine Signal Corps posts. They were situated every twenty miles between two isolated villages; one of them was where we were welcomed for having turned down the brigadier. We got to the first hut at 7.30 a.m., too early for anyone to be sung to, but we went in and had the first of the many cups of hot sweet tea in vast tin mugs that we were to be offered on that long day. Nine warm welcomes. Nine cups of tea. Sometimes we unloaded the piano and sang a few songs; sometimes we just had the tea and talked. Sid came to all our shows that day and every day. He laughed at every old joke, and asked for his favourite numbers. Afterwards he analysed the audiences. He drove us for three happy weeks.

In 1947 I was on tour with a revue called *Tuppence Coloured* and we were booked to play in Leeds. I wrote to Sid saying how much I'd like to see him again and I was looking forward to meeting his wife. After a long wait I got a letter from the manager of the firm Sid had gone back to after the war, telling me of his death shortly before my letter came. He had died after a lorry in the garage had pinned him against a wall. His marriage broke up and he had been wretchedly unhappy and hurt about it. The manager, who was also his friend, felt that life had lost all meaning after that, and Sid had lost the will to try and get well.

Our working conditions varied widely. The piano and the acoustics were the most important ingredients. Some warm lighting helped but we hardly ever got any. Acoustics and piano had to be endured more than enjoyed. I think I preferred the deadening effect of the tents to the swimming-pool resonances of high, bare wards. I hardly ever used a microphone on the tours because the few available were primitive and amplification was metallic and unpleasant. When the place was good for sound the shows went well from the start, but if I had to battle to be heard, articulating like a machine-gun with all consonants almost spat out, it took much longer to make contact. We spent two days in Algeria working in a tall T.B. sanatorium on top of a mountain, where all the beds, in wards measuring two hundred feet by ten, faced a panoramic view across a patchwork of agricultural fields, miles and miles of them, all the way to the sea, a pale strip in the far distance. Difficult to know where to put the piano – and me. We settled for somewhere in the middle and, although the place was good for sound, I had to stand with my back to the light and my face in shadow. By swivelling from time to time I managed to include all viewers. While I was singing Dick's song 'Nothing New to Tell You', I noticed, as I swivelled, that a straight curtain of grey rain marched across the land from right to left leaving bright sunshine behind it, while a great rainbow arched up clear over the whole panorama. I stopped singing and we all had a good look at the dramatic sight. And my heart leaped up.

Singing or speaking out-of-doors is always hard work. Nature and other hazards intruded in our concerts, indoors and out, particularly in hot weather. I often had to compete with birds, usually sparrows. The more I sang the more they sang too, piercingly and without stopping. They were always the winners. In India we had to play in a yard between two three-storey hospital buildings where the patients watched us from balconies above. It was a crick-in-the-neck occasion for me, not made any easier by crows and green parrots, both vocal and both raucous. That day every low-flying plane in the area came just over my head; ox-carts rumbled by, creaking, and an Indian carrying a letter scrabbled his big black boots on the asphalt path. Out of sight, just behind the trellis against which I stood, someone watered the flowers from a trickling hose. An uphill concert but good training for concentration. One day during a sandstorm, when stones on the roof of the Nissen hut made so much noise that we had to pause between gusts to be heard at all, Viola opened the piano and out fell a scorpion. The same night I was battling through a song at full voice when a mouse ran over my foot, but so diligent was my effort that I didn't notice it; Viola did and for the rest of the concert played without pedals, keeping her feet up on the rungs of her chair. Cockroaches of a kind I'd never seen before, enormous and bright brown, became a commonplace; I did not get fond of them, or of ants. We were warned to shake our shoes before we put them on in case of snakes. Thank heaven I never saw one.

In the Y.W.C.A. in Baghdad the warden kept a pet lamb, snow-white with a black face; very dainty as it tittuped over stone floors on tiny feet sounding like a miniature chorus girl in high heels. I saw it yawn. A tiny mouth with lips edged in black rubber; a small pink petal of a tongue. It had no sense at all and was wounded when a dog rebuffed its advances with a snap.

In an outdoor show on the island of Bahrein I had to compete with a gale. It wrapped my full skirt round my legs, blew my hair into my mouth and wafted away every note I sang, until I discovered that by standing sideways I could use the wind to carry my voice and some of my words to the audience. Viola's music blew off the stand and she had to sit on it and play from memory. As she had only moonlight to see by, we cut the programme short. It hadn't been much fun for the audience nor for us, and afterwards we went to the airmen's canteen and were warmed by hot drinks and a great many people crowded into a very small space. There we began all over again, and did requests till the early hours of the morning.

Another show outside our usual terms of reference was an outdoor concert for four hundred fighting troops waiting for orders to sail to Crete. It was a daunting prospect. They sent a guide in a jeep to lead us to the secret stronghold, and we left the main road and went across country over boulders and ditches till we reached the olive grove where the camp was, near Haifa. A small canvas-walled stage had been set up against the hillside, lit by the lights of a row of army vehicles focussed on to the platform. The men sat about on benches, on giant electricity cable-spools, in trucks and on the ground. It turned out to be a good place for sound, and the sight of all those sunburned young men in the evening light, before the car-lamps were switched on, has stayed vividly in my mind. They were tuned to concert pitch, ready to go into action. We had a marvellously lively and generous response that evening and we all sang together till the hillside rang. I didn't think the camp could possibly remain secret after that. The next day they sailed away.

In hospitals the last show of the day was usually the best and we enjoyed it most. The sun sank fast in all the countries we went to, and sunset was a time of release when shyness was forgotten and nostalgia became a pleasure and not an ache. The low sun, reflected from the shining ward-floors, lit the men's faces with a golden light as they sang with me slow sad songs of their own choice. In London, when I was going through piles of songs, trying to decide what to take with me, I had picked out a lot of cheerful, rhythmic dance-tunes and romantic numbers. Ignorantly I thought those were what were needed, but I found it was sad songs that did far more to restore homesick and depressed patients – sad songs, sung very slowly, were the thing. Spirits rose after a nice sentimental wallow.

It was moving to see the concern the men had for each other when one of them was very ill or low. In an eye-ward a recently blinded soldier, about twenty-two years old, was being looked after by two of his mates. It was a sunset show and the big ward was filled with its light. There were many walking patients in their bright blue hospital uniforms, as well as bed-patients. Some had come in on their way back from the canteen. The blinded boy wore his khaki greatcoat over his blues, with the collar turned up as if he felt he wanted to hide himself. He sat on a bed between his friends and they watched his every move. When I did a sketch they thought was funny they looked to see whether he laughed. When he did, they exchanged looks of relief over his head. After a time he relaxed a little and joined in the singing. One of his mates patted him on the arm. Then the boy wept a little, and his companions looked agonised and sang rather louder than before.

We were sent to an Italian monastery, then a hospital, where at least a hundred beds were squeezed into a big sombre vaulted sub-basement hall with very little light in it even by day. The battle for Cassino was on and casualties arrived from the front all through the afternoon. Blood-transfusions were given; delirious patients cried out; orderlies wheeled cases to and from the operating theatre. I was alarmed, selfishly, at the prospect of trying to perform under these circumstances, and I said to the sister-in-charge: 'You can't possibly want us here today. Shall we go away?' 'No,' she said. 'Just take your piano into a corner and sing a few quiet songs to two or three of the boys at a time. They'll like that.' I wondered. The Italian prisoners-of-war tried to carry the mini-piano without too much discussion, and we moved from place to place for about two hours. I sang, in the smallest voice I could find, gentle songs, familiar songs they might have known when they were children, and they asked for more. A very young boy with pale gold hair and a Devonshire accent lay very flat and still in his bed. He beckoned me over: 'Could you please sing a song about a mother?' I did not know one. Then I thought of a lullaby, 'Sweetest little feller', and I sang that for him. It proved to be a right choice, and after that I kept it in the repertoire. You learn as you go ... And you stop being afraid of sentiment.

We kept adding songs to our list as we learned them. I knew the tunes of most of the songs they asked for, and Viola could pick up an accompaniment by ear, but I did not know a lot of the words. An A.T.S. girl on the household staff at the Villa Desjoyeux taught me 'Nellie Dean' – essential, I found, for any communal sing-song. I learned 'Blaydon Races' from a Geordie jockey who wore his forage cap with his pyjamas. He sat on the side of his bed swinging his legs, and sang it to me over and over again until he was sure I had it by heart. Soon I could sing 'I'm a Lassie from Lancashire', 'Ilkla Moor bar t'at', 'My Old Man Said Follow the Van' and, for the Welshmen, 'All Through the Night'. In India a Cockney called out to me from his bed at the far end of a ward: 'Sing us "Deep Purple".' I wished I could; I knew the tune but not the words. I asked him if he wanted it for some special reason. 'Yes – my mother-in-law's varicose veins.'

When the atmosphere was right I invited volunteers to do turns. Orthopaedic wards were the most carefree, but a great many of the patients had to sing from a lying-down position. I remember a whole crowd of them egging on a man with his legs strung up to the ceiling – 'Come on, Joe – do us your Popeye!' He took out all his teeth and was cheered to the roof. In Malta a sailor-patient played the spoons all over his own body, on the end of the bed, on chairs and tables and up and down my spine. I sang duets with volunteers, did close harmony with groups and led the general singing. I always refused to sing the 'Ave Maria' because I didn't know it, and anyway I thought it wasn't my style. 'Oh, come on,' said a Scot, 'have a whack at it; it's a killer-diller.' There was often a volunteer to sing it. A very dark Indian from Mauritius, inevitably called Sambo by his ward-mates, sang it to us with a lot of feeling, and though Viola tried to follow him, the key-changes he made were so unusual and so frequent that she gave up and let him do it his way.

The last shows tended to run over the official finishing time, but understanding sisters joined in the singing and encouraged us to stay on, and our visit became a party. Whenever the sister of the ward offered to sing she was always the success of the day – with or without talent.

CHAPTER FIFTEEN

In India

WHEN we first arrived in India Ensa provided a bearer to look after us. He came from Bhutan and was called Ghulam Mohd. A handsome young man with an alternate grin and scowl. He always wore his grey astrakhan forage cap, in and out of doors. We grew fond of him.

India overwhelmed me. It was shocking, moving and sometimes enchanting, but I never felt at ease in the crowded cities where we saw so much poverty and wretchedness. Viola, too, was appalled by the streets of Calcutta where people in their cotton rags slept on the pavements. It was difficult not to get callous about beggars. They pursued us everywhere. When Ghulam was with us he shooed them away, scowling, but for some reason he wasn't there to dismiss the two we met on the road from Darjeeling when we stopped to look at the spectacular view toward Nepal. The first was a little boy about six years old and on his jersey was embroidered: 'Help this poor lame.' We did so. He was soon followed by an older man, also wearing a sweater, but his read:

Pleseh
elp this
Poor dumb

Irresistible.

I worried about Ghulam's attitude to almost everyone he met who wasn't in uniform or else in some way connected with us. He was always a great deal nicer to Viola and me than to anyone else. He despised most of the human race because, unlike him, they were not from Bhutan. I did my best to say that I was grateful for his protection against the hordes of beggars, but couldn't he do it in a more brotherly way? No, he said simply.

When we weren't billeted with nursing sisters we stayed in hotels, hostels or private houses, as well as, briefly, in Embassies and Govern-

Viola and I in India

ment House, Calcutta. It was a good idea to try and find out something about our hosts before we met them. I didn't always understand the information I was given: 'She's a dear,' said a W.V.S. worker driving us to stay with a couple in Central India, 'but he's a bit of an M.T.F.' I asked what that meant. 'Must Touch Flesh,' she said with a giggle. He wasn't all that bad but I think Viola and I were a disappointment to him. Ensa girls were expected to be younger and flirtier.

In 1944 there were still remnants of British insularity, but we had not expected to find deliberate refusal by some of the residents to know Indians as friends. When we were in Secunderabad we managed, with some difficulty, to meet a Muslim family, four beautiful young sisters and their brother, and they invited us to spend a day with them. In the morning they took us to meet a local Nawab in his crumbling cream-coloured palace, and to see his 'collections'. He had his own army, police force and postal service, and we saw small groups of soldiers in shabby uniforms (one elaborate with gold lace) sans the right number of epaulettes, or with none at all; some had boots, some had belts, but no one was completely accoutred. Gaunt men wearing co-respondent shoes and long dark Nehru coats turned out to be 'courtiers'. The scene was like a nightmare sequence in a foreign film shown in slow motion.

The collections included French furniture with its upholstery bursting out of rotting red silk covers; rooms full of guns, swords, daggers and four hundred walking-sticks, some like sugar-candy twist made of Venetian glass; exquisite bead-work pictures; and chandeliers, sometimes in working order, but more often standing on chairs or on the floor. In a small inner room, lit by a skylight, Viola noticed a Bechstein grand piano, probably quite new, but when she raised the lid the strings were orange with rust. 'But it is regularly tuned,' said our guide. 'And played?' 'No,' he said, 'not played.' Under the piano were piled leather gun-cases, unused but mouldy. There were also a great many pictures. Those that hung on the walls were large and probably Italian – a good many of 'the school of' kind – but the quality was so mixed and the condition of the canvases so diverse that it was not possible to assess them. The only common denominator was the subject-matter: the female form. I particularly remember an entire wall taken over by a picture of monks gazing at a pale blonde, naked as the day she was born, lying full length on a marble-topped table. Everything everywhere was thick with dust.

We came to the banqueting hall. The steps leading down to it were rocky with decades of pigeon-droppings. It was a high room with

French windows open to an inner courtyard where an old man in a plaid shawl was scratching at some defeated greenery. Skyed portraits of Queen Victoria and Prince Albert painted at various periods of their lives hung on the light green walls. Sofas and chairs shrouded in holland dust-covers had been pushed back from the middle of the room. There was no dining-room table; instead a ping-pong table, with two bats, handles crossed, arranged with ping-pong balls in a symmetrical design, took up the central position. Our guide, who was one of the palace secretaries, made an embracing gesture. 'Here where Nawab sleep.' It seemed unlikely; but beside the ping-pong table, only eight inches off the floor, was the Nawab's divan bed with a modest cotton paisley-patterned cover. The secretary turned back a corner and lifted out a tiny hard baby-pillow. 'He use this all his life. He cannot sleep without it. He has many rooms but he sleep here.' His bedside book was called *Love at the Courts of Russia*.

Finally, on a shady verandah, we met the Nawab. He was a pear-shaped man, about sixty, with ears that looked as if they had been taken off, ironed out, and put back like tea-pot handles. He wore his fez at an angle; a sad man with flashes of humour. After our grand tour we were grateful to be sitting down, in a curve of upright chairs around a low baize-covered card-table, to see his jewellery. Two wooden cases, copies of a child's toy chest-of-drawers, held most of the family's antique jewels. Our eyes widened as the ropes of Indian pearls knotted with emeralds and rubies, turban-pendants, chest-ornaments, rings for ears, noses and fingers, and ankle-bracelets for humans as well as elephants were taken out for us to see. Some of the pieces dated from the sixteenth century, and all of them were backed by enamel-work of great beauty. Diamonds the size of my thumb-nail were set in a gold device for elephants to wear on their foreheads. The Nawab allowed us to try on the jewels; and watched us closely as we did so. More boxes replaced the chests-of-drawers and we sat there for an hour looking at his family riches. Refreshments appeared; the icing on the stale Christmas cake was hard as concrete, and the coffee unrecognisable. I was glad to think the show was over. But it wasn't. Ten bearers, thin as pins and as poorly dressed as the army, came in, each with a battered black tin trunk on his head. These contained the modern jewels collected by the Nawab himself – ten trunks full. I can remember clearly only the cigarette-cases, dozens of them – simple grandeur from Cartier with square-cut jewelled clasps, and the rest an unenviable selection of cases encrusted with jewelled racing-cars, Felix the Cat, horses, the Eiffel

Tower, and one with a drunken man in a top-hat leaning against a lamp-post – all in diamonds. Square-cut. My eye fell on an unadorned plain wooden cigarette-case, and I was glad to see it.

At last we got away, but not before every box had been opened and everything in it shown to us. We were glutted with riches and dizzy with looking. It was kind of our Muslim friends to show us such amazing sights, and we were glad not to have missed them, but we were not sorry when the visit to the palace was over. Luncheon was ready for us when we got back to the family house.

It was good to be in such a pretty place, light and cool and uncluttered, with many coloured cushions on divans, and a dining-room table covered by unfamiliar foods and fruits in decorative dishes. The four sisters in pale saris, with flowers pinned to the back of their dark heads, moved gracefully about the room bringing us foods to choose from. I am unadventurous about new foods and decided on the saffron rice pilaff, but Viola, always braver, took something unknown. It turned out to be red hot, and she gasped. The more water she drank the more her mouth burned. Good manners mastered her pain, but she said later it had been a testing time and she would not want to go through it again. She asked for some of the pilaff.

After luncheon there was a pretty ceremony. The youngest sister sat on the floor in front of a low table and busied herself with a silver box full of betel-nuts and two kinds of spiced sauce in tiny silver mustard pots. She took a green leaf, pulled off the tip and the stalk, spread sauces on it with a little silver spade, sprinkled on chopped betel-nuts, folded the leaf into a neat square and skewered it by two cloves. We were advised not to try this delicacy unless we liked really fiery spices. The sisters told us how a famous English journalist had come to visit them to talk about India. They had not entirely liked his attitude, and after luncheon when the youngest girl packed the little green parcels she made his extra spicy and fastened it with three cloves. He ate it, panting, and when the family read his unfriendly book a year later they were not sorry about the extra clove.

India seemed to bring out eccentricity in the British women we got to know. We lodged with a middle-aged regular colonel and his unmarried sister in an airy house (rather too airy in winter) set in a garden thick with roses and sweet peas. Miss B. was warm-hearted and welcoming, and I took to her the moment I saw her standing in the doorway, hockey-playing legs wide apart, and her good big teeth revealed in a friendly smile. I thought of Disney's Thumper. She was like a caricature of an English Memsahib as evoked by Arthur Marshall, and it was easy to mock her enthusiastic team-spirit attitudes and her hearty laugh; but she was a dear woman and her straightforward simplicity and decent standards were somehow touching – and re-assuring. We stayed with her for only a week but long before it was over I had grown fond of her.

The house was full of objects, books, trophies and pictures: fretwork Bavarian gnomes climbed the drawing-room walls, and yard-high painted Negroes in blue tail-coats with red knee-breeches held out ash-trays. Aunt Marjorie ('Everyone calls me that, so *do*') sat with her feet in a cretonne bag held up to the knees by elastic against the intrusion of mosquitoes. She and her brother, we learned, were Theosophists, and her elder brother had X-ray eyes. Her sister, 'whom we never leave alone for long – she has no proper insides at *all*', lived nearby. As she talked about her family we built up a picture of minor monsters who exploited her. The colonel loomed largest. He was Number One Man in the house and had to have things done *properly*. He was passionately musical and sang bass. In a moment of disloyalty she said: 'I confess I'm not really in love with his voice. It could fill the cathedral in Calcutta quite *easily*.' She admitted that, alas, she was not musical, although she always sang her troubles away. Unfortunately her sister Enid, the one with no proper insides, and her husband (also Theosophists) could not bear anyone to sing about the house and Aunt Marjorie tried to remember this. In spite of not being musical she had once played in a ladies' mandolin band – 'Think of us, all wearing rosettes, with coloured ribbons hanging from our instruments!'

When he came home towards the end of our stay, we heard the colonel before we saw him. Roars of good-humoured chaff with his Indian butler and some rough-housing with his dog Tigger announced his return. ('Ever since A. A. Milne we've always had a Tigger.') I was wrong about his being a monster, he was a big overgrown Boy Scout with bare knees. He really did love music and sang to us in a growly voice, not fully under control, to his own accompaniment. His huge hands hovered over the notes and came down in sudden crescendos, the left hand half a beat behind the right. Aunt Marjorie didn't talk much when her brother was around because she wanted us to see him in his rightful place as Number One Man, bang in the centre of the stage. She was very proud of him. I expect he and Enid did take advantage of her good nature and willingness to serve but she throve on it and she gave no sign of martyrdom.

After the war I met another, older unmarried woman whose whole life had been devoted to her brothers, and it was she, together with the memory of Aunt Marjorie, who gave me the idea of writing a song with Dick Addinsell called 'Three Brothers'. Both women might have been pitied for what appeared to be wasted lives, but neither had any need of pity for they had been needed and honoured. I don't believe they suspected that they had been exploited; they were both fulfilled and felt blest.

Few luxuries compare with staying in a comfortable, fully staffed house when the owners are away, as happened to Viola and me at Christmas 1944. The Slaughters welcomed us to their official Railway Company house, The Gables, and then left Secunderabad for a week's holiday by the sea in Bombay. We liked the Slaughters and their three particularly attractive children and were glad when they came back home, but after weeks of being visitors it was good to be on our own for a few days in a cheerful house with friendly helpers and a garden full of birds, flowers and trees and green lawns. Every morning Ghulam brought breakfast-trays to our rooms with sprays of flowers tied with white sewing-cotton to slivers of bamboo – 'from the gardener'. Each day we were given luncheon at a table set on a carpet in a different part of the garden. We tried to identify the strange birds from a book we found in the children's room. Viola played the piano for hours on end before our day's work in the hospitals and after supper, when I lay on the sofa writing letters to Reggie. I particularly remember an arrangement of Grieg's Holberg suite. At night some large clumsy creatures clattered about in the big trees outside our end of the house. We hoped they were birds, but there was no sign of bird or beast when we looked in the daylight. For some whimsical reason I named them Mr and Mrs Albert Ross; there was an ancient mariner feeling about the size of the things, whatever they were.

Early one morning, while I was still lazing in bed, the butler, known simply as Butler, brought in a visiting-card. Mr Mohan, it said, was a lawyer from Bombay. On the back a message read that he would like an interview with Miss Grenvile. Viola went to the front hall and found a young middle-aged Indian in glasses, who said he wished to join Ensa. She urged him not to. He was ready, he said, to give up his career, for he hoped Ensa needed him and he was sure I could arrange it. Viola suggested that he should go away and write a letter putting in his qualifications and his aims, and bring it back the next afternoon when we had a free day and would give him tea. He arrived early, damp from his bicycle ride, mopping his smooth ageless face and greying straight hair with a big white handkerchief. He spoke fluent English but used it in his own way. 'In Bumbi [Bombay] they are putting up the *Doll's House*. I have studied Scandinavian drama but it is not appealing to the masses.'

We sat down to tea, which he drank slowly from a cup held in his left hand. Theatre was his 'craze'. He had produced sketches from Noël Coward, but they were for intellectuals; could *The School for Skendell* be appealing to the masses? I doubted it and asked him what other experience he had had in the theatre. 'I am watching it for three years.' I passed him another egg-and-tomato sandwich and he bit into it delicately, chewing as if it tasted of nothing. Now and then he raised his right hand and scratched his head slowly with an unbent finger. He wished to put up *Candida* in Hyderabad, but it was difficult to cast and would be a 'flup'. There were three or four Mohammedan ladies who were interested but, he said with scorn, none of them was *fit* to come on to the stage.

He had a lot to say about 'the Scandinavian drama' and the 'Ibsen-esque techniques' and I knew it would be kinder to be cruel and tell him straight out that he wasn't really the stuff to give the troops, but I didn't have the courage. Instead I asked if he had brought the letter I was to pass on to Ensa. After a page of autobiography, he ended: 'I presume that my services would be of some use to you in running shows. My birthday is Aug. 6 1911. In the circumstances I shall be much grateful if you would without going through much red tape kindly consider my case favourably for Appointment to Ensa.' Would I like to see what he called 'a certificate for me' written by the President of the Hyderabad Music Circle? I took it from his limp hand. 'Mr Mohan has been a precious asset to us as he has been personally acting in these plays – *Baby*, *Lapandas* and *Hach Mulacha Bap*, in which he played most exquisitely.' There was a great deal more, but already I was reeling slightly. In India I found it was sometimes hard to get things into clear focus. We waved Mr Mohan away and he bicycled slowly and erratically out of sight. Faithfully I forwarded his letter to Ensa as promised.

Soon after I arrived in Bombay I ran into Jack Hawkins. It was always comforting to run into Jack at any time but somehow, after a long time away from home, it was particularly encouraging, and we spent a congenial evening dining at the Taj Mahal Hotel where we were joined by George Devine. He and Jack were two of the most intelligent, articulate and pleasant men in the theatre; we spoke a good deal of one another's language and not only about the theatre. On and on we sat in the lofty dining-room until we were the last guests, and the staff, waiting to go home, had to turn off the lights in order to get rid of us. But not before we had discovered that all three of us collected items from Personal columns in Indian newspapers. One of mine survives: 'Engagement. Mr F. d'Cunha (Lallee) of Byculla is to get buckled up to Miss Valierien shortly.'

When Lord Curzon had Government House built in Calcutta he had it copied from Kedleston, his house in England, and painted white. When I saw it in 1944 it had been camouflaged with splodges of strawberry-jam colour and areas of Devon-soil red with green shutters. Viola and I spent four agreeable days staying there with the Caseys from Australia, who had made the place an hospitable centre and an oasis of charm and comfort. Mae Casey has a way with houses and had happily put her mark on this one. Government Houses at that time were used as hotels by travellers, and we were lucky to be asked to spend our first days in Calcutta under this friendly roof. When we were leaving Mae asked me where we were being billeted and when I told her it was with people we didn't yet know called Denham White, she said: 'That's good. You'll love them. She is the most fascinating woman in India.' No overstatement as we soon discovered. Bill Denham White was a very distinguished surgeon, and he and Evelyn had lived in Bengal for over twenty years. We drove to Asoka Road on a hot day and were glad of the cool rooms. I wrote in my journal that Mae Casey was right about Evelyn Denham White: 'She is hard to put on paper. Like a McEvoy water-colour, music by Delius and a poem by Yeats. She is faintly comic, too, but entirely kind, good, vague – but with moments of clear practicality. Everyone loves her. Her wispy hair is grey and brown, very soft; her eyes are the blue of French soldiers' uniforms – enormous, deeply set with heavy lids. Looks frail as lace but never stops bicycling in the heat wearing a big brown picture-hat; being kind; going to concerts; looking after Bill Denham White.' (And us.) 'The house is full of Chinese bits and pieces. Too many and general effect a little gloomy, but she has an eye for lovely things and some are beautiful. Books everywhere.' They both had many Indian friends.

I got used to the gloom and began to like the cool calm of her darkened rooms. Evelyn's conversation was a many-branched tree, with delicate branches continually sprouting in new directions. I wrote down some of her talk: 'You know Bill adores his work and he'll get up in the middle of the night to see decaying nuns without a murmur.' She remembered that she had been telling me about a friend of hers: 'She – the mother – was a brilliant creature – well, very clever – and *she* had a friend who had been head of a convent, my dear, and left. Got out of *the whole thing*. Odd. And her daughter – such a good simple sort of woman, straightforward with bones like Greta Garbo's – well, she couldn't bear any sort of fuss – not that it matters – and the Frenchman who dined with her last night – called Louis, with a face like a small monkey – was very pessimistic about *everything*. I do feel people ought not to be like that.'

I sat in a trance, feeling as if I'd been under water. I gave up trying to follow the thread and just floated. 'My brother is much older than the rest of us and rather difficult. I am not really attached to him. My father said he must Do Something and he said he was going to be an artist and went to the Slade. He wasn't too bad. But then he suddenly came to my aunt's and built a huge bonfire, my dear, of all his paints and brushes and pictures, right on the lawn. It was rather hard on my aunt. She was so fond of her grass.'

Of a missionary friend: 'She's an angel but never stops talking – but she *is* an angel. All those sick people and everything. She *is* an angel – but an annoying angel.' The missionary came to dinner that night, plump and garrulous, in brown *broché* satin with a brown net modesty-vest. She was obviously unselfish, gallant – and annoying.

We were given a week's leave at the end of three months' work, and the Denham Whites lent us their bungalow up at Darjeeling. There was a convalescent home for troops up there, so we went along to give them a short programme, and I discovered that the altitude ruined my phrasing. I had prided myself on singing the long opening bars of 'All the Things You Are' in one breath, but up there, over nine thousand feet above sea level, I could manage to do only a few notes to a breath – 'You are – the promised kiss – of spring time – that makes – the lonely winter – seem long.' It was also very cold at that height. Ghulam Mohd lit log-fires for us and we were glad of all the extra blankets on our beds. Every morning he called us early in the hope of showing us the sunrise on the far mountain of Kangchenjunga. We groped our way out of deep sleep; wrapped up in coats and blankets, we stood in the frosty air and hoped. But the clouds always hid the view, until one morning the whole range was clear, rose-pink above white cottonwool clouds, and I realised that I had never looked high enough before. The tops of the peaks were almost directly *above our heads*. The very roof of the world. Suddenly we seemed to be a long way from home.

Before I left England Noël Coward had talked of doing a new revue in 1945 and asked me to be in it. His confirming cable reached me in Darjeeling in February: 'Definitely planning revue to open May or June would like you home as soon as possible.' I cabled back that the tour was due to finish in the middle of March; was that soon enough? He said it would be, and I began to make notes for new material, in particular a sketch about an Ensa girl returned from doing an overseas job of entertaining troops. Not autobiographical.

Ghulam continued to look after us with devotion and asked me please would I take him with me when we went back to England. It was not easy to explain that I didn't feel his manner would go down well in London, and I had to say I was sorry we had no room for him to live in. (We had no rooms for Reggie and me to live in either, but this wasn't the time to worry about that.) I only once saw Ghulam without his grey astrakhan forage cap and that was when he was banging some washing on a rock in a river at one of our stops. I wondered what item of his wardrobe was undergoing such drastic treatment, and then I recognised my own pink nun's veiling dressing-gown Reggie had given me for the tour. It was never the same again. After the war, walking up Sloane Street in London, I saw what I thought was a familiar figure and then I recognised the grey forage cap. Ghulam had managed to get to England as bearer to a returned officer. He made low bows and salaams and was full of affectionate smiles: 'Oh Mem-sahib,' he said over and over, 'happy, happy days.' He looked back to our tour with longing. England was so cold, and the Captain had many many works for him to do. In the end he went back to India, promising to write, but after one sad letter telling me India was no good since the British army had left I heard no more.

CHAPTER SIXTEEN

Radio and Revues

IT took Viola and me five days to fly home from Delhi, for we only travelled by day, often by flying-boat, sleeping the nights on the ground. After working full-out for so long, feeling useful and well stretched, the return to England was difficult. The place looked grey and grim, and though daffodils and new leaves were out, winds blew cold and people looked tired and dreary. I realised I had become self-centred (more than usual) and spoilt. It was so very much easier working hard in far off places, without other responsibilities, than facing up to the day-to-day unglamorous life at home. On tour there had only been one job to be done and it had seemed important. I felt out of joint. I knew my wretchedness was wholly selfish and felt guilty at my lack of joy in being back. I also missed the ministrations of Ghulam, and the sun.

Reggie came to London for brief leaves and then went back to Belgium before being demobilised in October. Virginia let me use Cambridge Square as a base until I knew where we were going to live. (This turned out to be a walk-up maisonette at 149 Kings Road, Chelsea, over Mr Kent's toy-cum-confectioner's shop, bang on a bus-stop, where we stayed for ten happy but deafening years.)

Soon I was caught up in new projects and there was no time to mope. There were broadcasts booked with the B.B.C. Variety Department, and Stephen Potter, with whom I had collaborated earlier, was waiting for me to work on a new 'How' programme, and had more lined up to follow it. But my main job was to complete new monologues and write new songs with Dick for the forthcoming Coward review.

Has a revue ever opened without birth-pangs? I should think Bertie Farjeon's revues were probably the least painful ever produced because of his character and the high quality of the material. Of course there were endless conferences as there are in all revues; cuts, new items written and added; new running-orders tried out; heartaches, hearts restored; hopes dashed, raised, abandoned, until at last some sort of

'That is the End of the News'

whole emerged, marked with Bertie's own touch. There was always an indigenous unity about his shows. On the whole his company responded to him and respected his decisions. I did not find this was true of Noël Coward and *Sigh No More*.

The final production was mostly Noël's own work. Although Dick and I were invited to contribute, and had started off with seven or eight numbers, we ended with one song and my Ensa monologue. The revue as a whole was a thin brew, a disappointing patchwork amalgam of less than original ideas, and it only managed a run of six unsettled months.

Now I can put the whole thing down under the heading of Experience. At the time it seemed more of an endurance test than an educational adventure, but I probably did learn something from it – about true values for one thing. Brought up to believe in the good of the whole and concepts of team-spirit and brotherly love etc., I had some jolting moments, hitherto spared me in the Farjeon shows. It was a rough school. Noël alternately raged and praised; loved his company, liked it less; blessed it when laughter came, and blamed it when it didn't for a feebleness that sometimes stemmed from the frailty of the material provided. I found it difficult to decide what was the target he was aiming at. A good job well done? Personal success? A unified whole carrying on the Coward tradition of wit and sophistication? It did not appear to be clear. I don't remember tears, but I do remember some unhappiness and not only on my own account.

I found myself in the ambivalent position of Teacher's Pet, mainly because the Master fell out with his stars, and as a featured player I got pushed up a place. My ego was stroked and flattered, but I did not enjoy my position although it would be untrue to say I didn't respond to the audiences' welcome.

During his own overseas tours Noël had written a number for himself called 'That is the End of the News'. He cleaned it up for more general consumption and gave it to two young actors and me to do in the revue. After three or four performances in Manchester, where we opened in July, he gave the number to me to do as a solo. Dressed in a gym slip, pigtails and school hat on the back of my head, I belted it out with a maniacal grin and a shining morning face – no make-up, just a pale greasy moon. The song celebrated greeting bad news with a Pollyanna glee and was a success. My Ensa sketch, 'Travel Broadens the Mind,' begun out in India, was timely and went well enough. But 'Oh, Mr du Maurier', the song that I wrote with Dick for this revue still remains the song of which I am proudest.

The 'I' of the lyric is a fashionable young woman, much painted by the Pre-Raphaelite brotherhood, and admired by writers like Browning, Rossetti and Ruskin, who had failed to catch the eye of the novelist and *Punch* cartoonist George du Maurier; and his is the only eye she really wants to catch. Gladys Calthrop designed a becoming, tight-fitting white gown of the eighteen-nineties, gave me a black velvet neckband (like Granny in the Sargent picture) and long black gloves (*à la* Yvette Guilbert) and added extra curls to my fringe, and I felt very elegant indeed (see page 115.) For the only time in my life I was too thin, and the dress had to be padded to give me a period figure. Noël produced me in a stylised manner. I finally mastered the use of a fan, made my gestures sharper and larger, and I realise what a lot his direction added to the performance. 'Oh, Mr du Maurier' was one of those private gauges by which I rated audiences. It was put on very early, the second number in the show after the opening, and when it went well and the points were appreciated, I knew we had a listening and alert audience; when there was less reaction to 'du Maurier' the going was harder.

After *Sigh No More* closed in the early spring of 1946, I flew to America to see my mother. I hadn't seen her for nine years. Since her last visit to England in 1937 I had gone on the stage, appeared in four London revues, been overseas for two tours of hospitals and camps, made brief appearances in several films and done a lot of broadcasting.

The plane was delayed in Gander and the lavish American breakfast offered to us at the US air-base included such rarities as fresh orange juice, two eggs, strips of bacon, buttered toast and jelly – all on one plate – and made a change from austerity life in England. I spent three days with old friends in New York and was secretly amused by the complaints of hardship endured in that city during the war; the dim-out was *terrible*, and it had been almost impossible to find a man's plain white shirt.

Little Orchard, the house in Tryon that Aunt Nancy had given to my mother, built to my mother's own design, was as pretty and cheerful as she had described it in her letters; long, low and white, with a roof of weathered grey shingles, sitting on a stone terrace above a sloping field that ran down to the woods. A few miles away, over the tops of trees in their clashing spring colours, rose the Blue Ridge mountains. Light rooms in the small house bore many of my mother's special trademarks – the glass jars filled with green branches; low bowls filled with massed geranium flowers; gardenias; coarse white linen curtains and chair-covers. The living-room had a big picture-window (the first I had ever seen) and beneath it a long cushioned window-seat. In my bedroom, hung with crisp white organdie curtains, there were presents to welcome me – a house-coat, blouses, a nightgown and a dinner dress. Except for wishing Reggie could be there too it was a perfect holiday.

I was sad not to see Tommy on this visit, but his job in California kept him on the other side of the continent. Because he was born in America he had been able to claim United States citizenship and had lived over there since he was seventeen. We hadn't seen much of him until, in 1937, he brought his first wife, Elizabeth Brooks of Philadelphia, to London for eighteen months while he worked for Warner Brothers. When the marriage began to go wrong they sent their baby son, Wilton, to stay with us at Parr's, while they went back to America to try and sort things out. He was a beguiling little boy, just beginning to walk and talk, and he had an endearing illusion that when he shut his eyes he became invisible. Like his father at the same age he had a passion for *Peter Rabbit*, and we went through a daily read-through of the little book all the time he stayed with us. His fat forefinger prodded each

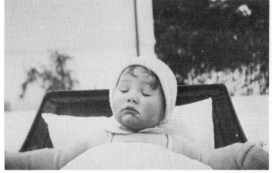

Wilton pretending to be invisible

Tommy and Wilton

picture of Peter as I turned the pages, and he pronounced its name with emphasis as the rabbit came into view. 'Pete-ah,' he said with relish. We missed Wilton badly when he sailed away to join his mother, and we saw him only once or twice after that until he was twenty and came to England on a 'cultural tour' with his college class. While he was in London he spent all his free time with us, and John Ward did an ink and wash drawing of him in our drawing-room, to add to the collection he has made for us that now includes pictures of Reggie, Walter de la Mare, Aunt Nancy, Hilda Grenfell, Mrs Gabe, Joe Dockery (stage door-keeper at the St Martin's Theatre where he worked until he was ninety-four) and me. John also drew Virginia and Tony, Dick, Victor Stiebel and Arthur Grenfell, Reggie's father.

A year after his college tour Wilton died in a boating accident in a sudden storm on one of the Great Lakes. He was with two other young men, one of whom survived and told Tommy that all through the ordeal Wilton had sung to encourage the others.

Tommy wrote for the films and then, in the heyday of American

Hilda Grenfell by John Ward

television drama, he contributed over seventy-five original scripts, many of them for the Robert Montgomery hour. He also wrote stage plays, one of which, *Four Winds*, was produced on Broadway. After the war he married Mary Chesebro from Texas, and they have a daughter, Sally, and a son, Lang, and live in New York. We love them dearly and wish the seas that divide us weren't so wide, but we keep in close contact by telephone and letter.

While I was in America a cable reached me: 'Clem says George wishes give you three-quarter length robe. Reggie.' I guessed that Clem must mean Mr Attlee, and probably George was the King, but what on earth was the three-quarter length robe? I cabled back: 'Mystified please elucidate,' and by return came Reggie's reply: 'Times crossword silly.' (Three-quarters of the word robe is O.B.E.) I was being honoured for my work in hospitals and camps, and the decoration reached me by post in London a year later.

All through the war I had done a lot of radio, usually as a guest artist in variety programmes. There were many of these – 'Monday Night at Eight', 'Henry Hall's Guest Night', 'Variety Band-box', 'Workers' Playtime' and others. Since 1943 I had also been writing with Stephen Potter his occasional series of 'How' programmes.

Reggie by John Ward

It may be immodest to say so, but I believe Stephen Potter and I antedated by some twenty-five years the improvisations of the Americans Nichols and May. It began for us soon after I met Bertie Farjeon at the Potters' house. A fortnight later the Potters and Grenfells dined with Cynthia and Alister Wedderburn at Rathbone Lodge in the Boltons. There was talk of the earlier party and Bertie's invitation for me to write for his new revue, and Stephen told about the Women's Institute lecture; and once again I illustrated it. Then without any preamble or warning we went into an improvised scene, Stephen as the author of an 'important' new novel and I as an enthusiastic young literary fan. This spontaneous combustion amused us and went well with the rest of the company. (Only now do I realise that that first improvisation of author and fan was the origin from which grew the sketch, 'Life and Literature', that I wrote and first performed at a party John Gielgud gave to the company at the Royal Shakespeare Theatre at Stratford-on-Avon in 1950, and which eventually went into the revue *Penny Plain*.) We did not know it at the time but it was the beginning of a collaboration that didn't materialise until four years later.

These 'How' programmes began as factual documentaries written by Stephen alone. Radio intercom and the preparation, rehearsal and performance of a symphony were two of the subjects I remember. Later he decided to add satire to the scripts, invited me to collaborate with him, and asked me to write and play in three or four short sketches about being interviewed, for a programme on 'How to apply for a job'. These illustrated how NOT to, and that became the general format of all subsequent 'Hows'. In the first two minutes we attempted to show the conventional and correct way to deal with the subject; the rest of the programme illustrated not only how NOT to but also how we usually do.

Rereading the scripts I am struck by the sharp way they reflected their own period. They are very dated. Much of human behaviour stays timeless, but the points of view from which we satirised some of the attitudes of the day are no longer mine and I don't think they would still be Stephen's. Or is it that I have become more self-conscious of the crime of being patronising? In those days we had no such fears. I still find it impossible not to observe differences in speech and thinking, but now one is no longer supposed to realise there are differences. There was a brief time after my initial success on the stage when any sketch I did in a cockney or rustic accent was criticised by the new young journalists for being patronising to the 'lower classes'. The fact that eighty-five per cent of my sketches mocked the upper classes was not noticed. I think super-sensitivity about class had begun to disappear, until the Labour Party chose to revive and whip it up for divisive political purposes, as they still do.

The 'Hows' were composed – that is made up, improvised, and only later written down. In the 1940s there were no tape-recorders available for us at the B.B.C.; instead, high-speed shorthand-writers came to Stephen's office at Rothwell House in Queen Anne Street, where the Features Department was housed, and there, in cold blood, we improvised scenes. It was not easy to forget the presence of a shorthand-writer, head down, painstakingly recording our hit-or-miss exchanges. The method didn't always work, but we were able to get the nucleus of an idea on paper and develop it afterwards. We also worked out of doors without the benefit of shorthand-writers, sometimes in Regent's Park and occasionally in Kew Gardens. I provided sandwiches and coffee and we sat on remote benches surrounded by sheets of paper, weighed down by my gloves, Stephen's cigarettes and the Thermos, until the pages escaped and took off in the inevitable breeze, and had to be run after. Concentration was made more difficult by wild life. Baby ducks ruined one Regent's Park session, and at Kew Stephen's enthusiasm for botany kept luring us round just one more corner in search of what might be blooming in the long grasses ahead of us. Later in our partnership more practical working sessions took place in the kitchen of our high flat in the King's Road.

We also worked separately. I have always been haunted by any writing job I had to do until it was finished. No virtue in this; it is an inborn urge that won't let me sit down until I have done the chores I know have got to be done. As a child I used to skimp my homework on Friday evenings to make way for a work-free week-end. I have been known to set the table for a dinner party twenty-four hours or more ahead of zero-hour; it means that Reggie and I have to eat off trays in between, but he doesn't seem to mind and I feel comforted by getting ahead with my preparations. It was not like that for Stephen. He was always a reluctant starter, a last-minute man, working up to the very edge of a deadline. It suited him to work that way; I never got used to it, and it was tough on his long-suffering secretary, Betty Johnstone, but she didn't complain. I don't think any of the 'How' scripts were completed until the day before transmission, and quite often Betty arrived at the studio just before rehearsals began, with extra scenes for the cast typed out on flimsy sheets of paper to be clipped into our scripts. So close was our collaboration on the final script that afterwards we were never sure which one of us had written which episode.

As the programmes developed certain characters emerged as regulars and were used again in different contexts. The Listener's Friend, a guide-compère, and Len, the technically keen radio-buff with his talk of baffle and woof, were Stephen's; so was the Practical Man ('I always carry a two-foot rule.'). Mrs Treubel, a refugee living in Golders Green who spoke of 've Britischers', was mine; so was Fern Brixton, vegetarian lover of Beauty and weaver of her own clothes. Gladys Young, a brilliant broadcaster, played Mrs Treubel, and I did Fern and the nursery school teacher, later to be developed as the central figure of sketches I wrote for my stage shows.

Rose Macaulay was a friend of Stephen's and sat with him in the control-room for one of the broadcasts. She was a fan of the 'Hows', and I was a fan of hers. She joined us in the studio after we came off the air, and I realised with a small shock of recognition that she spoke in the voice I had just been using as Fern Brixton. I had not consciously copied Rose Macaulay, but I suppose I must have remembered how she spoke from hearing her talk on radio. I wondered whether she had noticed the likeness. It was uncanny hearing her tell me in Fern's voice how much she had been amused by Fern.

At the read-through Stephen allocated parts to the cast sitting in a half-circle round him. He indicated how he wanted the character to be played and was so good at this that I wished he would play in the programmes more often. No one knew better than he how the part should be acted. This was not surprising because there was always a good deal of Stephen in what he had written, just as there is usually something of me in my monologues. The scripts he wrote were highly lit, often exaggerated expressions of himself. For myself, I know I could not have mocked some of the types I did unless I had been all too familiar with their frailties.

The cast knew each other well, and there was a reunion feeling about a 'How' broadcast. It was rewarding to watch the others as Stephen read through the script. They responded to new figures and welcomed old favourites. Regulars of the 'How' Repertory Company included Gladys Young, Betty Hardy, Carleton Hobbs, Roy Plomley and Ronald Simpson (who played golf with Stephen). Geoffrey Wincott, Deryck Guyler, Norman Shelley and Jonathan Field joined us for occasional programmes. Celia Johnson was our favourite guest-star. We wrote for her with the certainty of getting from her performance a

A 'How' programme in rehearsal (Carleton Hobbs, Stephen Potter, Joyce Grenfell, Betty Hardy, Ronald Simpson, Gladys Young)

great deal more than we had indicated in the script. In 'How to be Good at Music' Stephen gave her a stream-of-consciousness monologue; thoughts while trying to concentrate on a new work at a concert. She made it her own and played it to perfection.

Stephen was my idea of a good director. He never criticised or

Max Adrian and Laurier Lister

corrected us publicly over the intercom; he came into the studio and quietly explained to the actor the changes he wanted made. This may sound the obvious way for a civilised director to behave, but they are not all like that. He had an innate sense of rhythm and pace that gave the programme something of the freshness of improvisation – as now and then it was, when he and I played scenes together.

The first 'Hows' were always done 'live'. Immediacy was supposed to add quality and excitement, and there were some regrets when taping came in. But not from me. A performance is always a performance as far as I am concerned, and I find the necessary concert-pitch tension at a recording is as stimulating as at a live show. I think I give the same kind of performance whether I know it is instantly reaching millions or going into a recording device. But I am glad to be rid of the element of the irrevocable; I like being able to put mistakes right, as you can with tape.

In nineteen years Stephen and I wrote twenty-nine scripts, some of which were revived editions with up-to-date material added. We advised on how to talk to children; argue (with C. E. M. Joad as guest-artist); give a party; keep a diary; learn to speak French; woo; blow

Max Adrian and Elisabeth Welch

your own trumpet; be good at music; talk to young people; make friends; deal with Christmas; deal with the New Year; move house; be good at games (Stephen's book *Gamesmanship or How to Win Games Without Actually Cheating* brought to life); travel; cross the Atlantic First Class; know America really well and finally how to lead really full lives. There were in all four editions of 'How to Listen', the last one heard in 1962. The original one was the first broadcast to go out on the newly formed Third Programme.

Early in 1947 Laurier Lister suggested that I should star in a small revue to be written by me and my cousin, Nicholas Phipps, with Geoffrey Wright to do the music. (At that stage I had only written romantic songs with Dick.) This would be my first lead. I would be supported by Max Adrian and Elisabeth Welch. The show was to be called *Tuppence Coloured*, after the cut-out cardboard toy theatres of Regency days, and was to be financed and managed by H. M. Tennent Ltd.

To this day I know nothing about acting in plays. (I once rehearsed for the invisible part of the mother in a comedy called *Junior Miss* and withdrew, to the mutual satisfaction of the producer, director and myself, after three bewildering days.) My experience has been entirely in revue, and there cannot be a harder way of learning a craft and making a living. It is also great fun. On the whole. Humility is not one of the obvious virtues found in the theatre, but you certainly learn it in revue; songs and sketches change hands frequently and in the process egos get bruised.

I was involved in *Tuppence Coloured* from the beginning, and I should think it was a classic example of revue-making. Outside advice came from all sides: 'Beware of artiness.' 'Don't let in too much Beauty.' 'Insist on strong direction.' Yes, I said, of course; and hoped for the best in fluctuating moods of gloom and optimism. We aimed high and decided to ask Benjamin Britten to contribute a song. He kindly asked me to tea and wasn't very tempted by the idea but allowed us to have his arrangement of 'Sweet Polly Oliver'. Emmett of *Punch* agreed to design a backcloth and H. F. Ellis wrote a train-number to go with it. Our kitchen-dining-room at the top of 149 Kings Road was the scene of many conferences with Laurier, Nick, Geoffrey, the costume and set designers, wardrobe mistress, choreographers and me. Our spirits went up and down like yo-yos after the usual enthusiastic read-through when the material seemed so original and imaginative. Someone came up with a novel suggestion – a weather-vane number to be done by a dancer perched on a piano stool (manipulated by ropes) responding to the changes in the wind. Might be attractive. . . . Let's try it. We did and a lot of time it took with a minimum result. Oh! the eager response, the willingness to be wooed and won that always accompanies revue read-throughs.

I had written two new monologues for myself and rehearsed them up and down the flat. One was a view of England, in those austerity days just after the war, seen by a visiting American woman from the limited vantage-point of the Dorchester Hotel. I called it 'Odyssey'. 'It's *ghass*tly for them – you see they've got this Government that just *isn't* on their side . . .' The other, 'Artists' Room', showed four differently priced ticket-holders coming backstage to see a pianist after his recital. I took part in opening and closing ensembles, and a duet, 'Nice Song', with Daphne Oxenford. Dick and I had written a new song, 'The Countess of Coteley', and at last I found a chance to clown in a much broader manner, and invented an Echo song and dance for myself, to the music of 'By the Waters of Minnetonka', that liberated something

'Travel Broadens the Mind'   *'Echo Song'*

in me. The point of the number lay in my inability to locate the direction from which offstage yoo-hoos were coming at me. I listened, hand to ear, and hared off in the wrong direction, pausing when I got there to listen as the calls came from the opposite wings. A simple idea, pleasing in its idiocy. It gave me much joy to do and audiences giggled at my energetic galumphings across the stage.

We had been through a lot of ups and downs during the London rehearsals, but for the dress rehearsal at the Little Theatre in Cheltenham, in July, a new spirit was abroad – 'Let's see what happens tonight when we put it all together.' It was not an easy evening. Cheltenham sits very low, enfolded in deep hills, and there was a heat wave. The town was airless and the theatre stifling. Nothing went right. Contact between prompt-corner and the lighting-board failed. Voices were raised, patience began to run low, and the weather-vane number held things up. When all the costumes and sets were seen together there was a depressing preponderance of autumn colours. At 3 a.m. we still had not got to the end of part one. Laurier called a halt and sent us home to bed. Part two would begin rehearsing *sharp* at 2 p.m. the next afternoon.

Somehow we stumbled through the opening performance, and there was some laughter and a feeling that the audience responded, but afterwards a gloomy post-mortem with the London management went on in a corner of the half-darkened dining-room of the Queen's Hotel where most of us were staying. Reggie came down with Virginia and Tony, and they agreed with Winifred, Dick and Victor that the revue – 'in its present form' as they kindly put it to soften the blow – simply would NOT do.

For some reason I was not too depressed – I believed in the show and was sure we could get it right. The first weeks of any revue on tour are rough going. This is the essential trial-and-error period when different running-orders are tried out, the only known method of discovering what works and where. Perhaps the song that hasn't come off in part one may prove itself halfway through part two; perhaps if Betty wore a funny hat in the shopping sketch it might do something for the number. This hit-or-miss method seems to be the only one available; mysteriously the song from part one *does* work in its new position, the funny hat does seem to help Betty in the shopping sketch. Pitiful straws are clutched at, tried and abandoned. It takes time, courage and confidence on the part of authority to face up to the inevitable cuts and hurt feelings necessary 'for the sake of the show'. It is a decidedly wearing period that has to be lived through by all concerned. Not even the unexpected return the next morning of Virginia, Tony and Reggie with Winifred in command, after they had gone five miles on their way to London, upset me very much. Winifred had stopped the car and insisted they must go back and tell me yet again that until the show was entirely re-done it could NOT be allowed to come in to London. They stood round my bed at 9.30 in the morning and emphasised their reasons firmly – with affection – for my sake. Much as I loved them, I remember a weary sense of relief when they had gone and I had a feeling that now, rid of outsiders, we could really get down to business and clear up the problems.

Writing of my own confidence in *Tuppence Coloured* makes me seem smug. I don't think I was all that confident, but somehow the original impact of the numbers I believed in had lasted for me throughout the vicissitudes of experiments and discussions, and I still had faith in them. That is why I fought so hard for 'The Countess of Coteley' about

'Picture Postcard'

which Dick had begun to have doubts. It was a mild piece of social comment and perhaps it went against the mood of the time. Labour had just swept into power and to suggest that there was still some worth in the old order may have seemed risky, but I was ready to chance my arm and I'm glad I did. 'Coteley' was not everyone's favourite number, but it had its enthusiasts and one of them was Oscar Hammerstein who thought I should write an entire musical on the same subject.

After the suffocating week in Cheltenham, with immediate changes, cuts and searches for other material, we moved on to Leicester (gloomy but cooler) and Bournemouth (soggy but affable), and played our last pre-London date in Brighton. All the time we worked; items went in and out of the programme, and finally we came to the Lyric Theatre, Hammersmith, for the dress-rehearsal before our limited season of six weeks. We had done all we could, hoping – cheerfully in my case – for the best. Reggie came, again with Virginia and Tony, Winifred, Dick and Victor, and as they had been at Cheltenham (though they did not tell me this until after we had opened) they were *appalled* by the whole thing. They could find no sign of improvement anywhere and wondered what we had been doing during the long weeks away.

And then one of those inexplicable theatrical wonders happened – overnight the show jelled, tautened, took shape and flew. When the press and public came to the first performance twenty-four hours later they found a fresh, imaginative and entertaining little revue, and they welcomed it. Reggie was astounded and said if he hadn't witnessed the metamorphosis he would not have believed it. There was still plenty of room for improvement, but the Tennent management, convinced by the press and the 'House Full' boards outside the theatre, decided to transfer the show to the Globe when the Hammersmith engagement was finished. So we got down to work again; more conferences, more decisions, more rehearsals.

Just when we needed a new point of view a young American friend of Dick's, Leonard Gershe, came from New York to visit him, and immediately, fired by the situation, wrote lyrics that inspired Dick to write two splendid songs exactly suited to Elisabeth Welch. And I was told to write another song, not this time a comedy number but a straight song to be sung as myself, and this turned out to be a piece of personal philosophy called 'I Like Life', set to one of Dick's prettiest waltz tunes.

The revue ran for over a year.

Following the traumas of putting on *Tuppence Coloured* came the traumas of another revue with Laurier Lister, *Penny Plain*. This time we opened to very mixed notices, and without H. M. Tennent behind us we had no backing. Reggie worked a rescue operation, and in spite of problems we managed to jog along at the St Martin's Theatre for a perilous but long run, and ended with a successful provincial tour.

Touring after a run in London could not only be financially rewarding but also pleasant, and, because of the good company of Elisabeth

'Maud Won't Come into the Garden'

Welch, Max Adrian and others in the cast, I enjoyed the tours that followed both revues. Lis, Max and I usually stayed in the same hotel and spent our evenings together after the performance. We supped and sat up late talking in the colossal public rooms of most of the station hotels in the north, and I remember creeping along the high endless corridors of the Midland, Manchester, and the Central, Glasgow, on our way to bed, amusing ourselves by rearranging the shoes left outside bedroom doors to be cleaned. Today the management provides you with a little square of synthetic cloth to do the job yourself, but then it was done by a night-porter who collected the boots and shoes and polished them in some secret cubby-hole before returning them to the door of your room. We never muddled up the shoes, we simply put them in new positions *in situ* – toes turned in or out; one toe on top of the next; boots wide apart or going in opposite directions; up-ended on their toes – the variations were infinite. We competed to discover new ways of arranging them and found the silly game remarkably diverting. All of us were sober.

I relished hearing Lis and Max reminisce about their early touring days and other theatrical memories. Max made the most of a good story, and if he was, in Mrs Alington's Lytteltonian phrase about an imaginative story-teller, 'somewhat open-minded concerning truth,' he was certainly a beguiling *raconteur*. In Ireland his mother gave her first luncheon party in their new house. There was a long pause after the first course, so long that she had to investigate it. In the kitchen she found the cook, having the drink taken, leaning against the stove with arms spread in defence. 'Thim little birds is not comin' out of a nice hot stove to catch their deaths of cold.' Lis and I were an appreciative audience.

Once we three found ourselves in the same hotel as Elsie and Doris Waters and spent an evening hearing them tell of their childhood in South London, where they grew up in a rambling house beside their father's works. Mrs Waters, who modelled herself on Queen Mary – pastel colours, parasol, toques, winkle-picker shoes and all – provided a midday meal for the girls who worked in the family factory. From an early age Elsie and Doris helped to cut up the carrots and other vegetables that went into the nourishing stews. They also entertained the workers with songs and recitations. Doris remembered when she was about five standing on a table making up a long rambling song about wishing she was very pretty with golden curls and a frilly white party frock with a blue sash 'Just like dear little Jesus'. The song went well; she was modestly surprised by her success.

Max was not always the easiest character to work with, but as the years went on he and I had an increasingly companionable friendship. When he died in 1973 Laurier Lister invited me to speak at his memorial service and I looked back with affection to the tangy quality of his company and the rich and varied sounds of his voice, an instrument he used with great skill. He could make it purr or roar; whine and wound; cut the ear like a whiplash, or woo it like a cello. I best liked it when he spoke in his own Irish rhythms, and I have an indelible impression of him speaking 'The Fiddler of Dooney' that I much cherish. I enjoyed Max's glee, not always in the cause of charity, and his zest and enthusiasm for the job in hand, and for those he loved and admired. He was a versatile actor and a witty one. For me his most sensitive and telling performance was as Delius in Ken Russell's documentary for B.B.C. television.

While I played in *Tuppence Coloured* my dresser was Ida, a pale, pretty coloured girl, half West Indian and half Brixton, with a line in old army jokes that she brought out with a Cockney flourish as if they were freshly minted. Of a young man in the cast: 'See him sideways and you'd mark him absent;' 'Army cake – a day's march between currants.' If I was quiet and hadn't responded quickly enough to her cheerful, 'Hello love!' she asked if I was feeling 'dolcile', a word of her own, combining doldrums and docile. Interpreting some of her communications was like working out a puzzle. 'My Billy went in hospital for his sinus and come out on two sticks with trombones (thrombosis)'. 'Saw a lully film this afternoon with – you know that feller – Tinrow Prower.' 'Who, Ida?' By a process of elimination and a guess I arrived at Tyrone Power. Gladys Jones turned out to be Glynis Johns. I enjoyed Ida's company. This problem over proper names is not unknown. When Leslie Henson finally left the Winter Garden Theatre, after playing there for twelve or more years, the stage door-man, who daily had handled his letters and seen his name on posters and on the star dressing-room door, said to him on the last night, as he had said to him every other night: 'Good evening, Mr Henderson.'

Reggie and I have been truly blest, as my parents were before us, by the household helpers who have been involved in our lives. In my childhood Lucy, my nanny, dominated the scene; but there was also Doris Leslie, pretty as a Renoir, with pink cheeks, dark hair and bright blue eyes; Connie Jeffries, a dynamo of energy and drive, daughter of the number two on the garden staff of twenty-four at Cliveden; and Mary Edwards, the pillar in Tommy's early life.

I had never heard the word 'bugger' used until a new maid, May Bourhill from Yorkshire, came to waken us on her first day. She pulled up the blind too hard and it spun itself out of her reach. She stood looking up at it and said in one breath: 'Booger sorry madam.' May was the only properly trained, conventional – except for a certain freedom of speech – maid we ever had. She valeted Reggie like a Jeeves, wore stiff collars and cuffs, scoured and polished with energy, was cheerful and jokey, and we enjoyed having her in the house. She didn't stay with us long because we moved to the country, to Parr's, and she

'Mrs Gabe' by John Ward

'couldn't stand the idea of fields and that'. Rene Easden has been mentioned earlier.

It was just at the end of *Sigh No More* that I invested in the best six-pennyworth of my life by putting a postcard in the local newsagent's window advertising for someone to come and clean our Chelsea flat. Within an hour the street door bell rang and I went down from the fourth floor to answer it. A plump pretty woman with a friendly smile said: 'I have come because of the postcard.' We climbed up the long dark stairs and just outside our front door she stopped. 'In case you have a prejudice, I must tell you I am German.' The year was 1946 and the war was still very much in our minds. 'No . . .' I said at once, startled; even if I had any doubts I disapproved of them. 'No, I haven't.' This was my introduction to Anna Gavrielides who was to become our housekeeper for eighteen carefree years, and our friend for ever after. At first she came for the two hours specified on the postcard and added our jobs to others she was doing in the neighbourhood. But soon she gave up the others, took us over completely and not only cleaned and cared for our well-being, but also shopped and cooked special meals and played a central part in our lives. She came from Frankfurt, had worked for several years in Holland, was married to a Cypriot tailor's finisher and had British nationality. 'Call me Mrs Gabe,' she advised us. 'Nobody can pronounce Gavrielides.'

She is one of the world's givers; not only does she give us her love and her unstinting help but she includes our friends in the wide sweep of her affection. Some time after the death of her first husband, with whom she had a tragic and difficult time, she went on a coach tour of the Lake District and met a widower, Reg Brimm, who lived (and still lives) in a little house, with an orderly garden full of cared-for flowers, fruit and vegetables, at Burnt Oak, Edgware. They were married at Chelsea Register Office where I was her witness. At first we tried to remember to call her 'Mrs Brimm', but she was firmly entrenched as Mrs Gabe, and her Reg has accepted that the name is more of a loving nickname than anything else and he agreeably tolerates it. For a while Mrs Gabe tried to combine visits to Chelsea with running her own home, but the distance was too great, and she had to give up looking after us and passed the job on to her sister-in-law, Merope Gavrielides, whom we know as Mrs Agos. Happily for us she has been our housekeeper ever since.

Because of illness Mrs Gabe is now rarely able to come and see us, but we go there frequently on our way from staying with Virginia in her country flat. We never come away without bunches of flowers, lettuces and other bounty from Reg Brimm's garden.

All this time there were other activities running parallel to my theatre life. 'A Note with Music' was a weekly radio series commissioned by the BBC that I wrote and played in with George Benson; H. F. Ellis of *Punch* provided additional sketches. It was a gentle little half-hour programme that broke new writing ground for me, and in it I introduced a collection of American Negro songs that my mother sang to Tommy and me as children, and which Viola had arranged for me to sing in the concerts she and I were then giving in music clubs. Looked at now there is a naïve innocence about the scripts and not nearly enough entertainment. But we had some pleasant playing of light music, specially written; and as the BBC commissioned a second series a presumably narcissistic audience enjoyed listening to a reflection of its own middle-browed, middle-everything way of life.

'We Beg to Differ' advertised as a light-hearted radio discussion of subjects that divided the sexes, began in 1949. Roy Plomley took the chair, and, in those pre-Women's Lib times, it was accepted (but not by all of us) that a team of four women – Kay Hammond, Gladys Young, Charmian Innes and I – was needed to equal the two-man band of Kay's husband, John Clements, and Gilbert Harding. Kay's distinctive

voice added to her enchantment and wit. She had a way of not catching
the chairman's eye until a question had been thoroughly discussed and
then, only at the last moment, added her considered and well-timed
views. The rest of us had said our say on 'Would you rather be a bigger
fool than you look or look a bigger fool than you are?', when Kay
quietly scored by deciding it was not in her own interest to answer the
question. We soon had done with discussing obvious questions, such as
'Who should do the washing up?' and 'Are men the better cooks?' and
went on to more thoughtful subjects such as 'How would you answer
a child who asked "What is spirit?"' I remember this particular question because, as it was read out to us, I hoped no one would make a joke
about gin, although I had a private bet with myself that one of the men
might, and I was right. Both did. But once we had cleared that out of
the way there was an exchange of ideas that called forth more letters
than any other question put to us throughout all the years the series
was on the air. For the record, I said I would say to a child: 'You know
the feeling I have for you and you have for me – that is called love. And
love is spirit – the greatest power there is.' After the broadcast we all
had letters, and most of those addressed to me thanked me for putting
the writer's own view. They came from Quakers, Roman Catholics,
Jews, Anglicans, Baptists, Methodists and a Buddhist, and from all
manner of Nonconformists like myself, and I found it good to know
that we were all of one mind for once; and about something as important as spirit.

Gilbert Harding's irascible manner did not reflect the tender, not to
say soft-centred, heart of the gentle, insecure, courteous and intelligent
man he was. His tragedy, I believe, was his avoidance of challenges that
he knew he was fully capable of meeting. He despised his role of
Radio and TV Personality, knowing it had no real value, but he had
become trapped by his own public image and did not seem able to break
away from it.

I had also begun to get bigger parts in films, and in 1949 I appeared
as the first of the gawky overgrown schoolgirl types (a folk dance
enthusiast in Eric Linklater's *Poet's Pub*) that I was soon called upon
to repeat in many other pictures – Miss Gossage in *The Happiest Days
of Your Life*, and the unrequited policewoman, Ruby Gates, in several
disguises, in three of Launder and Gilliatt's successful St Trinian's series.
These films were fun to do; pleasant people worked in them, including
Margaret Rutherford who read poetry better than almost anyone I ever
heard, even better than she played those endearing caricatures she was

Glamour picture with my mouth shut

so justly famed for; and Alastair Sim, with his long sad face and heavy-lidded eyes. He is an essentially non-theatrical man and I think he was probably as surprised as I was to be in the world of films.

My mother wrote to me from America wishing I would, just for *once*, just now and then, look a little less unglamorous in the films in which I acted. Picture after picture reached her local movie-house with me playing those gawky girls and failing to get my man, and she did so wish her friends could see me in a more becoming guise. On her way over to visit us she told a new acquaintance at her table on board ship, that I was in the film they were going to see that evening. As usual I looked plain and awkward, and my ma's heart sank. When the lights went up at the end of the picture her companion asked, 'Which was your daughter?' 'I made a mistake,' said my mother. 'She wasn't in it.' Only after she saw *The Million Pound Note*, in which I had scenes with Gregory Peck and played an Edwardian duchess in beautiful clothes designed for me by Maggie Furse, did she feel like telling her friends to go and see me in a movie.

I remember getting a letter from Carley Dawson, my childhood friend to whom I have always written since she went back to America before the war, telling me that my cameo part of the hotel proprietress in the movie *Genevieve* had been well reviewed in her local Washington paper. The short scenes had been fun to do and were filmed in half a day. The notice Carley enclosed praised my performance generously, but the critic mentioned that I had a set of teeth 'only a horse could envy'. Glamorous publicity photographs taken for a new show had just reached me, and with regrettable vanity I sent one (mouth shut) to the critic. He wrote back what was nothing less than a love letter. I had always been told never to answer critics but this unexpected result made me glad I hadn't listened to advice . . . O vanity, vanity!

I have never minded looking funny – when it was intentional. But the public doesn't always realise that one is acting, and I've met with surprised reactions from people who are familiar with my movie image but have never before seen me as myself. I startle them by being much larger than they expect and evidently less peculiar-looking. In Leeds a friendly woman in an hotel said she hoped I wouldn't mind a personal remark. I braced myself for the blow; she touched me gently on the arm and whispered: 'You look so much better since you've had your teeth fixed.' All I could could think of in reply was 'I'm so glad.' At the time of writing I have not yet had my teeth fixed.

CHAPTER SEVENTEEN

Monologues, Ruth Draper and How
I Learned by Doing

WHEN I am interviewed I am often asked what made me decide to do monologues, and where do I find my characters. The answer to the first question is Ruth Draper, the greatest exponent of the genre that anyone now living has ever seen. I would not have thought of trying to do anything so peculiar unless I had seen her do it first.

Ruth was part of my life for as long as I can remember. She and my father shared mutual first cousins and had always known each other. She used to do her monologues for Tommy and me in our nursery; his favourite was 'Railway Accident'. It was not the most calming choice for a small boy of five to go to bed on, but it didn't do him any harm. I see him in his little blue dressing-gown, with white rabbits on the collar and pockets, standing at the end of his bed, holding on to the high bars that surrounded him, rocking to and fro with mounting excitement as the story went on. He was pretty familiar with 'Railway Accident'. It is a dramatic monologue in which Ruth played the girl in charge of the buffet. Jerry, the man she is going to marry, is the engineer on one of the trains involved in the crash, and we do not know whether he has survived. She is selfless and efficient in helping to look after the wounded passengers as they are brought in, organising hot water for the doctor, dispensing coffee and comfort; and only now and then do we see the strain she is under. It is a brilliant piece of work. The stage is peopled with passengers and neighbours she has telephoned to come and help. Every time the door opens gusts of icy wind and snow-flurries blow in. Tommy could hardly bear the tension. He stamped his foot, rocking to and fro, faster and faster. Towards the end of the sketch the girl looks up, sees her lover in the doorway and gives a cry of relief – 'Jerry', she cries as she flies into his arms. Long before she said this Tommy started to urge Ruth on. '*Please* say Jerry', he begged in a hoarse whisper, 'please, *please* say Jerry.' Ruth used to prolong the agony as long as possible. When she finally saw her lover and spoke, Tommy fell back on his bed and kicked his legs in the air. I doubt if she ever had a more responsive audience.

She came regularly to London and took a furnished house. We didn't always know exactly when she was coming because she liked to get here and settle in; then she announced herself over the telephone in a ringing voice that had no problem getting to the back of the dress circle: 'It's *Ruth*!' We had to remember to hold the receiver a little further off, but we were glad to know she was here. Until I was grown up I called her 'Miss Ruth', because she said 'Aunt Ruth' was false, 'Cousin Ruth' was prissy, and 'Ruth' was too familiar. We had to be on our best behaviour with her, but it was worth it.

My cousin Ann and I saw a good deal of her on her London visits and after she left school Ann went with her on some of her tours. From an early age we were allowed to sit in the wings on matinée days and watch the performance. (There was never an empty seat in the house.) I had been stage-struck since I was seven, and backstage visits were thrilling to boast about among school-friends. 'When I was behind the scenes yesterday with Ruth Draper . . .'

'Do you *know* Ruth Draper?'

'Heavens, yes. She's a *great* friend.'

When I went alone I had early luncheon first with Ruth in her rented house. Ruth loved her food. (Echoes of my grandmother come to me as I write that. 'You do not *love* your food, you enjoy it.') Ruth *loved* her food! Not to put too fine a point on it, she was plain greedy. She ate very fast with appreciative little noises as she spooned in, and she was always the first to finish and ready for second helpings before anyone else. I thought I had made a discovery when I told my father that Miss Ruth was a bit greedy. 'Well – yes,' he said.

After luncheon Fred and his Daimler took us to the theatre. He was an institution and whenever she was in England it was Fred who drove her everywhere, never too fast, always with loving care. Ruth was not one to get to the theatre hours before curtain time. I remember a season when she played at the Criterion. We arrived at the stage door about 2.10 p.m. for the 2.30 performance. The way into the back of the theatre is from Jermyn Street, and the journey is a long one, down, down to the bowels of the earth, before you get to stage level and the star dressing-room. Mr Marika, Ruth's manager, and the stage door-keeper were waiting for her a little anxiously, but both knew there was no need to panic; Ruth Draper was dependable as sunrise. She

Ruth Draper: 'Opening a Bazaar'

greeted them both, collected her letters and walked in briskly, down the endless stairs, calling back to Mr Marika to ask him what she was doing that afternoon. I trotted behind her with Mr Marika listing the items as we journeyed downwards. 'You are doing "Three Breakfasts", "In County Kerry", "In a Church in Italy", "Opening a Bazaar", "A Class in Greek Poise" and "Three Women and Mr Clifford".'

He left us when we got to the dressing-room. Her dresser hung up her street clothes as Ruth took them off, and to make up in she put on her familiar pale pinky-yellow kimono wrapper. I was told where to sit so that I could watch the preparations. She used a minimum of make-up; a little blue eye-shadow, a touch of brown eye-pencil, a spot or two of mascara and a little rouge. Rather dark lipstick was worked in with the tip of her little finger. No warm foundation, no clever shading, just those few additions and that was it. Her dark hair was kept neat in a fine net which she took off for the performance. A tail-comb raised the waves. She glanced at herself in profile in the hand-mirror and stood up, straightening her girdle and slip, getting carefully into her stage dress so as not to disturb her hair. I best remember a pale beige lace dress, sleeveless, with a two-tiered flounced skirt. Later there was a dark brown velvet made by Valentina in New York. All her props hung in the dressing-room – shawls, raincoats, various character hats, a feather boa, an overall, an office jacket, etc. She chose them with great care and they were an important part of her performance.

It was not until I was already on the stage, performing my own mono-logues, that I realised the genre was not familiar to everyone. The music-hall comedienne, Nellie Wallace, and I were doing a war-time concert in a small country cinema where there were no backstage facilities because there was no backstage. The only place for women artists to dress was the narrow space between the cinema screen and the back wall of the theatre; and the only surface available to hold our make up and props was on top of some big canvas-covered drums. We were each allotted a drum and left to get on with it by the light of a single bulb hanging high over our heads. We could hear the audience clattering and chattering as they settled down; far too near, I thought, just the other side of the screen.

Nellie Wallace was not pleased with the arrangements and in no mood to communicate with me. She nodded when we were introduced and then busied herself with the job of unpacking her stuff and setting it out on her drum. Before she took off her coat she had put on her little stage hat with the long feather and this made her look more familiar.

I struggled into my dress and could have done with a helping hand over the zip, but I didn't like to intrude because Miss Wallace put up a sort of wall between us by the bumbling grumble she kept going as she worked. When she got her dress off I was enchanted to see she was already wearing the vest made out of a knitted Union Jack, and I wanted to tell her how much I appreciated it, but this was not the moment.

She was top of the bill that Sunday afternoon and was going on last. I was in a much humbler position and followed the R.A.F. band (with its own drums) after it had nearly blown our heads off from only three feet away. The compère gave me a build-up, and I went out and did my first monologue among the music-stands left by the R.A.F. Nellie Wallace's mumbling monotone went on behind me, the other side of the screen, but it was low enough not to reach the audience and I tried to rise above it. At this time I was very new to the game and the least disturbance put me off, but I was beginning to learn something about concentration, and all was going fairly well when suddenly I heard Nellie Wallace say in a desperate sort of way, and clearly:

'What *does* she think she's doing out there on her own talking to herself?'

Somehow I knew she didn't really want an answer! For a second I lost concentration and went hot all over, but I managed to get back. I thought it was quite funny and tucked the incident away to be taken out and enjoyed later. But how do you explain what a monologue is to someone who *does* want to know and has no Greek. I would say: 'I'm not talking to myself, I'm pretending there is someone else on stage with me and I talk to him. If I pretend clearly enough I should be able to make you, the audience, accept the invisible character I'm imagining.'

Ruth Draper did this better than anyone has ever done it before or since. How can I describe her magic, even when she was elderly, alone on an empty stage convincing audiences that they saw not only a procession of characters, men, women and children, and their dogs, but also a variety of rooms, a church in Italy, the porch of a white clapboard house in Maine, a dressmaker's salon in Paris, a Court House in a poor part of New York, the waiting room of a hospital, and the inside of a large chauffeur-driven car in thick traffic, etc. See them is what we did. Producing these phenomena was surely a mammoth exercise in suggestion. A stage door-man at the Vaudeville Theatre where she was once playing told my father – 'She mass-hypnotises them.' In his book *The Art of Ruth Draper* Morton Dauwen Zabel quotes from one of the last interviews Ruth Draper gave: 'What I had as a child I've never lost

– the child's ability to pretend to be what he imagines he is. But it is the audience who must supply the imagination.'

She found that young people who had never seen anything but films and television realised when they saw her that they were expected to share in what she created, and to their amazement they discovered they could create too. It is the audience that does half the work.

Ruth could make you see objects as well as people and places. Miming is usually done in silence, as Marcel Marceau does it. Ruth was a hand-mime. She dealt with hairnets, hats and combs; knives, forks and glasses; telephones, buttons and scissors, and so clear was she that there was no possibility of confusing a fork with a spoon, or a button with a press-stud. When she cut the big pie to send out to the men on the snow-plough in 'Railway Accident on the Western Plains' she used a slicer to put the pieces on to a plate. I swear I saw it. Buzz, the boy who helped in the station buffet, had to carry it out. Before he went she scooped up the crumbs and popped them into his mouth, and when she told him to open wide the audience opened wide too. I remember the taste of those good brown crumbs.

As far as I know she never rehearsed before a season was launched, and I don't think she did much during it, except to refresh her memory. She told me that once she had begun a monologue 'it did itself'. Sketches that she hadn't played for some time had to be thought about, but I got the impression that her repertoire was safely stored in her memory, and she could probably have produced any sketch at any moment. I knew some of her monologues well enough to notice if she left out lines or added new ones, and I always told her what I had missed, and she'd say: 'Oh did I? I'm so glad you reminded me.'

Most artists seem to need a quiet pause, in silence, to prepare for a performance; I've been with musicians enough to know this is essential for them. But not for Ruth; she went on talking to me, or whomever else was in her dressing-room, until Mr Marika came to say it was time to start. Her technique was formidable, firm as concrete, but it never showed. Her sketches stayed fresh and she played them with a first-time quality. I don't think she had to re-think them each time. Nor was it necessary for her to suffer through a sketch in order to suggest agony – she was not at all a method actor. Sometimes she would come off stage and say she'd been thinking about what she would have for supper later. I was once in the wings, at the Haymarket this time, and Ruth was doing a dramatic piece in a three-episode sketch. I was so lost in the story and her performance that I forgot it was Ruth, acting out there in the lights, and I was startled, in a brief pause between episodes, when she ran off stage and said to me in a rush: 'I'm starving! Get someone to go and fetch me a ham sandwich. Get two.' Before she turned to walk back into the lights she was instantly the next character.

Ever since those early days of watching Ruth I have been fascinated to know how other actors work and whether they have to re-think as they go or, simply, as Ruth Draper did, start the reel and let the performance roll. One actress told me she made laundry-lists and planned menus while she played her scene. Perhaps they both relied on technique, and food, more than I supposed.

Ruth's 'dramas' (her word for them) had plots. Her work was composed at a period when there was plenty of time to introduce characters, establish them, allow them to develop, and finally reveal them as full-length portraits. What she wrote and performed with total mastery were little plays of great intensity, often dramatic. I was sure I could not manage drama, nor did I then want to. What I tried to do, because of the time in which I was writing, were brief, light-hearted, shorthand sketches of characters, suggested rather than detailed. They would mostly be English, but I felt free to do Americans, too, as long as they came from first-hand observation. From the beginning I was conscious that whatever I wrote should be kept well away from Ruth's territory – for instance, her portrayals of upper-class English women, including the débutante at a house-party and grand ladies showing their gardens and opening bazaars. By the time I had begun to write, these women were already a little out of date; that simplified any temptations I might have had to quarry where she had already mined.

When I was to appear in my first revue I asked Ruth for advice. This was a mistake. She would not play. It saddened me to discover that she thought I was out to compete with her. I could not have done so if I had tried. I found the situation ludicrous and incredible; it was like a goddess fearing a mortal. There was no possible threat. Gradually through the years she got used to the idea of my doing monologues too, and was generous enough about any success I had, but only once did she come to see me perform, in 1955 in New York, and she was genuinely pleased I was having a good season. There was a good *rapport*, she said, between the audience and me; but we did not talk about my sketches or my performance.

It was a long time before Ruth would make records or do broadcasts. She didn't like recording; I think she felt the microphone was an enemy. Using a script put her off; she had to give a performance as she would on stage or in a room, and she must have someone to play to, so she asked me to go with her to the B.B.C. It was like taking a reluctant child to the dentist. We were in a bleak little studio with strip-lighting, the producer was worried about time and Ruth was gloomy. She asked me how long my monologues took to perform; at that time my longest ran eight minutes. She was in despair; her shortest, she said, ran twice as long as that. As I remember it was decided to record her material without worrying about the clock, and later it was broadcast in a series of two or three sketches at a time instead of as a recital. She recorded well, but I felt that all her warmth was fully revealed only in her stage performances; then she was vulnerable, passionate, gentle, tender, loving and wholly approachable.

On stage she was dynamic and clear; off stage she had less presence. In spite of her good looks there was a faintly governessy air about her, a spinsterish order. (To see her pack a trunk was an education. There were special little linen bags for shoes, for hairbrushes, gloves, stockings. All her possessions dovetailed in. She folded skirts and blouses and dresses so that they came out the other end as smooth as they went in. String and boxes and rubber bands were saved. But she was very generous with her money.) I have been playing her recordings and again I am bowled over by the old magic. Her greatest *tour de force*, I think, is 'The Actress'. Much of it is spoken in her own invented Balkan sounds, but there is French, too, spoken with a Slav accent. I had always imagined she improvised the spoof language on the spot at each perfor-mance, but in the book of her published monologues there it all is, written down, so it had been carefully worked out and then learned. I am even more impressed!

I think her most attractive quality was her genuine humility. She really was surprised by her enormous success. She laughed when she told us of records broken at box offices and 'House Full' boards out for every performance at theatres where she played. It was real laughter. And she never got used to her repeated triumphs. 'Isn't it *crazy*', she used to say to my father, to whom she was devoted. 'Paul, they must all be crazy.' 'No,' said my father, 'Ruth' (for some long lost joke reason he pronounced the *u* in Ruth as in 'hut'), 'Ruth – you are a genius.'

I wish I could write down the fascination and involvement one had in a Ruth Draper performance. Perhaps it was because she made us work, too, that we left the theatre so well stretched and nourished. Today it is the straight sketches that interest me most. When I was young I found all her love scenes embarrassing, and I couldn't take them because I knew her too well. I squirmed all through the Mrs Mallory sequence in 'Three Women and Mr Clifford', and when she did 'The Return' about a brave young Englishwoman awaiting her wounded prisoner-of-war husband's return to their thatched cottage I didn't know where to look. Now I can take Mrs Mallory very happily and most of the other 'embarrassing' sketches; but 'The Return' remains a blusher.

The last time I saw her she was playing at the St James's Theatre, just before it was pulled down. She gave us 'The Italian Lesson' and 'The Actress', and I wrote in my diary on that night, 28 July 1956: 'An astonishing performance of really virtuoso proportions. Miracles of mime and observation; real skill, wit and timing. Absolutely perfect.' When I went backstage after that final matinée I was seeing her for the last time. I had been more moved by her performance than ever before, and I waited in the dressing-room (where Gerald du Maurier had always dressed) until the crowd had gone. Then I tried to tell her what the performance had meant to me. My diary records that I gave her a hug and said: 'I don't know how anyone dares mention my name with yours,' and she said: 'They don't!' I've been laughing ever since. But ruefully.

The way her life ended was most blessed. It was her farewell season and the most successful she had ever had in New York. The notices were enthusiastic and the houses booked solid. Until now her biggest successes had all been in London. She did well on Broadway, but there wasn't quite the same triumph she knew in England, where she was established, honoured, loyally loved, and had been for years. Only in her own city had she not completely found her true position as the great artist she was, but now in December 1956 she was fully recognised by a new generation of theatre-goers, and they brought their children to see her. She opened on Christmas Day, a common practice in New York. Older critics reaffirmed their praise and admitted they were at her feet. It must have been the sweetest kind of triumph to be recognised in this way at the age of seventy-one. A perfect Christmas present.

The following week was all glory. On the Saturday she did two shows and when the hired car came to take her home she asked the chauffeur to drive her back by way of Rockefeller Plaza so that she could see the illuminations and the Christmas tree. At her apartment house she said goodnight to the hall porter and the elevator man and let herself into her apartment.

The next morning her daily maid waited for her to come out of the bedroom. At last she knocked on the door. No answer. She went in and drew the curtains. Ruth appeared to be asleep, her hands folded like a child's under her cheek. The sheets were smooth, no sign of any distress or struggle to reach for the telephone by her bed. She had simply gone to sleep.

Later that day the United Press rang me in London and asked for a comment. My diary records: 'I said we should not see her like again. She was a genius.' Without time to think, clichés take over and often, because that is why they have become clichés, they tell the truth.

A flip answer to the second question interviewers ask me – 'Where do I get ideas for my monologues?' – is: 'If I knew, I would go there again.' In a very arid period, about fifteen years ago, I wondered whether I had come to the end of ideas for my work. I needed new material for a forthcoming season and my mind was blank. Then I had the sense to realise that ideas are never scarce; it is only one's panic sense of limitation that blocks the way. With this in mind I stopped fussing and when I next thought about it and looked back at the year's work, I found I had written more new songs and monologues than in any previous year. I have now come to see that ideas are not limited; it is simply a question of being open to them and ready to receive them.

When I was young I had a photographic and aural memory for detail. I took in clothes and facial expressions as well as accents and individual uses of language. I have a theory that I did most of my observing probably before I was twenty, stored it, and am still drawing on it. Now I am more interested in what people are thinking – and why – than when I only saw their funny hats and heard their chatter. I can no longer tell you the colour of their eyes, ties and whether they have moustaches or plucked eyebrows. But I do continue to notice voices and speech-mannerisms. If one is a commentator on the human scene, and that is what I think I am, it is as essential to listen with an ear open to speech-changes as it is to observe changes in modes, manners and points of view. Some of my contemporaries who write plays, and who had their biggest successes when they were young, seem to have stopped listening to how we now speak; and although their dialogue may be concerned with current ideas their talk echoes an older idiom. Nothing dates more quickly than everyday speech.

A writer once asked me what audience I had in mind when I wrote monologues; she said she wrote her books with the image of her worst enemy looking over her shoulder. It never occurred to me to think of an audience at all when I was working on material. Unless I managed to amuse myself I didn't think there was a hope of amusing anyone else. When I began I was amused by silliness, snobbery, lack of humour, pomposity and heartlessness; now I am more interested in people as individuals than in their follies. Perhaps I have grown more tolerant; or it could be that I become bored more quickly.

With one exception I don't believe I ever sat down to write a monologue. I always knew the character I was after; the way into it came through the voice and accent. It was the voice that brought the character into focus and with it instinctively came mannerisms and movements. I talked out loud to myself as I moved about the flat, thinking in the manner of the creature I was trying to bring to life. Sometimes I visualised backgrounds – bedroom, clothes, tastes (if any). The story-line was the last to be thought about. Throughout the building-up process – anything from two days to a month – I made notes of key-words and phrases, and so the piece took shape. Only then did I write it out in full.

The exception to my practice of working slowly and out loud happened one winter afternoon when Reggie, as always on a Saturday, had the television on to watch the sports programme. I do not like watching sport on television. For one thing it is so wearing. I run every race, jump every obstacle with the horse, and swim every length of the swimming-pool. I don't take part in football, I just recoil from it; particularly from the note of false enthusiasm in the voices of commentators. And I do not like massed men's voices singing and whooping through 'You'll never walk alone'. But Reggie and Virginia are both keen television football-watchers. When they switch on I move off.

On this particular Saturday Reggie and I were at home, and I was lazy about going upstairs to my work-room, and took a foolscap block and pencils into the dining-room with the idea of trying to think up ideas for a forthcoming concert-tour. I said to myself in my mother's Virginian accent: 'What you all goin' do this afternoon?', and at once I thought: 'I'll tell myself a story about an old woman in a rocking-chair, sitting on the back porch on a hot summer's night in Virginia.' I gave her a companion, Charlotte, and began to talk and write down what I said in the voice and idiom I knew so well from my ma – the story of Lally Tullett, a young school-teacher who had played a big part in the narrator's life fifty years before. The 'I' of the story is a very old woman and, as she reads aloud a notice of Lally Tullett's death, it unleashes memories of a dramatic incident long forgotten but now alive and felt again. At the end, with the merciful perspective of old age, she lets go of past pains and returns to tranquillity, rocking herself on the porch on that hot summer night.

For the only time in my monologue-writing life I had the idea and the way I wanted to do it, and wrote it down then and there, 'in one' as it were; complete. In performance I never told this story in exactly the same words because it was a memory, unrolling itself in the mind of the teller as she told it, and it called for a free style. But the paragraphs and sequence of events stayed exactly as they were in the original script. Lally Tullett remains one of my favourite sketches though not my favourite character.

Two other monologue-characters came into being through the looking-glass. Years before I went into the theatre I discovered, by putting my tongue in front of my lower teeth, I could alter my face into something I would not want to be stuck with if the wind changed. Speaking with my tongue in this position produced a plummy, rural sound, and I gave it a Buckinghamshire accent and loved it dearly. When Bertie Farjeon asked me to write additional material for *The Little Revue* I made up three different kinds of mothers – an American from the Middle West teaching her daughter a poem by Shelley; an understanding mother worrying about her sixteen-year-old daughter's infatuation for a middle-aged Portuguese conjuror; and a Buckingham-shire village mother with a funny face whose little boy got a conker lodged in his throat. About twenty years later I decided to revive the village mother, now an old grumbler, and I put her in a sketch called 'A Terrible Worrier'.

The second character appeared one night when I was cleaning my teeth. I looked in the mirror and curled back my upper lip to make sure they were clean and gleaming. (My teeth are large as tombstones and it is as well to keep them in good order for they are noticeable.) It occurred to me that I had found a new face and I wondered how it would speak. It spoke in a clear, clipped, educated manner and what it said was crisp and to the point. I went into the living-room where Reggie was still reading and I said: 'This is my new monologue face,' and talked to him in the new voice. He liked it. She is my favourite character in my gallery of 'monstrous women', the wife of an Oxbridge vice-chancellor. She has no name but I know her well, admire her intellect and wit and am devoted to her generous assumption, like Clemence Dane's, that everyone else is as well read and informed as she is. There is not much of me in this lady. I wrote three sketches about her called 'Eng. Lit.'

The character speaks in the same shape of phrase and with an unexpected use of words, as did one of my dearest older friends. Hester Alington, wife of the Dean of Durham, born Lyttelton and therefore attractively eccentric and individual. Mrs A., as she was known to me, had a deep, dark, rumbling voice that I could not reproduce for long without dislocating something; and I did not want to copy Mrs A. except in her unique way with a sentence. This was never straightforward. On a postcard addressed to a shoe-shop in Sloane Street she had written: 'Gently fussed about non-appearance of dim pair of shoes sent to you for heeling.' At lunch one day she warned the Dean of an impending Mothers' Union meeting: 'Dear Sir, at three o'clock this dining-room will be entirely deplorable for tonight.' And when Viola and I went to Durham to perform in aid of one of her charities she introduced the paying of our expenses: 'My dears, we have not yet touched on the sordid topic of coin.'

My vice-chancellor's wife was an entirely different shape from Mrs A. who was large and comfortable and moved quietly at a leisurely pace. The 'Eng. Lit.' character was taller, thinner and more deliberate, with a clear-cut precision, matched by Mrs A.'s mind and intelligence. I gave her a housekeeper called Mrs Kinton and invented Mrs A.-like lines for her to say. 'Mrs Kinton – is there a tolerable chance of your being in close proximity to a kettle?' I added to Mrs A.'s kind of phrase-building an inability to pronounce the letter *r*. I enjoyed doing the 'Eng. Lit.' sketches more than any others.

Of all the monologues I have written I suppose the 'Nursery Schoolteacher' is the most popular with the general public, because the special voice I used for talking to children is universally recognised – it is bright, not very confident and fools no one, particularly children. But the wretched woman is really not much of a character. Her invisible class of four-year-olds runs rings round her and she is always worsted by the low Sydney, who is a miniature wrecker. He and the teacher originated in the radio programme 'How to Talk to Children' some time in the 1940s. Sydney has remained four years old ever since; a disillusioned non-co-operator with a deadly aim for discomfiting.

I had never been inside a nursery school when I wrote the first sketch, but I knew from my own experience that an unnatural brightness crept into my voice when I spoke to children and tried to hold their attention, or distract them from pursuing undesirable ploys. At that time there was an educational programme on radio about music and movements for juniors, and I listened eagerly to a teacher dividing her class into Red Bunnies and Blue Bunnies and Brown Bunnies, and ordering them to go hoppity to the music *all* over the room, and then go *flop* when the music stopped. Out of all this came the nursery school-teacher. She has been recorded several times, with Sydney causing trouble in every episode. I am told Teacher Training Colleges use these records to illustrate how *not* to talk to children. A tribute I enjoy.

Methods may have changed, but not, I think, that special voice we all continue to use with the very young. After a concert in Toronto an earnest child-expert came backstage to tell me my methods were out of date and that no self-respecting nursery school would hire a teacher with such archaic ways. She was firm with me. 'You'll never get any-where with children if you go on running your class like that.'

Such suspension of rationality isn't rare. I have known unsophisticated audiences identify me with characters I am mocking. During the war I wrote, out of experience, a sketch about a lady of leisure then doing her bit by working – or rather not working very hard – in a forces' canteen. When I first did hospital concerts I started the programme with this limp woman – 'I'm *so* sorry but I'm afraid I'm *not* allowed to carry things' – and I didn't understand their reluctance to laugh or warm to me very much until I discovered the audiences thought I truly was that kind of woman. When I understood what was happening I began the programme with the village mother of the funny face and followed it with 'Canteen'; then all fell into place and the audiences twigged that neither of these people was really me.

Until I performed a new sketch I did not know where the laughs were going to be. After the war I was engaged to write a weekly episode for a radio series called 'Here's Wishing You Well Again'. intended to be heard in hospitals. I invented a new character, 'Shirley's Girl Friend', a cockney with a boy friend, Norm, 'the one who drives the lorry with the big ears.' I wrote endless scripts for her, and when I appeared in my own show I introduced 'Shirl' into the programme. One episode described how she went out dancing with a suave escort, Mr Lewis, whom she had met at her bus-stop.

'All of a sudden he leans acrorst the table and takes hold of my hand and he says: "Has anyone ever told you you got provocative eyes?" ' On the first night this got a good laugh, as I hoped it might. Then I added, out of a sense of truth and my own inability not to observe irrelevant details in moments of interest or drama: 'I see his cuff go in the beet salad but I dint say nothing.' I liked the line when I wrote it, but I never expected it to get a far bigger laugh than 'provocative eyes'. Ever afterwards I timed it carefully, holding back until the last second when it always topped the previous line. (After the first night at the Little Theatre Farjeon had told me I should go down on my knees in gratitude for a sense of timing, for it can't, he said, be taught; it's an instinct.)

'Here's Wishing You Well Again' was broadcast from the Paris Cinema in Lower Regent Street to an audience that included bus-loads of convalescent service-patients, still wearing hospital blue. Tea was provided and the cast stayed behind to help hand out cups and cakes and talk to the guests. One afternoon I had a pleasing little encounter with a very shy, withdrawn patient sitting by himself at the back of the hall. Someone told me he was uncommunicative and seemed isolated. I was asked to take him a cup of tea and, as I gave it to him, I noticed on the seat beside him there was a khaki bush-hat turned up on one side; this probably meant he had served in Burma. I have a good memory, but at that moment as far as I knew I had never seen the man before. I told him I had been on a tour of hospitals in India and wondered whether I had played where he had been a patient. Had he been in hospital in India? 'Yes.' Had we met? 'Yes.' My questions asked themselves. Was it at Comilla? 'Yes.' Had he been in the penicillin ward? 'Yes.' In the bed next to the door beside a man with red hair? 'Yes,' he said, smiling for the first time, 'I was.' I really hadn't remembered him before, but perhaps my wish to help him out of his shyness produced what seemed to be needed.

Only in the last years of my concert career did I write 'straight' sketches. Until then I was cowardly about risking anything except comedy, unless it was written as a song, like 'Three Brothers', or in loosely rhythmic free verse with an occasional rhyme. 'Boat Train' was written in that form, and the framework of verse made me feel one step removed and as if I were not directly involved. A quibble, of course, but it was then my only way of doing a more serious number. I had not set out to bring tears to the eyes when I wrote 'Three Brothers', the song about an unmarried sister and her life of devotion to her brothers; I found her gallant, and it was her unawareness of gallantry I found poignant; so did audiences. But 'Boat Train' was a tear-jerker, based on an incident I witnessed at Waterloo Station, with this difference: the real-life mother seeing off her grown-up son and his wife and family to settle in a far country was full of self-pity; the woman I wrote about was so distressed at the parting that she made light of it to spare her children. Gallantry again. Of all human qualities I find selfless courage the one I admire most.

'First Flight' was written much later. By that time I was braver and wrote it as a straight sketch. Like 'Boat Train' it was about selfless mother-love, a perilous subject for the theatre. Goodness is almost impossible to show on the stage. It calls for simplicity that is neither dull nor empty and for humility that is in no way false. Once again I knew that it could work only if treated lightly and with faint self-mockery. The sketch is about a woman in an aeroplane on her way to America to meet her son's black American wife and the grandchildren she has never seen. I couldn't find the right voice for it until I tried it out in an un-localised North Country accent. Then it fell into place. There is a directness in North Country speech that suggests honesty (though it can also suggest narrowness and that wouldn't do for the country-woman I was after). If the speech were too brisk it suggested smugness, so I worked on trying to get a gentleness that was at the same time sure and strong, but never dogmatic or opinionated. I wanted to show her as a woman of natural loving instincts, disturbed by her reaction to the situation, longing to be able to stand by the belief she holds dearly that all men are one in the sight of God, and much concerned that she may not be able to hide the ambivalence of feeling she hadn't expected to have and so longs to be without. 'I do want to do it right,' she says. 'I just want to do it right.' I hoped the audience would feel confident that she did.

'Nicodemus' was unlike anything I had ever seen on a stage or ever written before or since; and it was given to me on a plate. I was in South Africa; friends sent their car to fetch me to luncheon. Their driver was a young black African of twenty-five. I asked him where we were and he told me it was the University. 'Education is a wonderful thing,' he said, and tapped his forehead with the heel of his hand. He had not been able to finish his education because his family's money ran out, but he told me he read many, many books. 'What kind of books?' I asked con-versationally. 'I am finding W. Somerset Maugham is more easy for me than Stefan Zweig. It is in translation.' I sat up. 'What else do you read?' 'I am finding Chekhov is most poetical writer.' 'What else?' 'Guy de Maupassant and others.' He belonged to a Methodist Church reading club, where all the members read the same books and discussed them later with the head man, who was a wonderful teacher and read many, many, *many* books. We talked of the possibility of understanding through reading; of poetry, of love. He said: 'I am going to many places in books. All the time I am travelling in my head.'

When I got the chance (powdering my nose at my destination) I wrote down that last sentence Nicodemus had said before I forgot its precise wording.

Back in London I tried to make a song out of it and had the idea of using drum-beats as an accompaniment. I worked out a rhythm, two beats in the left hand against three in the right, slapped out on my knees with the flat of my hand. I read the lyric to Dick over the telephone. He asked me if I had a shape for the song in my head – a working tune? I told him about the drum rhythm and he asked me to tape the lyric with the drum-beats to give him an idea of what I wanted. When he heard the tape he said the piece had no need of music; it was complete, spoken against the drum rhythm, and I was to do it that way.

I first performed it at the Yvonne Arnaud Theatre in Guildford where Laurier Lister devised a lighting-plot that concentrated on my hands and knees and kept my face in darkness. I introduced the item by telling of the meeting with Nicodemus and explained that I had put his words into a formal shape, but the ideas were all his. I established the drum-beats, returning to the rhythm for the two choruses.

> I cannot leave my country,
> I cannot get a pass to go away.
> Money is something you must have also
> And money is something I do not have today.
> But I am making a discovery:
> Right where I am are books and books,
> And books are full of people and places
> And wide new ideas and poems
> On love, and other subjects,
> And I am going away, away,
> I am going away – in books.

(with
beaten
rhythm)

> All the time I am travelling in my head,
> All over the world I am going,
> I am travelling in my head
> And I am knowing different people,
> Different history,
> Different thinking – different mystery,
> And people, people talking –
> All the time I am travelling in my head
> Making discovery.

Johannesburg is my city,
I drive a big car for a business man.
Waiting is something I must do often
And when I am waiting I am reading when I can.
Since I am making my discovery
More I am reading books and books,
And books are full of terrible stories
And wonderful visions growing
Of man and what he can be.
And I am going away, away,
I am going away – in books.

All the time. . . . etc.

To my relief the piece worked on stage in spite of being done by a large middle-aged Englishwoman in a long evening dress.

Someone connected with the 'Feed the Minds' campaign, which provides books for emerging countries, asked me if I would allow them to have a recording of 'Nicodemus' to use in introducing their work around the world. I made a tape of it for them. It was also included in one of my long-playing records and heard in Australia by an Irish priest-schoolmaster who wrote to ask me for a copy for his school magazine. I wrote it out in longhand and asked him to acknowledge that the rights now belonged to 'Feed the Minds'. It says much for his broadmindedness, and my poor writing, that he unquestioningly agreed to give the credit to what he misread as 'Feed the *Druids*' campaign.

Music has sometimes been a stimulant when I was looking for ideas. I am loath to admit this because I thought that Viola's tuition had taught me to listen so that I actually heard what was being played. But not always. I went to a violin and piano recital of sonatas and thought I was paying attention to Brahms, when into my head crept the idea for a song about a quiet girl called Ethel whose character changed when she got to a football match. This was soon followed by the complete first verse. Going home in a taxi I wrote it out and never altered it. Thanks be to Brahms.

I don't understand Ethel,
I don't, I don't really.
She's one of my very best friends,
Just about the best nearly.
She's an awfully nice girl, Ethel is,

Dainty and refined.
I mean she'd never do or say
Anything unkind.
But get her inside of a stadium
And she seems to go out of her mind.

'KILL HIM!' she yells – 'Knock his block off'
(at hockey or football or what)
'Kill him!' she yells, turning purple,
'Kill the perishing lot!'
'Sh – Sh,' I say, '*Ethel,*
Sh – Sh,' and I die of shame.
'Kill him and bash his teeth in his face,'
She says
And calls him a dirty name.

Today when I look at old scripts of monologues I have been doing for years, I notice the original is very different from the sketches as I finally did them. New lines have crept in, and old lines I am glad to see again have been forgotten. I suppose there is always *some* improvisation in all I do, but I have never relied on it because carefully constructed material is always stronger and more telling.

I find most improvised theatre is an impertinence. It seldom works half as well as scenes written and rehearsed and looked at critically before they are shown to the public. However I have to admit that improvising is one of the most stimulating and inspiring experiences I know. It demands suspension of all conscious intention, all self-consciousness. In the musical improvisations in which I have taken part, it is as if, without any restrictions, doors open to stored memories and they take over. What comes out as parody is, I think, a sort of echo of assimilated material that becomes invention, in the manner of certain composers whose idiom is familiar.

I have done a good deal of improvising with William Blezard, with whom I worked through most of my show career; and from time to time with Joseph Cooper. With both collaborators the exercise has been entirely for our own self-indulgent pleasure – and amazement. We astonish ourselves by making unexpected key-changes and agreeable shapes in the music, and I find myself singing in a larger, freer, higher voice than I use in my own work. I believe the reason for this is that in improvisation the sense of responsibility vanishes and one has no fears or limitations; it doesn't matter if it goes wrong and, because it doesn't matter, one is free to let rip; or is it that the suspension of self-conscious-ness releases natural creativity? Bill and I once taped a long session of improvisations and, in the middle of a lot of meandering muddle, we did a song about a rose in the Roger Quilter manner that had form, charm, a pretty tune and made sense. We were glad to hear it. Making up the words is part of the game and sometimes, but only sometimes, the lyrics work as well as the music. I speak inaccurate French (accent good, grammar nil) but have no German, Italian or Russian. This does not stop me improvising in all these languages, using sounds approxi-mating to the original, phonetically passable and none of it making any sense at all.

Improvisation is heady stuff for the doer and must be severely rationed; unless it is truly spontaneous, patterns start to form, ideas are repeated, and it is no longer genuine improvisation. One or twice Joe and I have dared greatly and improvised in public. This is hair-raising. Because responsibility creeps in, I don't think improvisation in public can ever be as successful as it is when done entirely for one's own pleasure, without thought or worries about technique.

Technique is something you can learn from experts, or by trial and error; I learned mine that way. In my first revue I had almost no con-centration. A whisper in the wings or an unexpected movement or noise in the auditorium threw me completely. I lost my words and had to fight my way back into the sketch. But in the war the hospital shows helped me to build up resistance to disturbances. It was always impos-sible to get complete quiet in the wards. People came and went, bells rang, patients needed attention, and I had to carry on as if I were unaware of interruptions. I had to come to terms with the problem, and in the end if I was conscious of extraneous noises I could ignore them, and so I acquired a technique that is essential if one is going to be a professional. In one of the 'Shirley's Girl Friend' sketches I wrote a line that sums up what, in the theatrical or musical sense, I mean by pro-fessional: 'He can do it even when he isn't in the mood' – and when circumstances are far from ideal. A true pro has a technique of steel that carries him through thick and thin, through disturbances both of sight and sound – or very nearly.

When I began I felt secure only if I was safely behind footlights and couldn't see the audience. But in hospital wards there were no foot-lights and I had to learn to look just above faces, partly for my own sake and partly to spare the audience the embarrassment of being fixed by my gaze. It isn't always comfortable to be able to see one's public.

Monologues, Ruth Draper and How I Learned by Doing

Once in London an elderly man in the front row took out his watch at regular intervals, looked at it and put it back in his waistcoat pocket with undisguised boredom. It made me think of my father's story of Edward Marsh, who said he didn't mind if anyone looked at his watch when he was lecturing, but he didn't much like it when they looked at it a second time and shook it to see if it was still going. After the war I worked in music clubs and halls where lights were hardly ever powerful enough to blot out the first eight rows. (In the little Philip Theatre in Sydney where I played for thirteen weeks in 1959 I could see a long way back into the auditorium; on matinée days the ladies came in wearing hats, usually white, and when they laughed they bent forward from the waist and looked like a field of dog daisies bowing in the wind.) At first I found this visibility disturbing, but I came to like it when audiences were held by what was going on on the platform and gave themselves to the story or song as children do, mouths slightly open, eyes wide. They were transported out of themselves and came with me to the imagined scene, and between us we achieved an engagement of ideas. Their faces were wiped clean of personal worries and self-consciousness. It was as if one were seeing faces as they are meant to be: open, receptive and generous. I was moved by their innocence. The silence that goes with this kind of listening is lively and is the greatest reward a performer can be given, far more exciting than applause, because it is a kind of sharing.

I have come to believe that giving and receiving are really the same. Giving and *receiving* – not giving and taking. The receiver contributes his acceptance to what the giver is offering. Two halves of a whole. When there is an equal division of labour in a theatre the entertainer's ideas and the audience's imagination convert into one concept. Then programmes work. Like Ruth Draper I believe the reason audiences, particularly young audiences, seem to enjoy monologues is because, through their own imagination, they are also able to create.

CHAPTER EIGHTEEN

A Plan and a Poet

ALL through the spring and summer of 1953 I had talks with Binkie Beaumont about putting on a new kind of entertainment for me. For over a year I had been writing new material and there was a file full of scripts and lyrics, some already set by Dick, against the day when I would appear in a new programme. In New York *An Evening with Beatrice Lillie* had been a success and Binkie thought his firm, H. M. Tennent Ltd, might do something along the same lines for me; but although we explored ideas, had meetings and telephone conversations, and got as far as considering one or two possible performers who might join forces with me, none of the ideas flowered and I grew less and less confident about the project. In August I took a deep breath and withdrew from the enterprise. The relief was unexpectedly comforting. I felt set free; and I dare say Binkie, who had plenty of other undertakings to occupy him, felt the same.

Laurier Lister's latest revue *Airs on a Shoe-string* was a success, running steadily at the Royal Court, and on 2 September Reggie and I had supper with him in the restaurant above the theatre. He knew about the proposed Tennent project but not that I had just withdrawn from it. When I told him, he said at once: 'Why don't you do a new programme with me?' The reason had been a practical one: after the problems of putting on *Penny Plain* Reggie and I decided that next time I did a show it had better be backed by a bigger management. Tennent's had resources of capital and access to several theatres and Binkie's offer had looked safe and sound; but it had not matured. Laurier must have known my reasons. He had never before suggested that I might do the programme with him, but now he said he thought we could do an attractive small-scale show together, and I knew as he was speaking that was what I really wanted to do. Suddenly a small spark of hope rose in my heart and the whole project started to come to life for me.

Victor Stiebel with me in Switzerland

We decided to give ourselves six months to prepare the show. Laurier came to the King's Road flat to hear the material and we discussed whom to invite to share the programme. I wanted a dancer or a man singer, but preferred the idea of dancing as a better contrast to my songs and monologues. In the end we engaged three talented and diverse young dancers, Beryl Kaye (South African), Paddy Stone (Canadian) and Irving Davies (Welsh), who were doing an act together in the United States and would be ready to come back to England in time to rehearse for an opening late in April 1954. I was to write the words and Dick the music; William Blezard was appointed musical director; Victor Stiebel agreed to make me six dresses; choreography was to be by Wendy Toye, Alfred Rodriguez and the dancers themselves; the décor by Joan and David de Bethel and Peter Rice. The show was to be directed by Laurier Lister and called 'Joyce Grenfell Requests the Pleasure'.

It was in February that Laurier, Wendy, Rod and I got together with the dancers for the first time. We met in our kitchen, and Laurier outlined the shape of the programme – they were to dance solos, duos and trios – and I told them about the material already written. There was to be a Palais de Danse number in which I would be included. As a *dancer?* Yes. Intended to amuse? We hoped so.

By this time television had become an important part of our lives and was a good deal harder to resist than it is today. I had written an opening speech to welcome the audience to the show, and in it I thanked them for bravely taking the difficult step 'of leaving your television set, your radio and your book to come and have a look at real live entertainers, seen in the original size and natural colours – not tinned or canned or screened from here to there' (I indicated a gigantic movie screen) 'but actually here, breathing – more or less – and ready to do the show for you – NOW. It makes a change, doesn't it, and it's so *new* – you there, us here. . . . It makes An Occasion.' I read the draft of this as we sat round the kitchen table and the dancers responded favourably. An encouraging sign. We had more cups of tea mixed with mounting excitement about the show and parted full of enthusiasm. This time the project felt right and I could hardly wait for it to begin.

But before we were to start rehearsing, on 29 March, I had a diary full of engagements. The last weeks of preparation for the show coincided with the making of *The Belles of St Trinian's*, the first of the Searley Girls films I was in. When I wasn't at Shepperton Studios, dressed in a gymslip as Police Sergeant Ruby Gates (disguised as a games-mistress), I was working on songs with Dick; consulting with Victor about my six dresses; shopping for character-clothes and props with Jeanne Goddard, our wardrobe mistress; and, whenever possible, practising words and singing, wherever I happened to be. Any free moments I had at the studio were spent off the set in my dressing-room where I rehearsed out loud to myself.

Viola and I were still broadcasting and doing music club concerts together; but it was becoming clear that my future lay in solo performances, and she knew her way was in 'straight' music. Besides, she felt it was time for me to work with a male accompanist; it looked more professional and made a better balance. (I still don't agree with this conventional view but it seems a difficult one to break away from. As the two men accompanists I worked longest with were both expert and very congenial I have no complaints about the arrangement, but as a principle I question its truth.) Viola had always helped me with my singing. My tendency to sing flat is evident in early recordings and, although I wasn't all *that* flat, too often I sang just under the note, and Viola advised me to have lessons with Anne Wood. Anne agreed to take me on and from the beginning realised it was no good trying to turn me into a 'real' singer. What I needed to know was how to achieve a better performance of the kind of singing my programme demanded; and as, among other things, I was satirising the way 'real' singers sang in opera and on the concert platform, it was essential for me to learn to use my small voice in the right way before I took liberties with some of the odd manners in which 'real' singers used theirs. Mimicry came in useful. I found that imitating Anne (a good 'real' singer) helped me to find the right resonances. I liked the image she used to illustrate a *legato* phrase – 'smooth and rounded as beads on a long string.' I had my first lesson a few weeks before *Joyce Grenfell Requests the Pleasure* opened, and after that I continued gratefully to get very practical help from Anne throughout my career.

On the first day of rehearsals the dancers and I went to the Royal Court Theatre, where we were to do much of our preparation, met the stage managers, David and Penny Udy, and were given the week's schedule. The dancers left to work in practice-rooms and I had the stage to myself, with Laurier to set my numbers and give me my moves: 'When the curtain goes up you are discovered in your white organza dress with the broad pink satin sash, up stage right, with your left arm raised as you adjust the buttons on your long white gloves. Turn. See the audience over your left shoulder, come down stage centre and begin your opening speech.' I made notes on my script. It had been over a year since I had worked in a theatre and it felt strange but good to be on a real stage again after all the rough platforms in makeshift halls where I had lately been playing. I went through all my numbers and Laurier directed exits and entrances and marked where my table and chair were to be set. His direction was mostly concerned with presentation; interpretation came later and I did most of that for myself. But he was always the greatest help in showing me how to get the most out of my own material.

There were interruptions that day to look at revised designs for the set and costumes for 'Songs my Mother Taught me'. Viola had written some music based on one of them, 'Sit Down Sister', for Beryl and the boys to dance to before I came on to sing. Beryl as an Edwardian child was to wear a white frock with a big flat white hat; Irving and Paddy blue jeans (not yet fashionable). My dress was based on photographs of my mother as a girl – white leg-of-mutton-sleeved shirt-waist, buckram-belted piqué skirt and a big black taffeta bow pinned at the back of my head. We were pleased with it, and with the new drawing for the proscenium arch – bright dark red velvet outlined in white bamboo. I went home to tell Reggie I thought things were falling into place; I had enjoyed day number one. But a week or so later I wrote less happily in my diary about the first rough run-through on 10 April: 'I was *awful*. Forgot. Was woolly. Not in the *least* funny. But the dancers superb; really wonderful. Reggie was bowled over by them. A gruelling but useful day.'

On Good Friday, towards the end of rehearsals, I escaped to have tea with Walter de la Mare. There are certain people to whom it is sheer self-indulgent luxury to show one's work, and W.J., as he was called, was one of these. I had known him slightly since I was a child; he lived at Taplow only a few miles from Cliveden, but we had lost touch until the war; then we picked up the threads and became friends. For the last five years of his life I went often to see him in his roomy flat at the top of a big beautiful Queen Anne house in Montpelier Row, Twickenham. There he was looked after by 'N.' Saxton, a retired nurse to whom he was devoted. The house stood at the far end of the Row in the shade of an immense plane tree much admired by W.J. And me. (My favourite tree is a London plane. I have one outside my bedroom window in Chelsea, but it can't compare with the noble one at South End House. That is a prince of planes.) The views from W.J.'s windows gave on to playing fields and the distant Thames. Sometimes when I was there a rowing eight went by as if drawn by a string; unless the right light was on the water the river wasn't visible.

W.J. showed a flattering interest in my work and like my other octogenarian friend, Tom Jones, he took my early writing seriously. During the war he allowed me to send him poems to read. I rationed myself and very rarely sent him any, but I remember vividly the leap of joy when he returned one to me with 'Bull's-eye!' written on the margin in his fine clear hand. I've forgotten the lines that prompted this but not the emotion of reading that 'Bull's-eye!' At Twickenham I sang to him

'*Songs my Mother Taught me*'

(unaccompanied) new songs and performed new monologues as they were completed, and we talked about everything under the sun including the invention of characters. Could I account for mine; were they from another existence? No, I said, they arrive whole and I have no feeling of 'I have been here before'. He agreed about the completeness and said: 'If you invented a button it would have to be sewn on properly.'

On the Good Friday visit I found him, taking a day off in bed, in his blue-panelled bedroom wearing blue pyjamas with a red-and-blue silk handkerchief loosely knotted under his collar like a cowboy's scarf. After tea with hot-cross-buns he asked for news of the show's progress, and I described a new number, 'The Music's Message', and did it for him – with movements – in a corner of his room. It's a dotty sort of song, sung by an earnest, ungraceful, over-age schoolgirl type who joins a class in search of 'the rhythms of the earth and sea and sky'. The teacher tells her to listen carefully and see what message the music has for her. 'You must listen and listen and *listen*, my dear.' (I stood still, listening hard.) 'But the music said only one thing in my ear: "You're a horse." '

Like a child W.J. said: 'More, please,' and because I loved the opportunity of showing off to him I did half the programme and hoped I wasn't staying too long.

The first time I went to tea with him at South End House I was bidden for 3.45. At 4 o'clock Lady Hamilton, wife of another poet, Rostrevor Hamilton, arrived and looked surprised at finding me sitting there. At 4.15 Lady Cynthia Asquith rang the bell and when she saw two of us established on a sofa she looked even more surprised. I suspect we had each expected to be the only visitor. It amused me to discover that we had all been given different arrival times; I had the longest with the dear man and felt very favoured. Lady Cynthia produced a kitchen timer out of a paper bag, set it to sound off an hour later and put it in the middle of the tea-table among the scones and cakes, to remind us not to tire W.J. by staying too long. But he protested that the ticking was a disturbance and she had to put it away. It was always a temptation to stay on because he was an enchanter and time flew in his company. After a visit on 16 July 1954 I wrote in my diary: 'He affects me like a romantic beau. I want to shine for him, to please him. Egotism of course, but also it is because of a sense of being nearer to a vision. He is a prism through which light and colour come to change the view.'

Walter de la Mare

We often talked about images in the mind, and he asked me if I thought the tree we could see and touch is the reality, or is the tree we see in our mind the real tree? My diary does not record my reply. (If I was asked that question now I should say I believe I have found a yardstick for myself by which I measure reality. In the metaphysical sense, and I find this is the reliable one, only the infinite is real. The temporal eventually disintegrates, but the spiritual is eternal.)

In my diaries I always listed the subjects discussed with W.J. and we ranged far and wide. 16 July 1953: 'We talked about the Brontës, genius, children, innocence, eccentrics; about failure being more memorable than success. Of time. Of the Queen at Buckingham Palace last week when he went to be given his O.M. Said as usual he talked too much but she was SO NICE. Sometimes he got a sense of peace and then realised it was because he wasn't talking.'

31 July 1954: 'W.J. delighted by pomposity of his landlord below, who complained that W.J.'s load of firewood had been "untidily delivered". His letter said it might have been in the way of his Bentley. From the window we saw the landlord on the lawn – beetle-browed – holding a tin kettle. We talked of the child being father to the man. He thought the child arrives with a full portmanteau; an old man has only an empty bag in his hand.'

16 February 1956. 'We talked at length about poetry and why certain poems "come in one". He quoted his own "Jemima", and one he woke up knowing two years ago about a girl in a little green hat. He read me a poem of Hardy's about a bedraggled thrush and talked of memory and reminiscence. Said he loved reminiscing. Peace of mind means to him confidence outside one's own little mind. *Yes*.'

15 March. 'He talked about Edward Thomas. "I loved him," he said. "He never used slang but his conversation was rich and alive." W.J. didn't like *World Without End* (Helen Thomas's book about their marriage).'

8 April. 'Of homesickness. He described a room he had stayed in, as a small boy, near Shooters Hill where the pelmet above white muslin curtains was made of brass. He looked out of the window to a nearby railway line and counted signal-lights. If there were more green than red it meant omens were right for a speedy return home. He remembered standing on a carpet-stool between two old ladies who watched him while he ate jelly out of a glass. Then, he said, St Gabriel, in the form of a parlourmaid, came in and said someone had arrived to fetch him. He remembered the sense of release and joy that came with her words. (I told him of my homesick visit to Enfield.)'

W.J. had a taste for music hall songs and earthy jokes. He telephoned me one day and said: 'Hurry up and come over because I want to tell you a story I've just heard from Laurence Whistler.' When I got there later in the day he told me about an unfortunate woman badly handicapped by constipation.' I sit there hour after *hour*,' she told the doctor. 'Do you take anything?' he asked. She thought for a moment: 'Only my knitting.'

Joan Hassall the artist was there for tea one day. She brought a sort of table-harp with her and played and sang songs exactly right for the room and the instrument. It made a most innocent music and W.J. loved the size of the sounds she made, tiny, pure and clear, and the small songs she sang to match it. He had a great feeling for small things and showed us a cupboard full of miniature furniture, shells, cups and dishes. He wondered how small is the smallest audible sound. He once stood by an evening primrose and *heard* it open. I sang a bit of the 'Paradise Bird' carol and all three of us did Tallis's Canon. If he couldn't have music *very* loud (and he particularly liked the Bach Organ Toccata and Fugue played full up on his gramophone to remind him of his days as a chorister at St Paul's) then he liked it very small indeed. It was the same with flowers, only he didn't much like big flowers. The week before someone had given him a bunch of colossal chrysanthemums and he couldn't bear them in the room. We spoke of eternity, and Joan Hassall said the very thought of it made her feel giddy.

I once asked W.J. if he ever thought about death. He smiled with what I can only describe as enthusiasm and said: 'I hardly ever think of anything else.' Two weeks before he died he sat to John Ward for a drawing I had asked him to make for me. He is seen wearing a dressing-gown and a silk scarf, sitting in the window where he then spent much of the day. I was sure he and John would take to each other and I was right. The drawing is evidence of an afternoon well spent.

He died in 1956 on 22 June and after the service at St Paul's Cathedral I wrote in my diary: 'A huge company and a number of solitary figures on their own. One felt he had touched them all and their love and loss were real. When the organ roared the big Bach Toccata it finished me.'

CHAPTER NINETEEN

The Show Opens

In the last week of rehearsals, before we opened at Cambridge, I divided my time between the theatre, final fittings at Victor's and shopping for shoes and accessories for the show. Laurier had suggested I should get advice about my stage make-up. I had never had professional lessons in make-up, but now I made an appointment with an expert at Max Factor's and he scrutinised my face and suggested an entirely new way of painting it. The colours on the chart he gave me were very different from the pale tubes and sticks in my old make-up box, and I took the list to Frizell's in Leicester Square to buy a whole new set of ingredients. I was to look a lot 'peachier' and less doll-like, and I practised shading my cheek-bones, chin line and the area above my eyelids with a stick of umber. It seemed an improvement. From the start I hated using mascara on my eyelashes and took to outlining my eyes with a very soft black pencil and I've done this ever since; only, with the passing of time, I changed to soft brown; it is gentler. Max Adrian taught me to apply a fine line of bright green just above the pencil.

Bill Blezard, our musical director, was beginning to look a little less harassed by this time. He had his hands full because not only was he playing for rehearsals for the dancers, singly and together, but for me as well. He also had most of the orchestrations to compose for the whole show. There was a series of assistant rehearsal-pianists, and I did some work with Viola, but Bill had to be in command of the whole and he had looked frenzied as he bicycled from his flat near Earls Court to wherever rehearsals were going on. Sheets of manuscript music spilled out of his music-case and a perpetual frown-line crossed his forehead as he hurried in and apologised for being a little late. He was burdened by much responsibility, and on top of the show he was in process of trying to find a practical date, between final rehearsals, for his wedding to Joan Kemp Potter. Now that I know Bill so well I realise he uses a faint

William Blezard on holiday

pessimism as a kind of insurance against possible disaster. The gloom
never lasts and optimism takes over as soon as he feels in control of the
situation. This was a time of settling in for all of us. There were tussles
with dancers about tempi; there always are. I wasn't sure that some of
the accompaniments wouldn't drown me and nagged Bill about it. But
we got used to each other and I became and remain devoted. And he is
a superb accompanist.

For the first orchestral rehearsal he had the eight players assembled
in a dusty community centre near World's End. They had worked
during the afternoon and I arrived about six to go through my numbers.
I always find it strange to hear, for the first time, songs I have got used
to with the piano played by an orchestra. Parts have not always been

accurately copied; funny noises occur. That evening was no exception. The acoustics were horrible too, and my diary says: 'Terrible echo. Piano down and out. Clarinet off.' We got to my sad song about the unmarried sister, 'Three Brothers', and when I sang the lines about the old family house – 'the place was too big and too silent' – the clarinet gave two cuckoo-calls. Bill had warned me not to expect too much. Just as well. Afterwards I walked home along the King's Road summoning up confidence. It *must* be all right on the night. . . .

Next day a handful of people were invited to another run-through and this time we tried a new running order, ending part one with 'Palais Dancers'. This was my dancing chance. Beryl and I were two girls hoping for partners, and as she is small and slight and I am large and stand five foot eight in my stockings we made a funny pair. 'Me and my friend,' I sang eagerly, 'are mad on dancing, Me and my friend are. We've got dresses with sequins on and layers and layers of lace; We go to the Palais once a week, And keep up a terrible pace.' Wishful thinking on my part. Beryl, of course, played the successful girl who could dance the twiddly steps and immediately landed an expert (Paddy). My girl was both keen and willing but not good for more than an arm-pumping to-and-fro, straight up and down the dance-floor. (My pedestrian partner was Irving.) Having an audience of any kind at that stage of rehearsal was a boost to our morale and kind things were said to us, including an intended complimentary assurance from a couple of elderly journalists from Dublin, where we were due to do a week of the pre-London tour: 'They like *anything* in Dublin!'

At this point I must bring Victor Stiebel into closer focus because he played a very important part in the presentation of *J.G. Requests*. From 1946 until he retired in 1961 he made all my stage dresses and had long been a dear friend. He knew that this show was important to me and for it he produced some of his loveliest clothes. He was, I think, the most distinguished of the top London designers. He made deceptively simple clothes of great elegance, the result of an imaginative talent, taste, skill and an unerring eye for colour and texture; no gimmicks, no concessions; a quality couturier, one of the last in a disappearing trade. He also designed superbly for the stage.

Victor is not easy to describe because his vitality and quick intelligence come through so clearly that one is more aware of his presence than his appearance. When I stop to think about what he looks like I see a small-boned man with a well-shaped head; thick, dark, springing hair brushed back (it is white now), a fine-drawn profile with a small hawk-

'*Three Brothers*'

like nose, bright brown eyes behind glasses and a generous and ready smile. As a friend he is thoughtful, sensitive and affectionate; sympathetic and loyal. He can be critical too; caustic and quite demanding.

The loving care he always gave me over my dresses for the theatre, and for occasional off-stage clothes as well, turned every visit to his shops (in Grosvenor Street, when I first knew him, and finally in the scheduled Adam house on the corner of Cavendish Square and Wigmore Street) into a sort of treat. At the beginning I was apprehensive at the idea of going into such grand establishments. There was a commissionaire at the door; there were marble floors and sweeping staircases rising to the salons where aloof saleswomen waited, critically, I imagined, assessing my sophistication and poise. I felt inadequate; clothes wrong, figure hopeless. I always put on clean underwear for fittings, not, as I had been trained to do as a child, 'in case you get run over', but because I feared the scrutiny of the *vendeuses*. But as I got used to the place and the people, the staff became allies, and visits to Victor's shop became real treats, looked forward to.

I don't think I was a difficult customer but I had strong views, to the point of rigidity, about the kind of dress I wanted for working in on the stage – long-sleeved, trim-waisted, with a skirt wide enough to move and sit in with freedom. (I don't much like to see large women's upper arms bare when they are over twenty-five.) Victor probably found my basic demands tiresome, but he accepted them and produced endless original variations on my stipulated theme, with becoming results. With some justice he accused me of a leaning towards Augustus John peasant clothes and steered me away from the arty-picturesque to an elegance I never dreamed possible for me.

The whole ritual of getting clothes from Victor gave me pleasure. For *J.G. Requests ...* we talked about the programme in detail; I told him about the red velvet proscenium arch and curtains and described the numbers for which I needed dresses, and whereabouts in the programme they would probably be worn. He prepared drawings and sent them with patterns of stuffs for me to consider at home – several sketches for each number with alternative silks attached. There was excitement in opening the folder and studying sketches and patterns. I telephoned him to say they had come and we made a date for a work-session. At the shop a day or two later bolts of silk were brought to a fitting-room and draped over my shoulder to the ground so that we could get the general effect of colour and weight of material. For stage purposes we had to consider distance, and Victor went to the far end

Victor Stiebel

of the long salon while I stood under a light and tried to be helpful by turning in different directions to vary the effect. 'Stand still,' he ordered. He could be fierce when he was working. I stood still. 'Now let me see the green surah. . . .'

I think I must have a latent streak of Puritanism in me because whenever I sought clothes for private life or the theatre I began by looking for practical colours and durable stuffs, and it would never have occurred to me to choose for myself the dress Victor persuaded me to have for the opening number – a white silk organza crinoline, yards and yards of it, with a pale pink slipper-satin sash that turned into a sort of cross-over skirt at the back. I had never seen myself as the luxurious type, but that is what I would be on the first night, standing with my back to the audience, as directed by Laurier, wearing this delicate confection of a dress and rejoicing in it.

From the time I had my first Stiebel dress for the theatre, in *Tuppence Coloured*, I gained a new confidence. When a dress fits perfectly and is becoming, you don't have to think about how you look, you can concentrate on what you are doing, because you know the belt will stay where it is supposed to stay, the neckline sit in the right place and the hem be exact. And when you make the larger-than-life gestures that the theatre demands, you know you won't be impeded by dragging arm-holes. You can wave, reach, indicate and fling freely. (Sad memories of Madame Marthe and my constricting wedding dress.) Well-made clothes cost a great deal but, if you can afford them, they certainly pay off in terms of comfort and self-confidence. I was never shy but I have been self-conscious and I know what I am talking about.

I can list every one of the dresses, suits and coats that Victor made for me. All of them lasted for years and I wore most of them until they very nearly fell to pieces. As I added new stage dresses to my wardrobe I passed on wearable ones to friends in the concert world. There are still some Stiebel dresses in use, not always as originally intended. I know of cushions and a chair cover in Norfolk, made from two of my dresses for *J.G. Requests* . . . and I have a happy reminder of the show in the patchwork work-bag Victor had made for my first night present out of scraps from his six dresses. For sixteen years I kept a particular favourite stage-dress made for me in 1956, a grand black velvet gown with a full skirt and a *grosgrain* neckline. When Cecil Beaton mounted his fashion exhibition at the Victoria and Albert Museum in 1972 he asked me if I had a Stiebel dress to give to what was to become a permanent collection; and there it is, my most glamorous gown, worn first at the Lyric Theatre Hammersmith, then on tour in America, Canada and Australia; and, for the last time, at a private dinner-party Reggie and I were invited to by the Queen at Buckingham Palace.

On Saturday 24 April Reggie and I loaded the car with front-of-house pictures for the tour, our suitcases, my props, make-up case, picnic bag and Victor's six beautiful dresses, and we set off for Cambridge. Living on a bus stop made such departures complicated. We took it in turn to stand by the car, and journeys to the top floor to bring down all the luggage were long and slow. As we drove into Cambridge

I saw for the first time the pink posters announcing *Joyce Grenfell Requests the Pleasure* and, after a cup of tea, we went along to the Arts Theatre to make sure they were up there too.

The pre-London tour took off to a flying start. As usual the lighting rehearsal, the night before we opened, went on and on, and it was 4.30 a.m. and beginning to get light when we walked back to the hotel; but the theatre was already almost sold out for the whole week. The sets and Victor's dresses were as successful as I had hoped they would be, and I found my many quick-changes easier than I had feared. In the show I performed eight monologues, sang sixteen songs (some in groups) and changed my dress thirteen times. All the changes had to be made in an improvised quick-change room at the side of the stage, because once the curtain was up there was never time for me to get back to my dressing-room until the interval an hour later. Jeanne Goddard and I got the changes down to a minimum of time and effort. As she unzipped dress number one I stepped out of it and the shoes that went with it, and stepped into the shoes and dress for the next number, and so on. Ear-rings, necklaces, hats, head-scarves and gloves lay ready in the required order on the table. I had my longest rest between appearances after I made the change into the costume for 'Songs my Mother Taught Me'. After Jeanne had zipped me into the white shirt-waist and buckram-belted piqué skirt (made in one piece) I pinned the black taffeta bow to the back of my head, and I think I could probably have qualified for the *Guinness Book of Records* with the use I made of the three minutes left to me before my next number: I sat on a hard-backed wooden chair, closed my eyes and lost consciousness in a little cat-nap, until Jeanne gently woke me in time to recollect myself before, well-refreshed, I walked out on to the stage to sing.

We had a good time in Cambridge, followed by even greater enthusiasm and nightly House Full boards outside the Theatre Royal in Brighton. I began to feel perhaps we had a good show. Then came Folkestone. Laurier had warned me that things might be quieter there; it is not a theatre-minded town and interest in a new show was difficult to arouse. I was prepared for this but not for the forlornness of the mis-named Pleasure Garden Theatre; draughty, in need of paint, and not very clean. No stage doorman, and the two electricians appeared to be about sixteen years old; neither had ever before taken lighting-cues. Our show had dozens of lighting-cues. In the only backstage ladies' lavatory there were empty gin-bottles. I got there at midday on Monday morning to find that the advance for that night's performance was

£6 10s. It rose to £35 by the time the curtain went up, and though we did better than the despondent local management expected, we took under £500 on the week. Beryl's dresser was surprised at our disappointment. She thought we had done quite nicely really; the Christmas pantomime, a few months before we came, never had more than forty patrons in at any performance of its six weeks' season.

My father- and mother-in-law were living at Betteshanger nearby and came to see me, bringing with them a six-foot bouquet of magnolia-branches – not exactly a convenient sort of tribute at any time – and my heart sank as I looked through empty backstage cupboards for some sort of pot to put them in. The gin bottles were all that came to light, and the branches had begun to look tired before I struggled with them back to the hotel at the end of the evening. By that time it was too late to find vases, and the bunches of sticks they had become spent the night balancing in the wash-basin where the plug didn't fit. The Grenfells and a party of willing elderly friends sat in the front row and did their best to be a lively audience. The paying few were supplemented by the regular Monday free-list of local tradesmen, and though they were quiet, they seemed to enjoy what they could of an entertainment they never quite got to grips with. We played to small but friendly audiences throughout the week, and I hoped, as we packed up on Saturday night, that our next date, Dublin, would be more encouraging.

The Olympia Theatre, an old variety house, was battered, but freshly painted and full of character and atmosphere. Its bow-fronted boxes had exuberant plaster-work decorations and the whole house a period charm. Here we did a huge gala week and were made much of by packed houses and the Dublin press. On Saturday night five hundred people filled the gallery alone, and as they pounded their feet and cheered us after the final performance I wondered whether the rickety old building would stand the racket. It had been a stimulating visit and I couldn't help feeling hopeful for a programme that aroused so much friendly enthusiasm. But I remembered the successful tour we had with *Penny Plain* before it reached London, and the uphill struggle that went on after we had opened; and that gave me pause. All the same it had been a splendid week and Dublin was a real theatre city so perhaps . . .

An elderly chartered Wayfarer Transport plane flew the company with Bill, stage staff, orchestra, their instruments, scenery, curtains, costume-skips, props and our personal baggage to Whitchurch, near Bath, on a cold and frosty May morning. Reggie was at the airfield with good news of our advance booking in Bath, and the grey morning burned through to show us spring colours, fields of shining buttercups and blossom on the fruit-trees. The grass was almost as green as it had been in Ireland and there was a feeling of promise in the air.

The Theatre Royal in Bath is one of my favourites, and now that it has been modernised the faint smell of gas with which I always associated it must have disappeared from the auditorium, where the exit-signs over the doors were all gas-lit. Every evening when Bill and I did a warm-up practice on the empty stage, with the curtain up, I loved to watch the man on duty go through the darkened house with a lighted taper to illumine the signs with a hiss and leap of yellow light as he progressed round the stalls, up to the circle and on to the top gallery, in the same way as his predecessors must always have done since gas was first installed. My dressing-room was close enough to the stage for all my quick changes. I had to think hard about my make-up because the glass in the mirrors was so antique that it gave back a grey-green reflection, and care had to be taken not to overdo the new 'peachiness' in my efforts not to look ghostly. In spite of the penetrating damp cold backstage, and the primitive plumbing arrangements (a long walk from the dressing-room up stone stairs and communally used by everyone) I loved working in that theatre. It is beautiful for sound, pretty to look at and the auditorium seems to embrace the stage in a way few modern theatres manage to do.

In the theatre it is customary to give each other presents on first nights and Bath was a good place to find china, small gew-gaws and pieces of Georgian silver at prices I could manage. I explored the shops, assembled my presents throughout the week, and wrapped them ready for London, to celebrate this most important first night in my career. (I hadn't got a career when I went into *The Little Revue* and though that was a big moment because it was my début, this show that I had written meant a great deal. Perhaps it isn't so difficult to begin, but to continue and try new ways seems harder. I wasn't afraid, I never have been; but I had a pleasurable feeling of anticipation coloured by some hope.) The weather for our week in Somerset was summery and I drove the dancers and Jeanne round the crescents and terraces of eighteenth-century Bath, and we spent an afternoon in a may-scented field lying on rugs under a haystack, surrounded by frothing cow-parsley and the calls of cuckoos, talking of what lay ahead. Reggie had gone to London at the beginning of the week but was coming back to join me on Friday night. During the evening performance I saw his shadow outlined against the dress-circle door and recognised him by his ears; comforting to know he had arrived. His sister Mary Walde-grave lives in the Mendips and she was there on Saturday night with most of her seven children; and Reggie's cousin, Harold Grenfell, and Miriam his wife, brought friends over from Wiltshire. The dressing-room was crowded after the perfomance and they all wished me well for the opening at the Fortune Theatre.

There were two days in London before the first night on Wednes-day, 2 June 1954. I was glad to have a pause at home in the Kings Road flat with time to collect myself and catch up on letters and domestic jobs. Virginia had brought flowers to welcome us back, and Mrs Gabe was in and out a good deal to give me meals and generally spare my labours in the kitchen. Dick and Victor were both on holiday in Scotland and decided not to come south for the opening; Viola, too, was away, doing concerts. As these three of my closest friends all disliked first nights, particularly when they were concerned about the outcome, I was relieved to be spared the presence of their loving anxiety.

There was the inevitable lighting-rehearsal on Monday in an un-heated theatre. In the usual British way the management had turned off the heating because the calendar said 'summer', even though the tem-perature had fallen to wintry levels and the place felt like an ice-box. The Fortune was far smaller than any of us had remembered. The dancers shivered as they stood on the tiny stage and swore they'd never be able to dance in the space available to them. They were downcast and muttered. I looked at the close proximity to the footlights of the steeply rising circle and wanted to push it away from me. Backstage there seemed to be nowhere I could do my quick changes. I was low too. But by the end of a full dress rehearsal on Tuesday evening, given to an audience of orchestral wives and the men responsible for the enormous amount of electrical equipment taking up so much space in the wings, we had all begun to get used to the place. The heating had been turned on. It began to feel roomier and the dancers found they could cope with the small stage. The staff was efficient and seemed interested. I liked the atmosphere of the austere-looking little house. I knew I was going to enjoy working in it.

June the second, as well as being my all-important first night, was also Derby Day and I spent the morning supposedly resting in bed. I played with *The Times* crossword, talked to Virginia on the telephone, thought a great deal about the evening ahead and tried to stop my

'*The Music's Message*'

imagination running from success to failure, from failure to success, and settled on trusting to the work we had already done and in which, if I was honest, I had faith. Mrs Gabe came in at two to give me a late luncheon designed to last me through the rest of the day and evening. We listened to the race together and she decided that the winner's name, Never Say Die, boded well. A cup of tea after a fitful nap and Reggie drove me to the theatre and found a parking-place almost outside the door. The stage doorman said he had been taking in flowers all day long and more were being delivered as we arrived. My diary records that I had sixty-nine telegrams, including messages from Noël Coward, John Gielgud and Gladys Cooper. I had now been on the stage for fifteen years, but I was still stage-struck enough to be excited by attention from such stars. Dick had telegraphed twice, once early in the day, quoting from the title of one of our new songs: 'It's not an ordinary morning up here is it with you?' The second message, to the theatre, read: 'Don't suppose Myra Hess and Clifford Curzon ever feel like this do you?' He also sent me a pair of white-and-gold Crown Derby fruit-plates which were waiting for me, together with Victor's patch-work bag, in my dressing-room. Presents and flowers continued to arrive; I put on a careful make-up, sang some tentative scales, swallowed a lot and then I was called over the public address system. 'On stage, beginners please.'

I remember the dancers and I wishing each other and everyone else in the theatre all success and saying '*Merde alors*' and pretending to kick the behind of our fellow-artists in a ritual the origins of which I have never known. Laurier came on stage and kissed me his good wishes. I had had my wishes from Reggie earlier and hoped he was safely in his seat with Virginia and Tony and a great many of my relations and family friends. 'Places, please,' said Penny Udy, our stage manager. I went to my position up-stage right, turned my back to the curtain and adjusted my left glove. Before I had time to turn round and see the audience they had begun to greet me with first night applause. The show had begun.

My diary, written after supper at Virginia's, says: 'We still have to wait for the press but the reception was wonderful. I wonder what they'll say.'

When I woke the following morning I heard voices in the kitchen. I went in and found Reggie and Mrs Gabe sitting at the table waiting for me to appear. Open at the right page before them were all the London papers. Mrs Gabe had got up early to bring them in for us to see. I didn't have to ask if the notices were friendly. They both sat there smiling broadly.

The show opens

Poster photograph

Index

Figures in italics (*166*) indicate pages on which illustrations appear.

Index

Index

Index

London Has a Ruth Draper

Theatre : Little.
"The Little Revue."
Authors : Herbert Farjeon and others.

HERE is an intimate revue as near to perfection as any I have seen. So nearly perfect is it, that I will ....

Joyce Grenfell, who is new to me, is an artist of the Ruth Draper type, uniting quiet charm with a subtle eye and ear for character. Her "impressions" are delightful. ... with a ... sions" are of Left Wing flavour—here rather to the Left—should, unless it is miraculously excellent, be the perquisite of ... And little theatres in odd ... Joyce Grenfell. ... lenging Ruth Draper on her own pitch, pinks so many elusive targets that she must be said to carry off the acting honours of this gay and intelligent entertainment. ... loving Vienna has ... equently of late attracted the attention of the Serious Sunday Drama. It is depressing anyway. . . .

Agonisingly Funny

Two items that were given enough applause to—in theatrical parlance—"stop the show," were contributed by Miss Joyce Grenfell, who has never appeared on the stage before. ... genius, ... themselves when they showed us that that ancient revue-fodder—ridiculing the Russian Ballet ... funny, but excru... ly Also, there is Miss Joyce Grenfell, who looks like a tall and dignified young angel, and turns out to be as maliciously observant as Miss Ruth Draper herself ; her sketches of a women's institute lecturer and a Kensington mother are brilliant.

Miss Baddeley had previou... us, with Mr. Michael Anthony, the grimly diverting side of Torquay invalids, and Miss Joyce Grenfell's exquisite and subtle sketches of a trio of mothers of various types and of a lecturer on "Useful and Acceptable Gifts" showed that another Ruth Draper is among us.

The music is good, the lyrics are good, the company is good and the prospects are indisputably good. I can imagine no more useful or acceptable gift than a couple of seats for "The Little Revue." **P. P.**

Leigh with her positive genius for gentle, almost loving, caricature ; that fastidious artist, Miss Joyce Grenfell, and that endearing droll, Mr. George Benson.

By ARCHIE ...

Joyce Grenfell is another joy. She contributes two separate turns of her own composition, and hits off with gentle but deadly precision a whole series of well-meaning women. I think my favourite is the understanding mother coping brightly with an adolescent daughter who has fallen in love with a conjuror. ... ... to the top of this class. Cyril Ritchard also shows very marked development in this respect—so much so that he can now afford to forget the juvenile sentimentalities of his past.

George Benson and other members of the old gang again give grand support, and a new recruit. Joyce Grenfell, contributes a really brilliant burlesque interlude in a self-written monologue on beautifying the home.

ADDED effect is given to the excellent musical numbers by a small chorus with a large sense of humour, as well as by the personality and talent of Betty Ann Davies.

In suggesting that, on each of her Of the guest artist, Miss Joyce Grenfell, who provides her own material, it is only necessary to say that she is as funny as the Fish Man who was so outstanding in the last revue at this house.

It takes a woman to deal faithfully with the little foibles of her sex. You will remember Miss Gertrude Jennings upon the warpath, and there is a certain play now running at the Lyric Theatre which carries on the good work—but Miss Grenfell is not of these.

Her talents remind us of Miss Ruth Draper, and we fancy that she could probably hold an audience for a couple of hours just as securely as she holds them for ten minutes at the Little Theatre. Her main item is a cameo of a woman addressing a Women's Institute on the subject of those Helpful Hints which are found in the pages of the more feminine sixpenny magazines—how to make bed-socks for your husband out of the sleeves of his red flannel nightgown, and so on.

Actually, Miss Grenfell concentrates on the transformation of a biscuit tin into a waste-paper basket for "hubby's den," we must presume. We do not propose to give away her little secret—as critics say of a mystery play—but she exposes the pathetic little subterfuges of the synthetic home with a firm yet not unfriendly touch.

At a later appearance, Miss Grenfell takes a trio of mothers under her wing, and how she debunks the possessive parent is If we were a modern daughter, we should like to have a mother—or should we ? Mightn't she be up to our leave us shivering in the cool draught of maternal and mothers and all daughters should sit at the feet of compare notes as the Rolls-Royce is trying to wangle congested by-ways of the Adelphi.

" LI
By Herber

The Lit grow less. In the n riches wh that the p the runne winners. offends M contributic by Miss J logues are since Miss greatest p Farjeon, no Baddeley, come withi theatre! dozen ... recite Mis dance the strong, sta no country without w artistic. than supp leagues wi of which given exce leaders.

Miss Jo brings her tions, whi of a Wor types of mixture a lively Gifts is range of variations ... and the snobbery of bus ro he can re repeat hir ... ga ... o, ... l ... d ... could hav his show point and Revue.